fun with the family
Pennsylvania

Praise for the *Fun with the Family* series

"Enables parents to turn family travel into an exploration."
—Alexandra Kennedy, Editor, *Family Fun*

"Bound to lead you and your kids to fun-filled days, those times that help compose the memories of childhood."
—Dorothy Jordon, *Family Travel Times*

Help Us Keep This Guide Up to Date

We would love to hear from you concerning your experiences with this guide and how you feel it could be improved and kept up to date. Please send your comments and suggestions to:

editorial@GlobePequot.com

Thanks for your input, and happy travels!

FUN WITH THE FAMILY SERIES

fun with the family
Pennsylvania

hundreds of ideas for day trips with the kids

Seventh Edition

Christine H. O'Toole

travel

Guilford, Connecticut

All the information in this guidebook is subject to change. We recommend that you call ahead to obtain current information before traveling.

To buy books in quantity for corporate use or incentives, call **(800) 962-0973** or e-mail **premiums@GlobePequot.com**.

Editor: Amy Lyons
Project Editor: Lynn Zelem
Layout: Joanna Beyer
Text design by Nancy Freeborn and Linda R. Loiewski
Maps by Rusty Nelson © Morris Book Publishing, LLC
Spot photography throughout © Photodisc and © RubberBall Productions

ISSN 1539-8730
ISBN 978-0-7627-5722-0

Printed in the United States of America
10 9 8 7 6 5 4 3 2 1

To Jim, James, and Bill—great Pennsylvanians

—C.H.O.

Contents

Introduction ix

Philadelphia 1

Philadelphia Countryside 36

Hershey–Pennsylvania Dutch Country 68

Laurel Highlands Region 105

Pittsburgh and Environs 133

Northeastern Pennsylvania 157

Central Pennsylvania 185

Pennsylvania's Northern Tier 204

Index 229

Acknowledgments

A lot of people, young and old, helped make this book possible. Thanks to the kids who served as guinea pigs for this edition, and to those who recommended great new attractions. Bruno Lavoissier once again provided valuable fact-checking and boundless energy on the project.

About the Author

Christine H. O'Toole is an award-winning feature and travel writer based in Pittsburgh, Pennsylvania. Her work appears in the *Washington Post, the New York Times, International Herald-Tribune, Pittsburgh Post-Gazette, USA Today,* and online. She is the author of *Pennsylvania: Off the Beaten Path* (GPP Travel). A native of Newtown Square, Pennsylvania, she's also lived in Philadelphia and Harrisburg.

Introduction

In Pennsylvania it's easy to take our history for granted—we have a lot of it, dating back to 1681. But while the kids are young, it's a great time to explore Old City Philadelphia and Independence Hall, as well as places like Valley Forge, Gettysburg National Military Park, and pre-Revolutionary sites like Fort Necessity. Historic landmarks and living-history sites can be found in every corner of the state. There's no better time to discover them than now.

Seeing history in the present tense reminds us that our liberties (like our children) are a living legacy that requires regular care. The National Liberty Museum and the new National Constitution Center get kids thinking in new ways about the responsibilities of citizenship.

As a Philadelphia kid, I visited the Liberty Bell and the Franklin Institute with my parents. Later, I brought my own Pittsburgh kids to city sites and shared with them lots of rural adventures.

Whether you're looking for a place to hike, bike, camp, ski, horseback ride, or just take a Sunday-afternoon drive, Pennsylvania has a park for you. We've tried to cover the highlights of the state park system in this book, but to devote the space each deserves, we'd have to write another book on the subject. If you want more information about Pennsylvania state parks, call their special toll-free number, (888) PA–PARKS, or check the Web at www.visitpaparks.com.

Pennsylvania has nine major caves open to the public, including the only water-filled cave in the country. Many of the caves offer educational programs on such topics as geology, bats, and Native American history—all geared especially for children.

When I first experienced the spooky pleasures of the walk-through heart at the Franklin Institute, the exhibit was cutting-edge science education. Other "user-friendly" science centers include the Carnegie Science Center, Erie's expERIEnce Children's Museum, and Harrisburg's Whitaker Center, to name just a few. Some of the best family adventures can be adventures in learning.

Many parents are afraid to take kids to art museums, but my sons respond well to art museums as long as they experience them in small doses. The Westmoreland Museum of American Art in Greensburg helps by giving kids backpacks with clues to a "scavenger hunt" of art masterworks. Pennsylvania has some first-rate art museums, headlined by the Philadelphia Museum of Art and the Carnegie Museum of Art in Pittsburgh.

Pennsylvania also has places to go for just plain fun, with no hidden agenda. Amusement parks include Sesame Place, Dorney Park & Wildwater Kingdom, Hersheypark, Idlewild, Kennywood, Sandcastle, and many more. At two indoor waterpark resorts, Great Wolf Lodge and Splash Lagoon, families can enjoy all the thrills and fun of a waterpark—no matter what the weather.

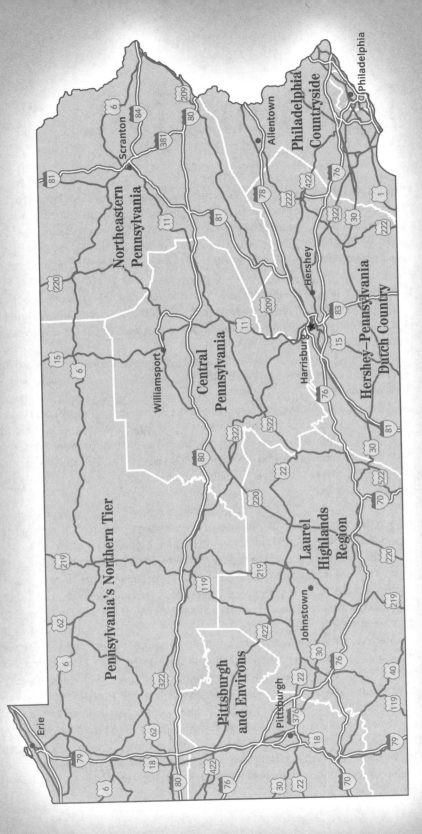

PENNSYLVANIA

Pennsylvania's rivers are another kind of amusement ride. Float down the Delaware on inner tubes at New Hope, kayak Pittsburgh's three rivers, or try white-water rafting on the Lehigh. Try a day of biking on safe, level trails at Pine Creek Gorge, Oil Creek, and Presque Isle. Hikers and bird-watchers will find plenty of other fun.

Looking for a place to start? The Web site at www.visitpa.com is a great jumping-off point for your adventure in Pennsylvania.

As you navigate through the commonwealth, make sure you have an up-to-date map. Exit numbers on major roads throughout the state have been changed and now reflect mileage from west to east as opposed to running consecutively. Double-check exit numbers on directions or call ahead to avoid confusion.

Accommodation, Restaurant, and Attraction Fees

Each chapter in this book gives a list of accommodations and restaurants for the area. This list is not meant to be complete, and we also recommend checking with the local tourist bureaus for other options. In general, we recommend advance reservations. Accomdation prices can vary depending on the season and other factors, so make sure you understand in advance how much you'll be expected to pay.

Because admission fees change frequently, we offer a general idea of the prices charged by each attraction. Keep in mind that even though many preserves and museums offer **free** admission, a donation is often expected to help the facility with the costs of keeping the lands and buildings open to the public.

Rates Used in this Guide

Rates for Attractions

$	up to $5
$$	from $6 to $10
$$$	from $11 to $20
$$$$	more than $20

Rates for Restaurants

$	most entrees under $10
$$	most $11 to $15
$$$	most $16 to $20
$$$$	most over $20

Rates for Accommodations

$	up to $100
$$	from $101 to $150
$$$	from $151 to $200
$$$$	More than $200

Attractions Key

The following is a key to the icons found throughout the text.

SWIMMING	**FOOD**
BOATING / BOAT TOUR	**LODGING**
HISTORIC SITE	**CAMPING**
HIKING / WALKING	**MUSEUM**
FISHING	**PERFORMING ARTS**
BIKING	**SPORTS/ATHLETICS**
AMUSEMENT PARK	**PICNICKING**
HORSEBACK RIDING	**PLAYGROUND**
SKIING/WINTER SPORTS	**SHOPPING**
PARK	**PLANTS/GARDENS/NATURE TRAILS**
ANIMAL VIEWING	**FARM**

Philadelphia

Families love Philadelphia's Old City, where three centuries of living history mix along the Delaware River. You'll see guides in tricornered hats leading tours, while kids whiz past them on skateboards. Uptown you'll find some of the best children's attractions in the nation—the Philadelphia Zoo, the country's oldest; the Franklin Institute; the Academy of Natural Sciences; and the Please Touch Museum. Fairmount Park provides plenty of room for families to picnic and play. Best of all, it's a walkable city, easy to explore and enjoy.

The Liberty Bell Center features groundbreaking exhibits that showcase the Bell's significance. The Independence Visitor Center provides a comprehensive gateway to the park, the city, and the region. And the National Constitution Center brings the Constitution

TopPicks in Phildelphia

- **Liberty Bell Center**
- **Independence Hall**
- **National Constitution Center**
- **Lights of Liberty**
- **Franklin Square**
- **National Liberty Museum**
- **The Franklin Institute**
- **Academy of Natural Sciences**
- **Betsy Ross House**
- **Philadelphia Zoo**

PHILADELPHIA

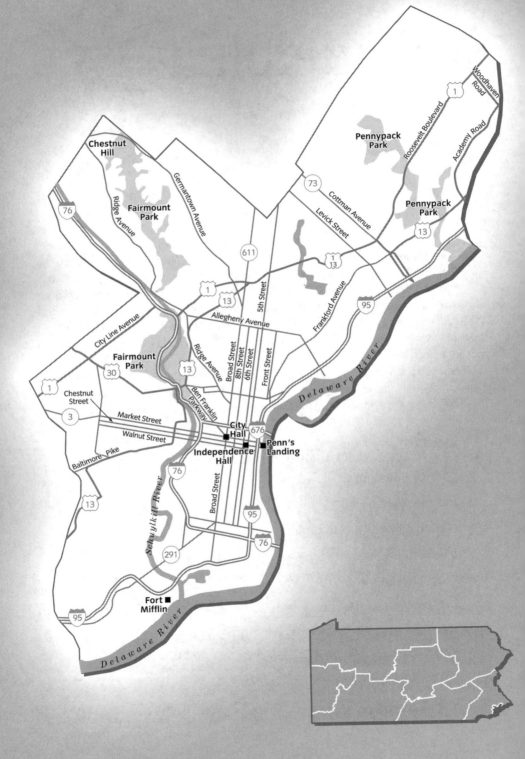

alive through dramatic and interactive learning experiences. Down the street, families can enjoy storytelling, mini-golf, and more at Franklin Square.

The Liberty Bell's move to its newest home became the occasion for a history project for the people of the City of Brotherly Love. Philadelphians have always cherished the Liberty Bell as a symbol of American freedom. It has also become an icon to abolitionists, feminists, and figures from Nelson Mandela to the Dalai Lama.

But recent archaeological research unearthed a startling fact: The new Liberty Bell Center was being built above the remains of the quarters where President George Washington once housed his slaves. The discovery sparked lively discussion. In the end, it was decided that the stark fact of slavery should not be "buried" but embraced as a teaching opportunity. Today's new Liberty Bell Center examines the Liberty Bell in its historical context, with the freedom it symbolizes seen as a process, as a goal both attained and not yet attained.

The Liberty Bell Center offers a video presentation and exhibits focusing on the Liberty Bell's origins and its modern-day role as an international icon of freedom. Taped presentations about the history of the Liberty Bell are offered in a dozen languages for the convenience of foreign visitors. The Liberty Bell itself is displayed in a magnificent glass chamber with Independence Hall in the background. Visitors can also view a new film on the Liberty Bell produced for the National Park Service by the History Channel.

The National Constitution Center features Freedom Rising, an excellent dramatic presentation, as well as exciting interactive exhibits that bring the Constitution to life in all its grandeur and complexity.

TopEvents in Philadelphia

- **Mummer's Parade,** Jan 1, summer version in June; (215) 336-3050.

- **Ben Franklin's Birthday Bash,** Jan; (215) 448-1200.

- **Philadelphia Flower Show,** late Feb or early Mar; (215) 988-8800.

- **Philadelphia International Children's Festival,** Apr or May; (215) 898-6791 or (215) 898-6683.

- **Penn Relays,** Apr through May; (215) 898-6145.

- **Philadelphia Orchestra Concerts at Mann Music Center (outdoor summer series),** Fifty-second Street and Parkside Avenue; (215) 893-1995 or (215) 893-1999.

- **Summer concerts at Penn's Landing,** June through Aug; (215) 928-8801.

- **Sunoco Welcome America! Celebration,** July; (215) 683-2200.

- **Army-Navy Game,** Dec, Lincoln Financial Field; (215) 336-2000.

- **AAMP Celebrates Kwanzaa,** Dec; (215) 574-0380.

Franklin Square (all ages)

At Sixth and Race Streets; (215) 629-4026; www.onceuponanation.org. Open daily except Christmas; extended hours in summer. Park access free, mini-golf $–$$, carousel $.

Franklin Square, one of the five public squares that William Penn laid out in his original plan for the city, has undergone a dramatic renovation. The shady park now boasts several all-new, family-friendly attractions. Philly Mini Golf offers eighteen holes decorated with some of Philadelphia's favorite icons. The classic Philadelphia Park Liberty Carousel pays tribute to the city's great heritage of carousel making. Local history comes to life on storytelling benches, where families can learn the lore of this famous neighborhood. And one of Philadelphia's most acclaimed restaurateurs, Stephen Starr, recently opened Squareburger, with an all-American menu of shakes, fries, hot dogs, and ice cream, on the square. Patrons can dine in or use the cafe tables anywhere in the square. Restrooms are located nearby.

Do your Internet planning ahead of your Old City trip at www.independencevisitor center.com, the Web site of the Independence Visitor Center. The Greater Philadelphia Cultural Alliance Web site, www.phillyfunguide.com, also offers useful tips. The Greater Philadelphia Marketing Corporation's site, www.gophila.com, offers itineraries, events, tours for special interests, and much more.

The Web site of the Philadelphia Convention and Visitors Bureau is www.pcvb.org. Another worthwhile site is http://philadelphia.about.com. You can take a virtual tour of the historic section at www.ushistory.org/tour and of City Hall at http://philadelphiacityhall willpennshomepage.org.

If you're visiting Philly for several days, I recommend the CityPass, which gets you into six attractions for one price and with no ticket lines. You can save about 50 percent off the combined box-office prices for the Franklin Institute, the Philadelphia Trolley Tour, the Philadelphia Zoo, the Academy of Natural Sciences, Independence Seaport Museum, and the National Constitution Center. Tickets are valid for nine days from first date of use. You can purchase a CityPass at any participating attraction, the Independence Visitor Center, or in advance at www.citypass.com.

Philadelphia is a great walking city. Most attractions are an easy jaunt from hotels and from one another. And when the feet get sore or the kids get cranky, the purple PHLASH bus, which travels in a loop from Penn's Landing to the Art Museum, is one of the best deals in town. To get to some of the attractions in the outskirts of the city, a car can be handy, but the one-way streets in Center City and cost of parking can be frustrating. Public transportation or walking is your best bet.

There are lots of companies that offer tours of Philadelphia, on everything from a reproduction of an old-time trolley or a horse and buggy to a streamlined coach. Here are some companies to contact: American Trolley Tours/Choo-Choo Trolley, (215) 333-2119; Big Bus Tour, (215) 965-7676 or (800) 537-7676; '76 Carriage Co., (215) 923-8516 (tours begin at Independence National Park); Riverboat Queen Fleet, (215) 923-4778 (cruises leave from Penn's Landing); Philadelphia Trolley Works, (215) 925-TOUR; PHLASH bus, (215) 4-PHLASH.

Philadelphia **Tours**

Try a themed tour to get an insider's view of the city. The Mural Arts program has introduced four alternating tours of some of Philadelphia's most wonderful murals. The Mural Arts bus tours depart every Wednesday, Saturday, and Sunday, April through November, from the Independence Visitor Center. Each Saturday of the month, you may tour the murals of a different Philadelphia neighborhood. There are also tours some Wednesdays. Advance reservations are recommended. Call (215) 685-0754, or check out the Web site at www .muralarts.org.

I-Glide Tours offers narrated introductions to Center City aboard Segway® Human Transporters. The tours, offered daily April through November, begin from the Philadelphia Museum of Art and take in Boathouse Row and the newly restored Waterworks. Reservations are required. Call I-Glide at (877) GLIDE-81, or visit www.iglidetours.com.

Historic Philadelphia

When most people think of Philadelphia, they think of its place in U.S. history. You'll hear the word first a lot while touring this historic city. In fact, the area that makes up Independence National Historic Park (from Second to Sixth Street along Walnut Street) is called "America's most historic square mile." Here you'll meander the streets walked by Benjamin Franklin, Thomas Jefferson, Betsy Ross, George Washington, Dolley Madison, John Adams . . . the list goes on and on.

Independence National Historical Park (all ages)
www.nps.gov/inde.

Forty-five acres in Center City containing more than forty different historic buildings make up Independence National Historical Park. Here you can visit the Liberty Bell Pavilion, Independence Hall, Congress Hall, Old City Hall, Second Bank of the United States, Carpenters' Hall, New Hall Military Museum, Franklin Court, Christ Church, Bishop White House, Todd House, Declaration House, and other sites.

Independence Visitor Center (all ages)
Sixth and Market Streets; (215) 965-2305 or (800) 537-7676; www.independencevisitor center.com. Most park buildings are open 8:30 a.m. to 5 p.m. daily. These hours are subject to some change; in summer some buildings are open into the evening. Admission is **free.**

The Independence Visitor Center is not just a spectacular building; it's the perfect introduction to the greater Philadelphia region.

Start by parking your car in the underground Autopark at Independence Mall. Inside the visitor center, make sure you visit its state-of-the-art theater for a brief video that gets you oriented. A second theater shows the excellent film *Independence!* directed by John Huston. Afterward, if you wish to tour Independence Hall, pick up a free dated-and-timed ticket here. You can also make reservations for restaurants in the area here, purchase tickets, or sign up for a Philadelphia heritage tour. You can even print out your own itinerary in visitor computer stations. You can get a snack at the Old Capital Coffee Bar or browse through the gift and book shop. A seventy-two minute AudioWalk tour is available for rent.

Be sure to pick up a copy of the *Historic Philadelphia Gazette,* a free newspaper that lists events, demonstrations, and current hours for many sites in Philadelphia. (At home, check www.historicphiladelphia.org.)

Most buildings within the park are free and open to the public, but a guide is required to tour some. For others, such as the Todd House and the Bishop White House, tickets are required. There is an admission fee ($) for persons age sixteen and older to enter the Second Bank of the United States. The urban park rangers of the National Park Service obviously love their jobs, and they'll make history come alive with their stories of colonial Philadelphia.

Security Procedures at
Independence Square and Liberty Bell

Visitors to Independence National Historical Park must be screened upon entry. First pick up your **free,** timed-and-dated tickets to tour Independence Hall at the Independence Visitor Center. There are no restrooms in the secure area, so have the kids go to the bathroom at the visitor center. (The visitor center is outside the secure area. A port-a-potty has been placed on the northwest corner of Fifth and Chestnut Streets, but this also is outside the screening area.) Since security procedures may take some time, it's a good idea to arrive forty-five minutes to one hour before your scheduled tour. The fewer personal items you bring, the faster you will move through security.

Visitors enter the screening facility on Market Street between Fifth and Sixth Streets. Here you are directed through the Liberty Bell Center. After viewing the Liberty Bell, you will cross the street to Independence Square. Once on the square you may visit the buildings there at your own pace, or you may leave the secure area if you choose not to see the other buildings.

You will not be able to return to the Liberty Bell once you cross Chestnut Street. You will be able to tour Independence Hall by timed-and-dated tickets only.

Amazing
Philadelphia Facts

Philadelphia is the largest city in Pennsylvania, the second largest on the East Coast (New York is first, but you knew that), and the sixth-largest city in the United States.

Also making history come alive are the Town Criers and other actors in period costumes that help transport visitors back in time. A special-events list distributed by the Town Criers gives a schedule of presentations, such as "General Washington's Call to Arms." Families are encouraged not only to watch these events but also to participate. Most events take place on weekends, with daily performances in summer. For more information call (925) 372-7721 or check the Web at www.ushistory.org.

Liberty Bell Center (all ages)

Sixth and Market Streets; (215) 965-2305. The Liberty Bell Pavilion is open from 9 a.m. to 5 p.m., with extended hours in summer. Admission is free. Wheelchair accessible.

Contrary to popular belief, the Liberty Bell's famous crack was not the result of overzealous ringing on July 4, 1776. In 1846 a thin crack was detected. It was repaired but cracked again when rung on George Washington's birthday. It has not rung since. To read the whole story, check www.ushistory.org/libertybell. The Liberty Bell's new home puts the bell into context with interpretive exhibits that examine it as an international symbol of liberty—both liberties attained and those not yet attained. The Liberty Bell first achieved iconic status during the 1840s, when it was adopted as a symbol of the abolitionist movement. Since then it has come to represent freedom and civil rights for many groups both in the United States and abroad. Viewing these exhibits makes seeing the bell, with Independence Hall in view just across the street, a moving experience.

Congress Hall (ages 8 and up)

Sixth and Chestnut Streets.

If you have some time to spare after viewing the Liberty Bell Center and before your tour of Independence Hall, stop by some of the other interesting sites inside the secured area. Please note that after you have crossed Chestnut Street, you will not be permitted to return to the Liberty Bell Center. You must exit the secured area at a marked exit.

Congress Hall served as the meeting place for both houses of Congress during those early years when Philadelphia was the nation's capital. Well-informed Park Service interpreters are available to answer any questions.

Great Essentials (ages 8 and up)

Chestnut Street, next to Congress Hall.

While waiting for your tour of Independence Hall, take a look at this moving display of historic documents that played pivotal roles in our nation's history. Here you can see surviving copies of the Declaration of Independence, the Articles of Confederation, and the Constitution. If you look closely, you can see handwritten notes in the margins, reminding us of the debates that shaped the final drafts. Here you can also see the Syng inkstand, which was probably used by signers of both the Declaration of Independence and the Constitution.

Old City Hall (ages 10 and up)

Fifth and Chestnut Streets.

Next to Independence Hall is Old City Hall, home of the first U.S. Supreme Court.

Independence Hall (ages 6 and up)

Chestnut Street between Fifth and Sixth Streets; (215) 965-2305. Open by tour only. Admission is free, but between Mar 1 and Dec 31, tickets are still required for all persons touring Independence Hall, including infants. The free tickets are timed and dated. You may get "walk-up" tickets at the Independence Visitor Center on the day of your visit. For a service charge of $1.50 per ticket, you may order tickets in advance through Spherix ticket reservation service at (800) 967-2283 or www.recreation.gov. Each individual may reserve up to six tickets.

It goes without saying that Independence Hall is a must-see for all ages. This building was originally known as the Pennsylvania State House, but in 1824 when General Lafayette returned to Philadelphia, he called it "the hall of independence," and the name stuck. The Declaration of Independence was adopted here, and the U.S. Constitution was written here. The Assembly Room has been restored to look exactly as it did in 1776.

Between 1790 and 1800, when Philadelphia was the capital of the United States, the Congress met in Congress Hall next door. On the other side of Independence Hall is Old City Hall, where the U.S. Supreme Court met from 1791 to 1800. Unlike many historic buildings, Old City Hall is wheelchair accessible.

Second Bank of the United States and Carpenters' Hall (ages 10 and up)
Second Bank is located on Chestnut Street between Fourth and Fifth Streets; (215) 965-2305; open daily 9 a.m. to 5 p.m. Admission $ for 16 and older. Carpenters' Hall is open Tues through Sun 10 a.m. to 4 p.m.; closed Tues in Jan and Feb. Admission is free. Carpenters' Hall information, (215) 925-0167.

The Second Bank of the United States and Carpenters' Hall, where the First Continental Congress met in 1774, are worth noting. Perhaps with kids you'd like to see the exterior only. Today Carpenters' Hall displays early carpenter's tools and chairs. The Second Bank houses the park's portrait gallery, featuring portraits of many early American heroes. The

City of **Murals**

On the corner of Seventh and Market Streets, across the street from the visitor center, you can see the mural *Tree Walk*. Driving on I-95 you can see the spectacular *Hanging Garden of I-95*. Philadelphia is the proud home of the largest collection of public murals in the country. Over 2,400 indoor and outdoor murals adorn the city, some sporting mosaic, sculptural, or fresco elements; some abstract; and many celebrating heroes both local and universal. This is all due to Philly's exceptional Mural Arts Program, begun in 1984 as the Philadelphia Anti-Graffiti Network.

This city-funded effort has not only brought art to the cityscape, turning graffiti-scarred walls into colorful vistas, but has also been a community-building experience. Each mural has its own story. Local communities get involved from the ground floor, requesting the mural, cleaning the space, choosing the artist and subject matter, often even picking up paintbrushes and getting hands dirty.

As you tour the city on your own, keep your eyes open. There may be a colorful surprise behind the next corner. If you want to see more, the Mural Arts Program offers bus tours every Wednesday, Saturday, and Sunday, April through November, departing from the Independence Visitor Center. Advance reservations are recommended. Call (215) 685-0754 or check out the Web site at www.muralarts.org. On the Web site you can print out your own self-guided walking- or driving-tour routes, which start at the Independence Visitor Center.

Walk down Thirteenth Street from Market to Lombard Street for a nice concentration of about seven murals, all within easy walking distance of the visitor center.

short biographies of each subject will interest children who are strong readers. For information call the visitor center at (215) 597-8974.

New Hall Military Museum (ages 6 and up)

Carpenter's Court between Third and Fourth Streets on the south side of Chestnut Street. Call the visitor center (215) 965-2305 for information or visit www.ushistory.org/tour/tour_milit.htm. Open daily 10 a.m. to 2 p.m., but hours may change seasonally. Admission is free.

The New Hall Military Museum offers a treasure trove for military buffs. On display are uniforms, dioramas, weapons, ship models, battle flags, and other memorabilia of the U.S. armed forces, going back to the Revolution. The museum features a gun deck preserved from an eighteenth-century naval ship, as well as interactive displays, such as one that allows visitors to control a ship's sails and rudder, and an honor roll of Marines who gave their lives in battle.

Bishop White House and Todd House (ages 8 and up)

Walnut Street between Third and Fourth Streets; (215) 965-2305. The Todd House and Bishop White House are open daily from 9 a.m. to 4:30 p.m. Tickets are $ for adults over 16 and may be purchased at the Independence National Historic Park Visitor Center.

The Bishop White House and Todd House offer contrasting early-American lifestyles.

Bishop White was the first Episcopal bishop of Pennsylvania and chaplain of the Continental Congress. Children may enjoy the boys' and girls' bedrooms, where initials were carved into the wood more than 200 years ago.

The Todd House, on the other hand, represents a middle-class Quaker home from the same period. Although well-to-do, this family lived more simply. After the death of John Todd, Dolley Todd married James Madison and became one of the most famous U.S. First Ladies.

Historical Reenactments in and around Independence National Historical Park (all ages)

Schedules are available in the visitor center. Or call (215) 629-4026 or visit the Web at http://historicphiladelphia.org.

Be inducted into the Continental Army. Sneak into Independence Hall at night. Hear strolling singers perform colonial ditties. The colonial actors from Historic Philadelphia, Inc., bring the past to life at selected sites in the historic district.

National Constitution Center (ages 8 and up)

Arch Street, between Fifth and Sixth Streets; www.constitutioncenter.org. Open 9:30 a.m. to 5 p.m. Mon through Fri, 9:30 a.m. to 6 p.m. Sat, and noon to 5 p.m. Sun. Admission is $. *Freedom Rising*, the theater show that begins the visitor experience, runs every half hour.

The National Constitution Center features *Freedom Rising*. This dramatic presentation uses both a live actor and a surround-screen to explore the meaning of the words of the Constitution and how they have been interpreted throughout our history. When you exit the Kimmel Theater, you'll enter the DeVos exhibit hall, where you can enjoy interactive exhibits and high-tech fun. Your children can enter a voting booth and vote for their all-time favorite president. Here's your chance to take a photo of your child being sworn in as president of the United States. But in Signers' Hall, where your child can mingle with life-size bronze sculptures of the signers of the Constitution, they're likely to linger a bit longer. The Delegates Cafe offers a kid-friendly menu. This stirring experience of the National Constitution Center will help you "enter as a visitor, leave as a citizen."

Declaration House (Graff House) (ages 8 and up)

Seventh and Market Streets; (215) 965-2305. Declaration House is open daily 9 a.m. to 1 p.m. Hours may change seasonally, so call ahead for information. Admission is **free.** Wheelchair accessible.

A couple of blocks away from the Liberty Bell is Declaration House (or Graff House), also part of the National Historic Park. In 1776 the Virginia delegate (Thomas Jefferson) to the Second Continental Congress rented rooms in this building, and it was in these rooms that he wrote a little document called the Declaration of Independence. School-age kids will be especially interested to see the exact place where the Declaration of Independence was penned.

Atwater Kent Museum (ages 6 and up)

15 S. Seventh St.; (215) 685-4830; www.philadelphiahistory.org. Open daily, except Tue, from 1 to 5 p.m. (bookstore, 10 a.m. to 4:30 p.m.). Closed on major holidays. Admission is $. Wheelchair accessible. **Free** admission on Sat.

On the same block as Declaration House, but not part of the park, is the Atwater Kent Museum, which tells the history of Philadelphia, a city whose story parallels that of our nation as a whole. Children under twelve enjoy the low-tech, hands-on approach. Special family programs include hatmaking or a visit from the "candy man," as well as exhibitions such as the annual Toys of Holidays Past, Trains and Trolleys, and Children Turning the Centuries.

Lights of Liberty (ages 6 and up)

Shows depart from PECO Energy Liberty Center, Sixth and Chestnut Streets, and take place throughout Independence National Historic Park. Tues through Sun dusk to 11:15 p.m., up to six shows per hour, May through Oct. Additional shows may be added during holiday seasons. Purchase tickets ($$$) at the PECO Energy Liberty Center, or reserve in advance by calling (215) LIBERTY or (877) GO-2-1776.

Your family can be a part of the Revolution! Lights of Liberty, the world's first walking sound and light show, uses the latest technology to immerse you in the Revolution as it happened and where it happened. Walking along these historic streets, you'll see five-story projections on historic buildings. Wireless headsets equipped with surround sound make you feel as if you're a member of the crowd surrounding Independence Hall as the Declaration is read. Headsets are available in a children's version, as well as several different languages. Since each person gets an individual headset, everyone can choose the version that's most appropriate. This is an excellent introduction to the city's historic district. There is some walking on cobblestone streets, which may be difficult for toddlers and parents using strollers.

U.S. Mint (ages 8 and up)
Fifth and Arch Streets; (215) 408-0114; www.usmint.gov. Sept through May, open 9 a.m. to 3 p.m. Mon through Fri; June through Aug, open Mon through Fri 9:30 a.m. to 4:30 p.m., Sat and Sun 10 a.m. to 4 p.m. Closed major holidays. Admission is **free.**

The U.S. Mint is the world's largest coinage operation. Visitors can take a forty-five-minute self-guided audiovisual tour and watch money in the making from a glass-enclosed gallery.

African-American Museum in Philadelphia (all ages)
701 Arch St.; (215) 574-0380; www.aampmuseum.org. Open Tues through Sat 10 a.m. to 5 p.m. and Sun noon to 5 p.m. Admission is $$ for adults; $ for seniors, students, and the physically challenged.

The African-American Museum houses 500,000 objects, images, and documents, including fine arts, folk art, photography, and more. Call for information about current exhibitions.

Betsy Ross House (ages 6 and up)
239 Arch St.; (215) 686-1252; www.ushistory.org/betsy. Open seven days a week Memorial Day through Labor Day, 10 a.m. to 5 p.m. In the off-season, open Tues through Sun 10 a.m. to 5 p.m. Open on Monday holidays including Martin Luther King Day, Presidents' Day, Columbus Day, and Veterans Day. Closed Thanksgiving, Christmas, and New Year's Day.

Just 2 blocks away from the U.S. Mint, on Arch Street between Second and Third Streets, is the Betsy Ross House. Yes, Betsy Ross really lived here at 239 Arch St. And, yes, she really did sew flags for the Continental Congress, although nobody is certain how active a role she played in the design of the American flag. Her renovated house is an excellent example of a colonial artisan's home. Greeters are in colonial garb, and tours are self-guided, with kid-friendly signs. The tour itself is brief, but there is continuous family-friendly entertainment on the stage in the courtyard. For example, you might meet Betsy Ross, Ben Franklin, or an eighteenth-century magician.

Elfreth's Alley (all ages)
Between Arch and Race Streets on Second Street in Old City; (215) 574-0560; www.elfreths alley.org. Mantua Maker's House Museum and Windsor Chairmaker's House are open Thurs through Sat 10 a.m. to 5 p.m. and Sun noon to 4 p.m. Admission is $ for adults and children 5 to 18; kids under 5 are **free.** Maximum admission per family, $$.

To get an idea of what Philadelphia may have looked like in the 1700s, take a walk down Elfreth's Alley, the oldest residential street in America. Families still inhabit this cobblestone alley tucked between Arch and Race Streets on Second Street in Old City. Walking down this charming street, you can imagine what life must have been like when these thirty houses were built between 1728 and 1836, when carpenters and other artisans lived here.

Number 126, the 1762 Mantua Maker's House Museum, and Number 124, the Windsor Chairmaker's House, are open to the public. (A mantua was a type of gown made by

Amazing
Philadelphia Facts

Philadelphia is America's number-one city for African-American tourism.

the house's first residents, a pair of seamstresses.) A guide will show you around. Other houses are open during special open-house events. On weekends in summer there are demonstrations of traditional crafts, such as basket weaving, broom making, needlework, and candle dipping. In June the Elfreth's Alley Association hosts Fête Days, when many of the houses and gardens are opened to the public and colonial crafts are demonstrated. On the second Fri of Dec, the alley hosts "Deck the Alley," a candlelight open-house tour. The garden and Windsor Chairmaker's House are wheelchair accessible. People still live in these houses, so remind your children to use their manners.

Fireman's Hall (all ages)

147 N. Second St.; (215) 923-1438. Open Tues through Sun 10 a.m. to 4:30 p.m. Admission is free.

Just about every family has somebody who wants to be a firefighter when he or she grows up. Fireman's Hall will fascinate that somebody. Ever since Benjamin Franklin founded the city's first fire department in 1736, Philadelphia has had fire equipment and firefighters. You'll see old-fashioned leather buckets, hand pumpers, three fire wagons that date from 1730, a spider hose reel from 1804, fire helmets from around the world, and a memorial wall for firefighters who died in the line of duty. Aspiring firefighters can try out the re-created living quarters of real firefighters or take the helm of a fireboat. Fireman's Hall is in the historic district, half a block from Elfreth's Alley.

Christ Church (ages 8 and up)

Second Street between Arch and Market Streets; call (215) 922-1695 to check winter hours and for group reservations; www.christchurchphila.org. The church is open to the public from 9 a.m. to 5 p.m. Mon through Sat and from 1 to 5 p.m. on Sun. In Jan the church is closed on Mon and Tues.

At Christ Church you can find the pews formerly occupied by George Washington, Benjamin Franklin, Betsy Ross, and other characters out of your history books. Kids will be interested to learn that this is also the birthplace of a character from a children's book: Amos, the mouse who befriended Ben Franklin in the classic Ben and Me. "The Nation's Church" has been an active Episcopalian parish for 300 years, with Sunday morning services at 9 and 11 and communion services on Wed at noon. All are welcome to attend.

Seeing Independence National Historic Park with Limited Time

If you have only time for a half-day visit, use your time wisely. Don't miss these highlights:

- Independence Visitor Center
- Independence Hall and Congress Hall
- Liberty Bell Pavilion

If you have a little more time, try:

- Elfreth's Alley
- Franklin Court

National Liberty Museum (ages 6 and up)

321 Chestnut St.; (215) 925-2800; www.libertymuseum.org. Open Tues through Sun 10 a.m. to 5 p.m. Closed on Mon in the winter. Admission is $$ for adults and $ for seniors and students.

The National Liberty Museum was created to celebrate our nation's history of freedom and the wonderfully diverse society it has produced. After your family has seen the places where our liberty was born, bring them here to learn how to preserve our liberty.

Using artwork, dioramas, displays, and hands-on experiences, visitors are encouraged to think about the responsibilities we all share. Visitors can "vote" on real contemporary issues and learn about more than 350 modern-day heroes of all backgrounds. They can see a model of Nelson Mandela's cell or Anne Frank's attic. (For parents of younger children, it is easy to bypass the more disturbing images.) First, view the introductory film, and then go up to the third floor and work your way down. Doing this, you'll end your experience at the shredder machine, where kids are encouraged to write down "mean words" they've heard or used and put them into the shredder, where they are ripped into colorful shards. A walk across the "Bridge of Forgiveness" completes the experience.

Highlighted in the museum are many beautiful glass sculptures. Glass is used as a metaphor for, and illustration of, liberty because once broken, it cannot be put back together the same way. This is an inspiring trip, especially for older children who are beginning to be aware of social issues.

Franklin Court (ages 6 and up)

Market Street between Third and Fourth Streets; (215) 965-2305. Open Mon through Fri 10 a.m. to 4 p.m., Sat and Sun 10 a.m. to 5 p.m.

Historians know very little about the appearance of Franklin's house, which once stood on this site. Today an oversized "Ghost Structure," designed by world-famous architect Robert Venturi, marks the spot. Here you can also see the Franklin Print Shop, U.S. Postal Service Museum, and the Franklin Museum. The underground exhibits include Franklin's many inventions and a great twenty-minute filmography.

"Ben Franklin" and Franklin's Friends (all ages)

For details contact "Ben Franklin" at P.O. Box 40178, Philadelphia 19106; call (215) 238-0871, fax (215) 238-9102, or e-mail Ben1776@aol.com. For Franklin's Friends call (215) 238-0871; www.ben1776.com. Free.

"Ben Franklin" performs at Franklin Court daily, Memorial Day through Labor Day, at 11 a.m. His "Friends" perform a program called "Meet America's Founders" from Carpenters' Hall Tues through Sun, Memorial Day through Labor Day, from noon to 2 p.m. Another friend demonstrates the music of the glass armonica, which Franklin invented, Tues through Sun, Memorial Day through Labor Day also at Carpenters' Hall.

City Tavern (ages 6 and up)

138 S. Second St.; (215) 413-1443; www.citytavern.com. Open Sun through Thur 11:30 a.m. to 9 p.m., Fri and Sat 11:30 a.m. to 10 p.m.

Now that you're completely steeped in history, why not eat a historic meal? Dining here gives a real feeling of the past. This historic gathering place, now part of the Independence National Historic Park, was opened in 1774. Paul Revere came here in May of that year to announce that the Port of Boston was closed. General Washington set up headquarters here, and Benedict Arnold slept here. John Adams called it "the most genteel tavern in America."

The building was rebuilt in 1975 to look exactly as it did in colonial times. The tavern serves Thomas Jefferson Ale, brewed exclusively by the Dock Street Brewing Company, along with colonial specialties such as turkey-thigh stew and beef and pork pie. More tame entrees are also available, but this is not the place to bring picky eaters.

City Tavern is in the heart of the Historic District, a short walk from Elfreth's Alley.

ALSO IN THE HISTORIC DISTRICT

Other sites within the Historic District include **Congregation Mikveh Israel** and the **National Museum of American Jewish History** at 55 N. Fifth St., which tells the story of the American-Jewish experience. Open daily except Sat and Jewish holidays. Admission is $. Call (215) 923-3811 or visit www.nmajh.org for more information.

The Waterfront/Penn's Landing

New things are happening all over Philadelphia, and the site that once hosted William Penn's arrival in 1682 bustles with activity, including a new Hyatt Regency hotel, with an outdoor waterfront cafe and Keating's River Grill, and a state-of-the-art amphitheater with new festival space encompassing the area from Walnut to Market Street along Columbus Boulevard.

On the Philadelphia side of the river, you can enjoy RiverRink (in season), the Independence Seaport Museum, Dave & Buster's, and lots of shops.

April to September you can take the RiverLink ferry across the river to Camden, New Jersey, to see the Adventure Aquarium and Children's Garden or attend a concert at the Tweeter Center. To find out more about these attractions, check the Web site www.pennslandingcorp.com. For information on RiverLink call (215) 925-LINK or visit www.riverlink.org.

The *Spirit of Philadelphia* cruises leave from Penn's Landing at Lombard Circle, near the Chart House Restaurant. For information call (866) 455-3866) or check www.spiritof philadelphia.com.

Independence Seaport Museum and Historic Ships (all ages)

211 Columbus Blvd. at Walnut Street; (215) (215) 413-8655; www.phillyseaport.org. Open daily 10 a.m. to 5 p.m. Admission to the Museum and Historic Ship Zone (Olympia and Becuna) is $$ for adults; $ for children ages 5 to 12. Children under 5 enter **free.** The museum offers **free** admission on Sunday morning from 10 a.m. to noon.

Start your visit to Penn's Landing with the Independence Seaport Museum, which uses exciting family-oriented interactive exhibits to tell the story of four centuries of maritime history. The collection of nautical artifacts and ship models that were formerly housed in the old Philadelphia Maritime Museum have been enlivened at every turn by audiovisuals and multimedia computers. Kids can try out an immigrant's steerage bunk or a rowing machine or learn about the history of underwater exploration. This is a great place for any folks with a taste for the nautical.

In exhibits like Home Port Philadelphia, children can chart a course for Penn's Landing and navigate underneath the three-story replica of the Benjamin Franklin Bridge. Protecting the Nation features the bridge of the guided-missile destroyer

USS *Lawrence,* most recently used in the Persian Gulf Conflict. Divers of the Deep explores the development of diving technologies such as helmets and scuba gear.

The Independence Seaport Museum also includes Historic Ship Zone, where you can see two real vessels: the *Olympia* and the *Becuna* (319 Delaware Ave., at Spruce Street; 215-922-1898). Step aboard the *Olympia,* flagship of Admiral Dewey's Asiatic fleet, and see the bronze impressions of the admiral's feet in the exact spot where he stood in 1898 and said, "You may fire when you are ready, Gridley." Then take the kids aboard the *Becuna,* a guppy-class submarine from World War II, where sixty-six men shared the tight living quarters.

If you purchase a RiverPass ($$$), it includes round-trip passage on the RiverLink ferry from Penn's Landing to Camden, New Jersey (a twelve-minute trip), plus admission to the Independence Seaport Museum on the Philly side and Adventure Aquarium on the Jersey side. The recently revamped aquarium features "breakfast with the hippos" in the West African River exhibit and a "swim with the sharks" encounter. For RiverPass tickets call (215) 925-LINK or visit www.riverlink.org.

Blue Cross River Rink (ages 3 and up)

Columbus Boulevard and Market Street; (215) 925-RINK; www.riverrink.com. Seasonal hours late Nov through Feb: Mon through Thurs 6 to 9 p.m.; Fri 6 p.m. to 1 a.m.; Sat 12:30 p.m. to 1 a.m.; Sun 12:30 to 9 p.m. Admission: $$, skate rental $; skate sizes from toddler size 9 (single blade) to adult 14. Skating lessons are available on Sat morning from 10 a.m. until noon. Special sled skating sessions for people with disabilities are offered every Sun from 9:30 until 10:30 a.m. Reservations required for lessons and sled skating.

This popular Olympic-size attraction overlooks the huge Benjamin Franklin Fridge—er, Bridge—and the Delaware River. If your little ones get too chilly, they can take a break in the heated pavilion, which offers a snack bar and game room. Live evening DJs and karaoke nights on weekends attract an older crowd. Parking is available on-site ($$).

Tip: download coupons from the rink's Web site to take advantage of discounts.

Dave & Buster's (ages 6 and up before 10 p.m.)

Pier 19 North, 325 N. Columbus Blvd. (formerly Delaware Avenue); (215) 413-1951. Open to children 11:30 a.m. to midnight.

Older children or young adults will probably enjoy Dave & Buster's. This unusual attraction bills itself as a family entertainment center with something for everyone.

Parents should be aware, however, that not all activities are appropriate for all ages. For example, many of the video games have violent content. There are also bars here. Dave & Buster's has taken over all 70,000 square feet of Pier 19 on the Philadelphia waterfront and filled it with Skee-Ball, hoop toss, video games, a variety of bars and restaurants for different tastes, music, and virtual-reality games. You can play golf on a virtual golf course. There are billiards, shuffleboard, and an outdoor deck with a view of the Ben Franklin Bridge.

All games are activated by a "power card," with additional charges for food, beverages, billiards, and the turbo-ride (and these can add up for a group). No one under twenty-one is permitted unless accompanied by a parent. Clean and neat clothing required; no tank tops. No more than three children to one guardian over twenty-five years of age.

Parkway Attractions

Philadelphia has a tradition of excellence in museums. On Benjamin Franklin Parkway, sometimes called "Philadelphia's Champs-Elysées," there's something for everyone—from toddlers to teenagers. We've found that for most of the museums on the parkway, it's best to beat the crowd by arriving in the morning right when the museum opens.

Academy of Natural Sciences (all ages)

Nineteenth Street and Ben Franklin Parkway; (215) 299-1000. Open Mon through Fri 10 a.m. to 4:30 p.m., weekends and selected holidays 10 a.m. to 5 p.m. Admission is $$; under 3, free. Wheelchair accessible.

You really should not miss the butterfly exhibit, which can only be described as "magical." One six-year-old insisted on walking through twice! On the third floor, Outside In is a hands-on exhibit for children twelve and under. Kids can touch mice, snakes, "legless lizards" (skinks), frogs, turtles, and enormous cockroaches from Madagascar. Enthusiastic and well-informed volunteers are available to answer questions. Near Outside In is a robotic dinosaur not to be missed. It roars! (Very little children may be frightened.)

The Academy of Natural Sciences is the oldest continuously operating natural-history institution in the Western Hemisphere. Some of the oldest residents in Dinosaur Hall are *Tyrannosaurus rex* and *Gigantosaurus,* one of the largest meat-eating dinosaurs ever discovered. In The Dig, visitors can be paleontologists and dig for real fossils with real tools.

Make sure you check the schedule when you arrive at the academy, because there are live animal shows and films at regular intervals. Family memberships are available.

The Franklin Institute (ages 5 and up)

Twentieth Street and Benjamin Franklin Parkway; (215) 448-1200; www.fi.edu. The Science Center is open daily 9:30 a.m. to 5 p.m. The Mandell Center is open daily 9:30 a.m. to 5 p.m. The Tuttleman IMAX Theater is open museum hours, plus until 9 p.m. on Fri and Sat evenings. Call for prices and IMAX and planetarium showtimes. Admission starts at $$ for children 4 to 11, $$$ for adults.

If you visited the Franklin Institute as a child, you'll probably remember walking through the model of the human heart, following the path that the blood vessels take, hearing the sound of the heartbeat. The popular model has received a complete renovation and upgrade. Now the heart has more elaborate sounds and special effects and is enhanced by other exhibits, including video of actual cardiac surgery.

The Franklin Institute was founded in 1824, and pioneered the idea of hands-on museum displays. In 2010 two perennial favorites reopen after a complete overhaul. Our Changing Earth examines climate change and weather forecasting, while Electricity includes a sustainable dance floor. The museum has continued its tradition of forward-looking exhibits. The Sports Challenge uses interactive devices and virtual-reality technology to teach kids about the physics, physiology, and material science behind their favorite sports. In Kidscience, children ages five to eight can explore a cave, turn the crank of a waterwheel, and have a lot of fun while learning basic science concepts. In The Tram Factory you can visit the Franklin Institute's beloved Baldwin steam locomotive, as the centerpiece of the Railroad Hall. And don't miss the indoor Sky Bike.

Be sure to also check out the Science Center, which includes exhibits about flight, optical illusions, and the Fels Planetarium.

The Tuttleman IMAX Theater showcases popular movie experiences on its huge screen, giving a 180-degree field of view. Check to see what movie is currently playing, but the short feature *Philadelphia Symphony,* which usually precedes the main show, presents an excellent introduction to Philly.

The gift shops offer an unusual assortment of educational and scientifically oriented toys, books, posters, and so forth.

Amazing
Philadelphia Facts

Founded in 1812, Philadelphia's Academy of Natural Sciences is the oldest scientific research institution in the Western Hemisphere.

Wachovia Science Park (all ages)

Twenty-first Street, between Winter and Race Streets; (215) 448-1200. Admission through Franklin Institute. Open seven days a week 9:30 a.m. to 5 p.m. May through Sept, weather permitting.

This family-centered outdoor learning area includes more than twenty elements, such as miniature golf, swings, sundials, sand pendulums, hide-and-seek tunnels, and more.

Free Library of Philadelphia (all ages)

Nineteenth and Vine Streets. Call (215) 686-5322 for hours; www.library.phila.gov. Admission is **free.**

The Free Library of Philadelphia stands across Logan Square from the Franklin Institute and the Academy of Natural Sciences and down the parkway from the Art Museum and Rodin Museum. It houses more than six million books, magazines, newspapers, and other printed items and frequently hosts special events and exhibits. The library is open daily in winter, closed Sunday in summer. On Sunday there are tours of its remarkable rare books department.

Rodin Museum (ages 6 and up)

Twenty-second Street and Benjamin Franklin Parkway; (215) 568-6026; www.rodinmuseum .org. Open Tues through Sun 10 a.m. to 5 p.m. A per-person contribution ($) is suggested. **Free** guided tours are available at 1:30 p.m. on Tues, Thurs, Sun, and on the first and third Sat of the month.

Everybody knows Rodin's *Thinker*. You can see this popular sculpture at the Rodin Museum, along with the most complete collection of Auguste Rodin's work outside Paris. This museum is administered by the Philadelphia Museum of Art, down the parkway.

Philadelphia Museum of Art (ages 6 and up)

Located at the end of Benjamin Franklin Parkway at Twenty-sixth Street; (215) 763-8100; www.philamuseum.org. Open Tues through Sun 10 a.m. to 5 p.m., Fri until 8:45 p.m. Admission is $$ for adults and students age 13 and up; children to age 12, **free.** On the first Sunday of each month, the rule is "Pay what you wish, all day." **Free** guided tours are conducted hourly between 11 a.m. and 3 p.m. Tours are also available in foreign languages (215-684-7923) and sign language (215-684-7601). The Museum Restaurant is open for lunch Tues through Sun 11:30 a.m. to 2:30 p.m. and for dinner Wed 5 p.m. to 7:30 p.m.

Sunday brunch is available from 11 a.m. to 3:30 p.m. The cafeteria is open 10 a.m. to 4:30 p.m. Wheelchair accessible.

At the far end of the parkway, on the other side of Eakins Oval, are some steps that many people will recognize. Who can forget that memorable scene from *Rocky* when the boxer runs up all these steps? But the collection inside the Philadelphia Museum of Art is even more memorable—with a permanent collection of some 300,000 works, including one of the largest and most important collections of European art in the United States. The art museum takes a somewhat unusual approach, juxtaposing the painting, sculpture, furniture, ceramics, textiles, and architectural elements from the same period to convey a sense of that time. The museum is also known for its outstanding collection of rural Pennsylvania crafts and works by Thomas Eakins. A seven-year-old boy could spend all day in the Arms and Armor collection.

The art museum's neoclassical facade stands at the end of Benjamin Franklin Parkway at Twenty-sixth Street, within walking distance (unless your children's legs are very short) of the Franklin Institute, Free Library of Philadelphia, Logan Circle, and other parkway sites. The Perelman Building, just across Fairmount Avenue from the main building, extends exhibit space for the collections (it is not open on Friday evening).

"Something every Sunday" is how the museum describes its family activities. Different programs are offered, usually on a walk-in basis, for families with children ages three to thirteen. Most of the programs take place on Sun at 10:15 a.m. or 1:30 p.m. Programs range from storytelling to hands-on art activities, with titles like Tales and Treasures, Try a Technique, and Gallery Games. Many of these programs are **free,** and the rest are $. Accompanying adults are free. Children especially like the Japanese teahouse, Chinese palace hall, and the thirteenth-century French cloister. Every day of the week, you can pick up a family-oriented self-guided tour brochure at the West Information Desk. For information about family activities and children's art classes, call (215) 684-7605. Wheelchair accessible, with changing tables in the restrooms.

Fairmount Park Waterworks Interpretive Center (ages 4 and up)
640 Waterworks Dr.; (215) 685-0723; www.fairmountwaterworks.org.

If you've ever driven the Schuylkill Expressway in Philly, you may have noticed the striking colonnaded building below the art museum. This is the Waterworks, the nation's first municipal water center. The Waterworks Interpretive Center is a humorous, approachable combination of environmental education, architectural history, and cultural heritage. Combine a visit here with a walk along Boathouse Row, a stroll through the azalea garden, and a tour of the art museum.

Eastern State Penitentiary (ages 7 and up)
Fairmount Avenue at Twenty-second Street, 5 blocks from the Philadelphia Museum of Art and the parkway; (215) 236-3300; www.easternstate.org. Open Apr through Nov, Wed through Sun 10 a.m. to 5 p.m. Closed Mon and Tues and the months of Dec through Mar except for private tours. Guided tours are available every hour from 10 a.m. to 4 p.m. Chil-

Amazing
Philadelphia Facts

Fairmount Park is the nation's largest landscaped city park.

dren under 7 are not admitted. **Admission: adults, students, and seniors $$; children ages 7 to 17 $.**

When Charles Dickens visited the United States in 1842, there were two sights he didn't want to miss: Niagara Falls and the Eastern State Penitentiary. It has been called the most influential prison in the world because its design was grounded on the nineteenth century's most modern ideas about civic responsibility and criminal behavior. Instead of using physical punishment, this prison was designed to encourage solitude and penitence.

The History Channel and the *New York Times* have featured the prison, and the number of visitors has tripled in recent years.

Al Capone did time here, as did "gentleman bandit" Willie Sutton. An operating prison for more than 140 years, until 1971, the building has been reopened as the Eastern State Penitentiary Historic Site Society makes plans for its future. At present there are special art exhibits here, and sometimes dramatic productions.

The building has been made safe for tours but has otherwise been left "as is." Visitors must wear hard hats and stay with tour groups. Most people won't have to be reminded; the decaying plaster, dampness, and remnants of prison life make this a pretty eerie place—great for teenagers! The Halloween Ghost Tours are very popular; call (215) 763-NITE. The gift shop offers T-shirts, posters, and books with a prison theme.

Fairmount Park

At 8,700 acres, Philadelphia's Fairmount Park is one of the world's largest city parks and an amazing source of activities. The park includes: Andorra Natural Area, Bartram's Gardens, Boathouse Row, Japanese House and Garden, Smith Playground and Playhouse, the newly relocated Please Touch Museum, and the Philadelphia Zoo. Of lesser interest to families with children are the following sites: Horticultural Center, Ryerss Library and Museum, and the ten colonial mansions of Fairmount Park. Although the Philadelphia Museum of Art and the Fairmount Park Waterworks are technically part of Fairmount Park as well, they're found here under "Parkway Attractions."

The Fairmount Park Conservancy (215-988-9334 or www.fairmountparkconservancy .org) offers maps and event information. For a guided tour of the mansions, please contact Mansions of Fairmount Park, Park House Guides Office, Philadelphia Museum of Art, or call (215) 684-7926. Trolleys circulate around the park, stopping at all the historic mansions so that you may tour the houses on your own. For information call (215) 925-TOUR.

Andorra Natural Area (all ages)

Between Ridge and Germantown Pikes on Northwestern Avenue; (215) 685-9285. The park is open daily dawn to dusk. The visitor center is usually open on weekends noon to 4 p.m. **Free;** some educational programs have fees.

Andorra Natural Area offers many wonderful programs for children including nature trails, exhibits, and special events. Most activities begin at Treehouse Visitor Center, a one-hundred-year-old home where you can explore a touch table and other exhibits. Even when the visitor center is closed, there are maps, activity sheets, program calendars, and other information available.

Two annual festivals emphasize hands-on participation. In Oct, you can pick apples and make them into apple butter at the Harvest Festival, and in Feb you can tap a tree at the Maple Sugar Festival.

Historic Bartram's Garden (gardens: all ages; house: ages 8 and up)

Fifty-fourth Street and Lindbergh Boulevard; (215) 729-5281; www.bartramsgarden.org. The garden is open daily from 10 a.m. to 5 p.m.; admission is **free.** The home is open Tues through Sun noon to 4 p.m. There is a charge ($) for the house tour.

The oldest surviving botanical garden in the country includes the pre-Revolutionary home of botanist John Bartram, as well as forty-four acres of gardens. Now it's a verdant plantation surrounded by industrial sites. Boat rides connect the gardens to the Schuylkill Banks, a downtown greenway; check www.schuylkillbanks.org or call (215) 222-6030.

Boathouse Row (all ages)

A lovely place for a stroll along the Schuylkill River, Boathouse Row consists of twelve nineteenth-century buildings where Philadelphia's rowing clubs keep their boats. The outline of each boathouse is trimmed with lights to create a luminous view of the boathouses from across the river at night.

Amazing Philadelphia Facts

More Revolutionary War battles were fought within a 50-mile radius of Philadelphia than in all the New England states combined. It was also the capital during the Revolution, except for nine months when it was occupied by the British. It then served as the nation's capital from 1790 to 1800.

Baby Loves **Disco**

Founded in Philly, Baby Loves Disco is an afternoon dance party featuring real music spun and mixed by real DJs blending classic disco tunes. Kids and parents can shake their booties at Shampoo Nightclub, 417 N. Eighth St. Get tickets online at www.babylovesdisco.com or call (215) 922-7500.

Japanese House and Garden (ages 5 and up)

Near the Horticultural Center, at Belmont and Montgomery Avenues; (215) 878-5097; www .shofuso.com. Open May 1 through Oct, Tues through Sun 10 a.m. to 4 p.m. Admission is $; children under 6 enter **free.**

Now in its sixth decade, the Japanese House and Garden offers many events that your family might enjoy, including a Japanese tea ceremony presented in the Japanese House. At the annual Children's Festival, held in May, kids can learn about origami, kimonos, Japanese crafts, dolls, and armor. They can also see a traditional tea ceremony, hear traditional music and stories, and try Japanese food. This event is modeled after the Japanese celebrations of Boys' Day and Girls' Day. At the Summer Festival in June, kids can participate in the beautiful custom of launching lantern boats.

Please Touch Museum (ages 2 to 8)

Memorial Hall, Fairmount Park, 4231 Avenue of the Republic (formerly North Concourse Drive; enter 4231 N. Concourse Dr. for GPS directions); (215) 581-3181; www.pleasetouch museum.org. Hours are 9 a.m. to 5 p.m. Mon through Sat, 11 a.m. to 5 p.m. Sun. Admission is $$ for ages 1 and over; children under 1 are **free.**

Named one of the best children's museums in the world by the *Observer of London,* and rated one of the "Top 50 Attractions by Child Appeal" by Zagat's *U.S. Family Travel Guide,* the Please Touch Museum is gathering even more honors in its new home. Memorial Hall was the grand site of the 1876 Centennial Exhibition, and gave the museum plenty of growing room. While other museums cater to school-age children, the Please Touch Museum is perfect for kids ages one to seven. Your child can visit again and again, always discovering something new.

There are six major exhibit areas. Each offers hands-on exploration: City Capers lets kids pretend to be neighborhood helpers. Flight Fantasy features a human-powered hamster wheel. Roadside Attractions will lure your favorite little motor-head, while Wonderland and River Adventures offer more thrills. The Centennial Exploration shows kids what the 1876 fair looked like, and the giant Liberty torch and arm in the museum's vast atrium is a colorful sculpture composed entirely of cast-off toys. Please Touch offers a full calendar of special events and a Playhouse Theater with live performances. Outside, an antique Dentzel Carousel ($ additional) offers gentle rides.

All those great new features have attracted great big crowds. The museum offers a few tips to avoid them: Come on Monday, when groups can't visit; choose afternoons instead of mornings; and remember that rainy days are always the busiest.

Adults must accompany children into the museum and are encouraged to play just as much as their young companions. Wheelchair accessible. Strollers are not permitted on the gallery floor.

Smith Memorial Playground and Playhouse (ages 2 to 10)

Kelly Drive; (215) 765-4325; http://smithkidsplayplace.org. Enter the park at the statue of Ulysses S. Grant on Kelly Drive and follow the signs to the playground. The playhouse is open year-round Tues through Sun 10 a.m. to 4 p.m. Birthday parties may be held for children age 5 and younger on weekends (two weeks' advance reservations required). The playhouse is open to children ages 5 and under, and the playground is open to ages 10 and under. Admission is free.

Smith Memorial Playground and Playhouse in Fairmount Park has hosted an average of 1,000 children daily every summer for nearly 105 years! After its famous giant wooden slide was renovated, the playground added Swing City, a giant net climber, seesaw, and climber/spinner that can entertain 200 children at a time.

Inside the playhouse there are three floors of activities for preschoolers. The train on the first floor was donated by the singing group Boyz II Men, whose members played here as children. In Smithville (on the basement level), little kids climb into the kid-size cars and "drive" on kid-size roads, with delightful details like traffic lights and parking meters.

During the summer months, there is an outside carousel for preschoolers, two swimming pools (including a wading pool for little ones), and a concession stand. Adjacent to Smith Memorial, on its property, is the only Frisbee golf course in the city. Free and open to all ages.

Smith offers a Story Time for preschoolers every second Wednesday of the month at 10:30 a.m. Each thirty-five-minute session features the reading of a special story followed by a small related activity. Story Time is open to children three to five years old (preregistration required).

Winner of several "Best of Philly" awards for birthday parties and the Giant Slide and dubbed "Best Playground for Children," Smith's is partially wheelchair accessible. There are restrooms in the house, and a concession stand is open seasonally. There is also plenty of free parking.

The Rest of Center City

Former Philadelphia mayor Edward G. Rendell realized the importance of tourism to his city. One of his first actions upon taking office was to start renovating the amazing City Hall (at the intersection of Broad and Market Streets, ground zero of William Penn's original plan for the city) and open it for free tours.

City Hall (observation deck, all ages; tour, ages 8 and up)

Broad and Market Streets; (215) 686-2840. Tours available daily at 12:30 p.m. Tours are free, but donations are welcome. The observation deck is open daily 9:30 a.m. to 4:15 p.m.

See the courtroom where the film Philadelphia was made and the 548-foot-tall tower that is topped by a statue of William Penn. The bronze statue was designed by Alexander Milne Calder, grandfather of the twentieth-century mobile creator Alexander Calder. The statue is 37 feet tall. Billy Penn's nose alone is 18 inches long.

A virtual tour is available at http://philadelphiacityhallwillpennshomepage.org. Volunteer guides from the Foundation for Architecture conduct real tours departing from Room 121, the Tour Office, Mon through Fri at 12:30 p.m. There are tours of the tower only Mon through Fri every fifteen minutes from 9:30 a.m. to 4:30 p.m. All tours are free.

The observation deck (at William Penn's feet) affords a spectacular view of the city.

Claes Oldenburg's Clothespin (all ages)

Located in Centre Square Plaza at Fifteenth and Walnut Streets.

Either you love it or you hate it. Either way, Claes Oldenburg's public sculpture of a giant clothespin is one you're not likely to forget.

Robert Indiana's *Love* (all ages)

Located at Kennedy Plaza, Fifteenth Street and JFK.

This public sculpture became famous in the 1960s and 1970s. It has been cleaned and looks better than ever.

Pennsylvania Academy of the Fine Arts (ages 8 and up)

118 N. Broad St. at Cherry; (215) 972-7600; www.pafa.org. The museum is open Tues through Sat 10 a.m. to 5 p.m. and on Sun 11 a.m. to 5 p.m. Closed Mon and New Year's Day, Thanksgiving, and Christmas. Admission is $$ for adults, seniors, and students with ID; $ for children under 5 to 12; and free to members and children under 5.

Walking up Broad Street near Cherry, you can't miss the graceful facade of the Pennsylvania Academy of the Fine Arts, home of the nation's first art museum and its first art school, the Academy School. The building, with its Gothic arches and lacy ironwork, is a masterpiece of High Victorian Gothic architecture. The galleries in the historic landmark building have been completely renovated and include American masterworks by Charles Willson Peale (one of the academy's founders), Thomas Eakins (who served as the academy's director during the 1880s), Mary Cassatt, Winslow Homer, Andrew Wyeth, Alexander Calder, Louise Nevelson, and many others.

You can make your visit more lively with Family Inform, an audio-guide system. Look around the galleries to find numbers that you key into the audio machine's keypad, and you can hear messages about the works of art.

Academy of Music (ages 10 and up)

Broad and Locust Streets; call (215) 893-1935 for information or to make reservations. Tickets available through www.anytickets.com or www.rpac.org.

That spectacular opera house seen in the movie The Age of Innocence is Philadelphia's own Academy of Music. You can see the landmark if you attend a concert by the Philadelphia Orchestra (the "Sound All Around" series for kids ages three to five is held here) or a performance by the Opera Company of Philadelphia. But by reservation only, you can take a one-hour afternoon tour of this beloved building on Broad and Locust Streets, including a peek backstage and into the artists' dressing rooms.

The Kimmel Center for the Performing Arts (ages 3 and up)

260 S. Broad St. on the Avenue of the Arts; (215) 790-5800; www.rpac.org.

The Kimmel Center joins the Academy of Music to become one of the nation's largest performing arts complexes. The Kimmel Center and Academy of Music are home to eight of Philadelphia's premier ensembles: the Philadelphia Orchestra, the Opera Company of Philadelphia, the Pennsylvania Ballet, American Theater Arts for Youth, the Chamber Orchestra of Philadelphia, PHILADANCO, the Philadelphia Chamber Music Society, and Peter Nero and the Philly Pops.

Tickets to any of the theaters in Kimmel Center and Academy of Music are available at the Web site above, which also lists many **free** family-friendly performances.

Reading Terminal Market (all ages)

Twelfth and Arch Streets; (215) 922-2317. Open Mon through Sat 8 a.m. to 6 p.m. year-round. The Amish merchants occupy the northwest corner of the market and are open Wed 8 a.m. to 3 p.m. and Thurs through Sat 8 a.m. to 5 p.m.

If you're hungry and you don't know what to eat, or if you're planning a picnic, stop by the Reading Terminal Market, where farmers and merchants from around the Philadelphia area (many of them Amish) sell very fresh produce, cheese, fish, meats, baked goods, and much more. There are over forty different restaurants and lunch stands, offering everything from cheesesteaks to sushi.

While you're in the area, head across the street and up the stairs to the old Reading Terminal, which has been converted as part of the Pennsylvania Convention Center. This cavernous hall was at one time the main train station in downtown Philadelphia.

Chinatown (all ages)

Between Arch and Vine Streets, Eleventh to Eighth Street. For information about Chinatown call (215) 922-2156.

Go 1 block east of the Reading Terminal, and you're in the heart of Philadelphia's Chinatown. Stop here for authentic Chinese cuisine and products.

Edgar Allan Poe National Memorial (ages 10 and up)

532 N. Seventh St.; (215) 597-8780; www.nps.gov/edal. Open Nov through May, Wed through Sun 9 a.m. to 5 p.m.; June through Oct, daily 9 a.m. to 5 p.m. Closed Thanksgiving, Christmas, and New Year's Day. Admission is **free.**

A couple of long blocks north of Chinatown is the house where Edgar Allan Poe lived with his wife and mother-in-law in 1843–44. There is a brief slide presentation about the author's life.

Rosenbach Museum and Library (ages 10 and up)

2010 Delancey Place, on Rittenhouse Square; (215) 732-1600; www.rosenbach.org. Open Tues through Sun 11 a.m. to 4 p.m. (last tour, 2:45 p.m.). Closed Mon, national holidays, and Aug 1 to the second Tues after Labor Day. Admission is $$; seniors, students, and children $.

To get a feeling of a traditional, stately Philadelphia neighborhood, stroll around the blocks surrounding Rittenhouse Square. On Rittenhouse Square, the Rosenbach Museum and Library houses an astounding collection of rare books, manuscripts, antique furniture, silver, porcelain, and works of art in the beautiful home of the Rosenbach brothers, who lived here from 1948 until their deaths in 1952 and 1953. This wonderful museum used to appeal strictly to adults and literary folks, but its exhibits changed when beloved children's author Maurice Sendak donated his illustrations and manuscripts for his famous children's books to the Rosenbach. With expanded exhibit space, the Maurice Sendak Gallery now mounts shows related to Sendak's work and characters. The museum owns more than 3,000 original drawings by Sendak. On display may be originals from *Where the Wild Things Are, Higglety Pigglety Pop!* or *Chicken Soup with Rice.* The Rosenbach Museum Shop offers books and prints signed by Maurice Sendak, as well as an assortment of unsigned Sendak books, prints, toys, and more.

In the adjoining town house are more than 30,000 rare books and 300,000 manuscripts, including letters penned by George Washington, Thomas Jefferson, Benjamin Franklin, and Abraham Lincoln. You may also see Lewis Carroll's own copy of *Alice's Adventures in Wonderland,* the manuscript for James Joyce's *Ulysses,* and the notes for Bram Stoker's *Dracula.*

For information about wheelchair accessibility, call (215) 732-1600, ext. 25, or visit www.rosenbach.org.

Avenue of **the Arts**

Broad Street south of City Hall has been renamed the Avenue of the Arts. Already home to the Academy of Music, Kimmel Center, the Merriam Theater, and the University of the Arts, several new theaters have been added: Wilma Theater, Freedom Repertory Theater, and Prince Music Theater.

Mutter Museum and College Gallery of the College of Physicians of Philadelphia (ages 10 and up)

19 S. Twenty-second St., between Chestnut and Market Streets; (215) 563-3737; www.coll phyphil.org. The Mutter Museum and College Gallery are open Mon through Sat 10 a.m. to 5 p.m. Admission is $$ for adults, seniors, students, and children 6 to 18; children under 6 enter **free.**

For years the College of Physicians of Philadelphia (not an educational institution but the nation's oldest private medical society) has maintained the Mutter Museum of medical anomalies. Begun as a teaching collection for medical students in a time when students had little access to clinical situations, it has become known for its wall of more than one hundred skulls, the tumor removed from President Cleveland's jaw, and the preserved body of an eighteenth-century woman.

The college's exhibits, however, are now moving into the twenty-first century by taking on some of the hottest issues in current medicine. The College Gallery features temporary exhibits that examine important issues. The C. Everett Koop Community Medical Information Center (CHIC) is a free library on health, with books, CD-ROMs, Internet access, and videos.

North Philadelphia

Philadelphia is home to a huge number of colleges and universities. Besides adding to the rich cultural diversity of the city, these institutions offer some unusual museums.

Temple University Dental Museum (ages 8 and up)

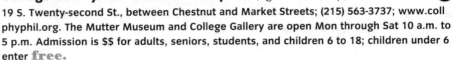

Broad Street and Allegheny Avenue; (215) 707-2816; www.temple.edu/dentistry/museum .htm. Open by appointment only.

The Victorian dental office, on the third floor of the dental school, is open full-time, no appointment necessary. By appointment only, you can also tour an unusual collection of dental memorabilia going back to the 1700s. Its best-known piece is the first dental chair in the United States, dating from the 1790s.

Wagner Free Institute of Science (ages 8 and up)

1700 W. Montgomery Ave.; (215) 763-6529; www.wagnerfreeinstitute.org. Open Tues through Fri 9 a.m. to 4 p.m. for self-guided tours. Special programs are offered on Sat; call for schedule. Admission is **free.**

The Wagner Free Institute of Science presents an unusual opportunity to visit a science museum that looks pretty much the way it did in about 1890. This is a great place for amateur naturalists and paleontologists.

Amateur scientist William Wagner founded the institute in 1855 to provide free science education to all, regardless of race, gender, or financial resources. He used his personal collections to illustrate the lectures, and these objects now form the core of the museum's exhibits, which were given their present arrangement after Wagner's death in 1885.

More than 100,000 specimens, including fossils, minerals, shells, mounted animals, skeletons, and insects, are displayed in the Victorian cherrywood cases. (Very young children may have difficulty seeing into some of the cases.) All children under eighteen must be accompanied by an adult. The institute also offers evening and Saturday-morning science classes (off-site) for ages twelve and up.

Shoe Museum (ages 10 and up)

Eighth and Race Streets, at the Temple University School of Podiatric Medicine. Free tours must be arranged in advance by calling (215) 625-5243; http://podiatry.temple.edu.

A unique diversion, the Shoe Museum at the Temple University School of Podiatric Medicine displays footwear belonging to celebrities such as Ringo Starr, Julius Erving, Lucille Ball, Mamie Eisenhower, and Ronald and Nancy Reagan. There are also shoes from around the world, tiny Chinese shoes for bound feet, huge shoes for circus giants, tap shoes, ballet slippers, and many more.

West Philadelphia

There is an abundance of learning opportunities throughout West Philadelphia. The University of Pennsylvania and Drexel University are just two of the must-see sights in the area.

The Philadelphia Zoo (all ages)

3400 W. Girard Ave.; (215) 243-1100; www.philadelphiazoo.org. Open daily 10 a.m. to 5 p.m. Mar 1 to Nov 1; 9:30 to 4 p.m. Nov 2 through Feb 28; closed major holidays. Admission: adults $$$, seniors and children ages 2 to 11 $$, members and children under 2 free. Additional fee for Zooballoon.

That tethered hot-air balloon you see rising over the Schuylkill Expressway is the Philadelphia Zoo's Channel 6 Zooballoon. For an additional fee you can ride up 400 feet above the trees and view the animals from above. Each voyage lasts fifteen minutes.

One annual feature is not to be missed. From Apr to Oct, weather permitting, the Birds of Australia exhibit is open. Even bigger kids are wide-eyed with wonder when these colorful birds drink nectar from the children's hands.

The zoo offers a treat for all ages—a chance to meet more than 1,800 animals housed in naturalistic settings, all surrounded by beautiful trees and plantings.

The newest attraction at the zoo is Bank of America's Big Cat Falls, featuring snow leopards, pumas, and jaguars, along with lions and tigers. The endangered species share a habitat that's open year-round (timed admission required), with tunnels connecting exhibit areas and the animals' "swimming pools."

University of Pennsylvania Museum (ages 8 and up)

Thirty-third and Spruce Streets; (215) 898-4000; www.penn.museum. Open Tues through Sat 10 a.m. to 4:30 p.m. and Sun 1 to 5 p.m. Closed Sun in summer. Admission is a

donation of $$ for adults, $ for students and children; children under 6 are free. For information on Family Fun Days, call (215) 898-4890. For children's workshops call (215) 898-4015.

The University of Pennsylvania Museum is a treasure trove for your budding archaeologist or anyone interested in sphinxes, mummies, African sculpture, or ancient Mayan, Greek, or Polynesian culture. The three floors of this museum are loaded with a wealth of artifacts unearthed by the University of Pennsylvania Museum's own world-renowned archaeological and ethnographic expeditions.

Kids will be awestruck by the genuine Sphinx of Ramesses II, weighing in at twelve tons of solid granite. They will be mystified, and perhaps a little unnerved, by the real mummies. The huge Chinese crystal ball is a favorite. Other ongoing exhibits include Raven's Journey: The World of Alaska's Native People.

The annual Chinese New Year celebration and the Celebration of African Cultures, both popular family events, are held in winter. Please note that while the large marble halls keep pretty cool, the building is only partially air-conditioned. The Cafe offers a kid-friendly multicultural menu, especially on weekends. The Pyramid Gift Shop has educational and inexpensive items for children. Wheelchair accessible, with diapering facilities in some bathrooms.

Penn's campus is also home to the Penn Relays, the largest track and field meet held in the United States. Held the last weekend of Apr or the first weekend in May each year, the meet draws thousands of participants, from high school runners to Olympic stars to 90-year-old sprinters. Little athletes will be impressed by the speed of the stars, and the crowds are big and enthusiastic. For tickets and schedules, check (215) 215-898-6145 or www.thepennrelays.com.

ALSO IN THE AREA

Also on the Penn campus, kids might enjoy a look at **College Hall,** one of two Philadelphia structures reputed to be a model for the Addams Family house. (Charles Addams went to Penn and was well acquainted with this building. The other candidate is the

An O'Toole **Family Adventure**

Philadelphia's Penn Relays always said "spring" to our family. Our son James, a competitive runner, loved to see his heroes in action at this annual event, held at the University of Pennsylvania's Franklin Field. Runners from age 14 to 90 compete in track and field events over three days. On Saturdays, we'd arrive early and spend the whole day in the sunshine. Our favorite event—a real crowd-pleaser—was the "U.S. versus the World" relay race, where the country's fastest 400-meter runners sprinted around the track, each running one lap against their international competitors. The whole stadium roared at the finish.

Ebeneezer Maxwell Mansion in Chestnut Hill.) There are also some interesting sculptures on this campus, such as Claes Oldenburg's oversized button and the statue of Benjamin Franklin.

South Philadelphia

South Philadelphia is home to many of the city's ethnic neighborhoods, as well as the world's largest outdoor market, the Italian Market.

Italian Market (all ages)

Ninth Street, between Wharton and Christian Streets; (215) 334-6004 for Italian Market tours. Open Tues through Sun 9 a.m. to 4 p.m.

The country's largest daily outdoor market, the Italian Market is a great place to find unusual cheeses, fresh fruits and vegetables, homemade pasta, exotic spices, and unusual kitchenware.

FDR Skatepark (ages 10 and up)

Pattison Avenue and South Broad Street; (215) 683-0200; www.fairmountpark.org. Open daily during park hours (until 1 a.m.).

Philadelphia's premier skateboard park, in South Philadelphia's Roosevelt Park, is a concrete paradise, designed and built by skateboard enthusiasts. With features like the "Dome," a 4-foot wall of concrete that climbs up into a burly overhang, and the "Bunker," a 60-foot-long, 11-foot vertical brick coping, this park is a serious challenge for skateboarders of all skill levels. The park is situated under the I-95 highway overpass, right off Broad Street, protected from rain and snow. To get there use the Pattison Avenue stop of the Broad Street subway line.

John Heinz National Wildlife Refuge (all ages)

8601 Lindbergh Blvd., in the Tinicum section; call (215) 365-3118 for information; http://heinz.fws.gov. The Cusano Environmental Education Center (CEEC) is open 8:30 a.m. to 4 p.m. daily. The trails are open 8 a.m. to sundown daily. The programs, facility, and grounds are free.

The 1,200-acre John Heinz National Wildlife Refuge near Philadelphia International Airport is managed by the U.S. Fish and Wildlife Service for conservation of habitat and promotion of environmental education. The refuge is alive with 281 species of birds and healthy populations of mammals, reptiles, and amphibians. Ten miles of hiking and biking trails meander along the Tinicum Marsh and Darby Creek. Don't forget your binoculars to enhance the view from the Observation Tower.

The Cusano Environmental Education Center (CEEC) was built using sustainable design techniques. The building includes a resource center, classrooms, Tinicum Treasures Bookstore, and a "living-marsh machine." The center houses many interactive exhibits and displays highlighting wetlands and wildlife.

Concerts for Kids

At the Mann Music Center in beautiful Fairmount Park, kids perform for kids. The popular weekday concerts have way-cool performers, like young Chinese acrobats, the Five Browns (piano-playing siblings), or Caribbean steel bands. Best of all, it's absolutely **free,** with no tickets required. Mann seats 4,000 under cover and an additional 10,000 in the open. Feel free to bring lawn chairs, blankets, or your own picnic. Get the lineup by calling (215) 893-1999 or visiting www.manncenter.org.

Mummers Museum (ages 8 and up)

1100 S. Second St.; (215) 336-3050; www.mummersmuseum.com. Open Wed through Sat from 9:30 a.m. to 4:30 p.m. and Sun from noon to 4:30 p.m. It is closed on Mon, and on Sun in July and Aug. Admission is $; guided tours are available by reservation.

No Philadelphian can hear the tune of "Golden Slippers" without picturing the sequined costumes, the feathers, and, of course, the distinctive strut of the mummers. But non-Philadelphians may need a few words of explanation.

Philadelphians have created a mummers tradition all their own in the annual Philadelphia New Year's Day Parade, when the string bands, fancy brigades, and clowns strut up Broad Street. The Mummers Museum surrounds you with the spangles, the colors, the history, and the music of the mummers. You can see videos of past parades, learn how the costumes are made, and practice your "Mummers' Strut." In nice weather, the string bands appear for concerts on selected Tues evenings at 8 p.m.

Fort Mifflin on the Delaware (ages 8 and up)

Fort Mifflin Road; (215) 685-4167; www.fortmifflin.us. Open Apr through Nov, Wed through Sun 10 a.m. to 4 p.m. Closed Mon and Tues. During the off-season prebooked tours may be available. Admission is $$ for adults, $ for seniors and children 2 to 12, and **free** for children under 2.

Fort Mifflin played a strategic role in the Revolutionary War. In 1777 more than 200 British warships sailed up the Delaware River with needed supplies for British troops occupying Philadelphia. For seven weeks the little fort held back the mightiest navy in the

Amazing
Philadelphia Facts

The Benjamin Franklin Parkway has been called "Philadelphia's Champs-Elysées."

world. Although it was almost completely destroyed in the process, Fort Mifflin never surrendered.

On Sat and Sun afternoons, in addition to tours there are militia-guard drills. A blacksmith also demonstrates how weapons were made in this period.

Manayunk and Chestnut Hill

Although located within Philadelphia's city limits, the Manayunk and Chestnut Hill sections feel more like small towns than urban neighborhoods. Manayunk, one of the country's oldest villages, has a reputation as an artists' community. Main Street in Manayunk is lined with art galleries, boutiques, and unusual shops. Chestnut Hill has a different atmosphere, with its beautiful old homes and elegant shops. Both offer wonderful restaurants (see the Where to Eat section of this chapter).

Ebeneezer Maxwell Mansion (ages 8 and up)

Greene and Tulpehocken Streets, Chestnut Hill; (215) 438-1861. Open Fri through Sun 1 to 4 p.m.

Rumor has it that the Ebeneezer Maxwell Mansion is the model for the *Addams Family* house, as depicted by Philadelphia's own Charles Addams. It is unclear how much cartoonist Charles Addams was influenced by the Victorian buildings he saw, but it is known that he was familiar with both College Hall (on the Penn campus) and the Ebeneezer Maxwell Mansion, and both may have shaped the architecture of the *Addams Family* house. This eighteen-room Victorian mansion in the Chestnut Hill section was built in 1859. Young children will love the children's bedroom, filled with games and toys of the period. The gadgets are also wonderful, including an apple corer and a sausage stuffer. The gardens include a grape arbor and a small lake. At Christmas there's a Dickensian Christmas celebration and in fall a ghost walk.

Morris Arboretum (all ages)

Germantown Pike at 100 Northwestern Ave., Chestnut Hill; (215) 247-5777; www.upenn .edu/arboretum. Open Mon through Fri 10 a.m. to 4 p.m., Sat and Sun from Nov through Mar 10 a.m. to 4 p.m., and Apr through Oct 10 a.m. to 5 p.m. During June, July, and Aug, the gardens offer extended hours on Thurs evenings until 8:30 p.m. Guided tours are given Sat and Sun at 2 p.m. Admission: adults $$, students $, and children under 6 free.

The Morris Arboretum, the botanical garden of the University of Pennsylvania, is filled with exotic plants and picturesque vistas. The arboretum fills ninety-two acres in Chestnut Hill, including Japanese gardens, rose gardens, the only Victorian fernery in the United States, and a charming pond complete with swans.

For kids, the real highlight of the Morris Arboretum is definitely the Tree Adventure, which allows visitors to cross a swaying suspension bridge to reach the Bird's Nest, a shelter 50 feet above ground. Its Squirrel Scramble lets kids race from limb to limb, and a canopy walk traces a path atop the mature forest. The Garden Railway, open from

Amazing
Philadelphia Facts

Philadelphia is known for its distinctive foods, including cheesesteaks, scrapple, snapper soup, and soft pretzels with mustard.

mid-June until early Oct, is a G-scale model railroad with six trains and three trolley lines, operating on a layout of thirty-four miniature Philadelphia landmarks constructed from acorns, moss, bark, twigs, and such. There's even a waterfall.

In season, the Garden Railway display is open daily 10 a.m. to 4 p.m. and until 8 p.m. on Thurs. It is wheelchair accessible. Nearby, the Arboretum Cafe is open daily 11 a.m. to 2:30 p.m., Apr 30 through Oct 31. It's also open on Thurs evening during the summer, when the Arboretum hosts concerts for kids.

Northeast Philadelphia

Insectarium (all ages)
8046 Frankford Ave. in Northeast Philadelphia; (215) 335-9500 or (215) 338-3000 (to inquire about educator availability); www.myinsectarium.com. Open 10 a.m. to 4 p.m. Mon through Sat. Admission is \$\$ per person; free for anyone younger than 2 with a paying adult.

Steve's Bug-Off Exterminating Co. has assembled the Insectarium, a collection of live insects in naturalized settings, mounted specimens, and interactive displays. This one-of-a-kind museum is designed to teach the importance of insects as part of the diversity of nature—but mostly it's a lot of fun. You won't be able to forget the "cockroach kitchen," the "glow-in-the-dark" scorpion, the live termite tunnel, or the tarantulas (no matter how hard you try).

Fox Chase Farm (all ages)
8600A Verree R. in northeast Philadelphia; (215) 685-0470; www.foxchasefarm.org. Admission \$ for special events.

This 112-acre working farm is a cooperative project of Fairmount Park and the Philadelphia School District, which means its weekend programs for children are both fun and educational. Outdoor movies, hayrides, maple sugaring, and more provide hands-on fun for city kids.

Where to Eat

IN PHILADELPHIA

City Tavern, 138 S. Second St.; (215) 413-1443; www.citytavern.com. Award-winning children's menu, booster seats. In the heart of the Historic District.

Italian Market, Ninth Street between Christian and Dickinson; (215) 922-5557.

KatManDu, 417 N. Columbus Blvd.; (215) 629-7400. High chairs, booster seats, children's menu. Great view of the Ben Franklin Bridge. Voted best restaurant in Philadelphia by the City Paper.

Marathon Grill; (215) 561-1818; www.marathongrill.com. With five downtown locations, fast, friendly service, a vast menu, and a full bar, Marathon is a favorite of adults and kids. Brunch is served on weekends.

Mulberry Market, 236 Arch St.; (215) 928-9064. Deli-style food, sandwiches, hoagies. Across the street from the Betsy Ross House.

Reading Terminal Market, Twelfth and Arch Streets; (215) 922-2317.

IN MANAYUNK

Le Bus, 4266 Main St.; (215) 487-2663. Children's menu, high chairs, casual atmosphere. On weeknights, kid's meals are just $1 with an adult meal.

Derek's, 4411 Main St.; (215) 483-9400. "Italifornia" food. Small portions and special menu items for children. High chairs, booster seats; babies and toddlers welcome.

Where to Stay

IN PHILADELPHIA

Best Western Center City Hotel, 501 N. Twenty-second St.; (215) 568-8300 or (800) 528-1234. Convenient to major museums and other attractions. Restaurant, outdoor pool.

Crown Plaza—Philadelphia, 1800 Market St.; (215) 561-7500; www.crownplaza.com/philadelphia-centercity.

Holiday Inn—Express Midtown, Thirteenth and Walnut; (215) 735-9300.

Holiday Inn—Historic District, (Historic Area), 400 Arch St.; (215) 923-8660 or (800) HOLIDAY. Seasonal outdoor rooftop pool.

Sheraton Society Hill, 1 Dock St.; (215) 238-6000.

For More Information

Greater Philadelphia Tourism Marketing Corp., (888) 999-3790; www.visitphilly.com.

Philadelphia Convention and Visitors Bureau, (215) 636-1666 or (800) 537-7676; www.pcvb.org.

Philadelphia
Countryside

The countryside surrounding Philadelphia offers many opportunities for family fun and learning. For sheer fun, pick Sesame Place, the Crayola Factory, Giggleberry Fair, and Dorney Park, with its floorless roller coaster, Hydra the Revenge. Sesame Place, an amusement park based on the beloved PBS TV show, offers rides and activities designed for the whole family, including waterslides that even older children will enjoy along with their younger brothers and sisters. The Crayola Factory gives young imaginations a place to run wild. And Giggleberry Fair offers a colorful six-level climbing structure and thousands of soft foam "berries." If you prefer nature's roller coasters, try tubing the Delaware River at Point Pleasant with Bucks County River Country outfitters.

TopPicks in the Phildelphia Countryside

- **Sesame Place,** Langhorne
- **Crayola Factory,** Easton
- **Giggleberry Fair,** Lahaska
- **Valley Forge National Historical Park,** Valley Forge
- **Dorney Park and Wildwater Kingdom,** Allentown
- **Mercer Museum,** Doylestown
- **Tubing at Point Pleasant,** Bucks County River Country
- **Elmwood Park Zoo,** Norristown
- **Chanticleer Garden,** Wayne
- **American Helicopter Museum,** West Chester

PHILADELPHIA COUNTRYSIDE

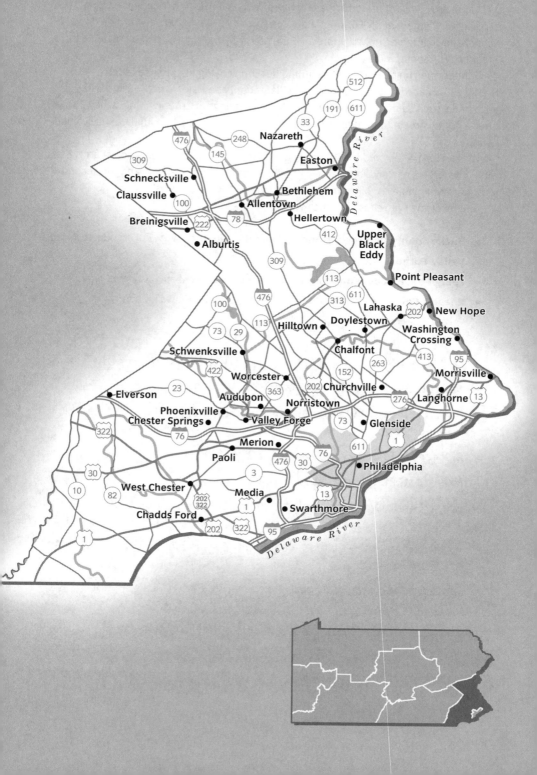

There are plenty of opportunities for more serious fun as well. Younger children especially love the friendly Elmwood Park Zoo, with its playful otters and prairie dogs. School-age children on up will appreciate the quirky Mercer Museum and West Chester's American Helicopter Museum.

Other opportunities for family learning beckon at living-history sites such as Hopewell Furnace, Colonial Pennsylvania Plantation, and Peter Wentz Farmstead. Historic parks such as the Brandywine Battlefield, Washington Crossing, and Valley Forge offer a great combination of history and outdoor fun, all in the beautiful Pennsylvania countryside.

Art can be fun too, and the Barnes Foundation's collection of Impressionist art is dazzling. The streets of New Hope teem with art—in galleries, craft shops, and the second location for the James A. Michener museum.

The following Web sites introduce you to this area:

- **Bucks County Conference and Visitors Bureau, Inc.:** www.buckscountycvb.org
- **Valley Forge:** www.valleyforge.org
- **Lehigh Valley Convention and Visitors Bureau:** www.lehighvalleypa.org
- **Chester County's Brandywine Valley:** www.brandywinevalley.com

TopEvents in the Phildelphia Countryside

- **Mercer Museum Folkfest,** May; (215) 345-0210.
- **Devon Horse Show,** ten days surrounding Memorial Day weekend; (610) 964-0550.
- **Blobfest** in Phoenixville, July; (610) 917-1228.
- **Musikfest,** Bethlehem, Aug; (610) 861-0678.
- **Great Allentown Fair,** (starts on the Tues before Labor Day); (610) 433-7541.
- **Philadelphia Folk Festival,** weekend before Labor Day; (215) 242-0150 or (800) 556-FOLK.
- **Scarecrow Competition and Display** at Peddler's Village, Sept; (215) 794-4000.
- **Battle of Brandywine Reenactment,** Sept; (610) 459-3342.
- **Great Pumpkin Carve** in Chadds Ford, Oct; (610) 388-7376.
- **Longwood Gardens Christmas Display,** Nov to Jan 1; (610) 388-1000.

Brandywine Valley

For a trip that includes historic homes and battlefields, art, and gardens, all within easy distance of one another, contact the Chester County Tourist Bureau (800-228-9933). You may wish to make a weekend visit to the towns of Kennett Square and Chadds Ford.

The fields, mills, and farms of rural Pennsylvania have found their way into the art of Chadds Ford's most famous artist, Andrew Wyeth. Here you're surrounded by Wyeth's landscapes and his art. You can visit the historic Brandywine Battlefield, eat lunch in a historic inn, shop, and take a walk along the Brandywine River.

Paddling the gentle Brandywine is another wonderful family adventure. Several outfitters rent kayaks, canoes, splash boats, and inner tubes for floating downstream. In Mortonville call Brandywine Outfitters (2096 Strasburg Rd.; 610-486-6141; www.canoepa .com). In West Chester try Northbrook Canoe Company (1810 Beagle Rd.; 610-793-2279; www.northbrookcanoe.net).

Longwood Gardens (all ages)

US 1 in Kennett Square; (610) 388-1000; www.longwoodgardens.org. The outdoor gardens and conservatory open at 9 every day of the year. Both close at 5 p.m. from Nov through Mar and at 6 p.m. from Apr through Oct, although both are frequently open later for special events and holiday displays. Call ahead for a complete schedule. Admission is $$$ for adults ($$ on Tues), $$ for youths ages 16 to 20, $ for children 6 to 15, and free under age 6. Prices subject to change.

Longwood Gardens is a place to enjoy the variety of nature, both indoors and out. In a four-acre conservatory, Longwood's visitors can see orchids, roses, bonsai, exotic jungle plants, and waterfalls, even on the coldest winter days. On warmer days you can tour the outside gardens and the fountains. No matter what the weather, don't miss the annual holiday display.

Longwood caters to kids with the indoor Children's Garden, which features a secret cave with a drooling dragon and a bamboo maze. Seventeen fountains mean you'll probably want to pack an extra towel or T-shirt. The outdoor Bee-Amazed Children's Garden focuses on the busy honeybees and their important role in pollination. The Honeycomb Maze is full of surprises: tunnels, a beehive arbor, and the Queen Bee's Throne.

The Garden Railway, open seasonally, depicts the Brandywine Valley. Longwood's admission fees vary seasonally. All admission fees are discounted on Tues. The Terrace Restaurant includes both a cafeteria and a sit-down dining room. Reservations are recommended for the dining room.

Brandywine River Museum (ages 6 and up)

US 1; (610) 388-2700; www.brandywinemuseum.org. Open daily 9:30 a.m. to 4:30 p.m. Admission is $$ for adults; $ for senior citizens, students with ID, and children 6 to 12; free for children under 6. N. C. Wyeth House and Studio open Apr through Nov; $ additional admission.

Andrew Wyeth came from a family of distinguished artists. The Brandywine River Museum, in a converted gristmill on US 1 in Chadds Ford, has the world's largest collection of Andrew Wyeth's work, as well as that of his father, N. C. Wyeth; his son, Jamie Wyeth; and other family members.

Children especially go for Jamie Wyeth's painting *Portrait of Pig* and the life-size animal sculptures along the riverbank. Many visitors will recognize the illustrations of N. C. Wyeth for such swashbuckling classics as *Treasure Island* and *Kidnapped.* The Brandywine River Museum has a children's audio tour of its permanent collection as well as selected exhibitions. This lively tour answers questions such as, "How did Jamie Wyeth convince a pig to pose for a painting?" Works by other artists from the Brandywine region hang near still-life paintings, landscapes, and an unparalleled collection of American illustration.

Surrounding the museum are stands of wildflowers, trees, and shrubs indigenous to the Greater Brandywine Valley. For an additional fee, visitors may tour the N. C. Wyeth House and Studio. The museum also offers tours of the Kuerner Farm, inspiration for over 1,000 of Andrew Wyeth's paintings.

John Chads House (ages 8 and up)

PA 100; (610) 388-7376; www.chaddsfordhistory.org. Open May through Sept, Sat and Sun from 1 to 5 p.m. Admission is $$ for adults, $ for children. Combination ticket to both John Chads House and Barns–Brinton House is $$ for adults and $ for children.

Often you can watch bread being baked in the beehive oven. On the weekend after Labor Day, the Chadds Ford Historical Society, which administers both John Chads House and Barns–Brinton House, hosts the annual Chadds Ford Days with pony rides, music, art, and games. The society also hosts a display on the history of the Underground Railroad in the area.

Barns–Brinton House (ages 10 and up)

US 1; (610) 388-7376; www.chaddsfordhistory.org. Same hours and admission fees as the John Chads House.

At the Barns–Brinton House, guides in period costume demonstrate colonial crafts and give tours of this early eighteenth-century Quaker home. Just past the herb garden you'll find the Chaddsford Winery.

Brandywine Battlefield Park (ages 8 and up)

US 1; (610) 459-3342. The battlefield park grounds are open, free, year-round Tue through Sat 9 a.m. to 5 p.m. and Sun noon to 5 p.m. The visitor center is open Tues through Sat 9 a.m. to 5 p.m. and Sun noon to 5 p.m. Closed Mon. Admission for house tour only: $. A family rate ($$) is available.

After retreating at the Battle of Brandywine, George Washington's troops moved on to camp at Valley Forge. At Brandywine Battlefield Park you can tour the house where Washington and Lafayette set up their headquarters. The visitor center offers an audiovisual introduction to the park, along with maps for a self-guided driving tour that includes twenty-eight historic points of interest. A reenactment of the battle is held every Sept. Soldiers in colonial costumes fire real muskets and march across the fields—a thrilling spectacle. There is a museum shop, and picnic areas are available.

Elverson

Hopewell Furnace (ages 8 and up)

2 Mark Bird Lane; (610) 582-8773, TDD 582-2093; www.nps.gov/hofu/. Open daily 9 a.m. to 5 p.m., except New Year's Day, Martin Luther King Jr. Day, Presidents' Day, Veterans Day, Thanksgiving, and Christmas. Entrance fee is $ per person. For living-history events an additional fee ($) per person is charged. Annual passes, family passes, and senior passes are available.

Watch a real blacksmith hammer a shape from white-hot iron. Visit a cast house where iron weapons were made for the Continental Army. Learn how colonists prepared food and clothing. Hopewell Furnace National Historic Site gives you a chance to see what life was like in a colonial iron-making town. Although open year-round, the site is most active in summer, when authentically costumed artisans demonstrate their crafts. Mother's Day is sheep-shearing day. The visitor center and restrooms are wheelchair accessible. Some of the historic structures are accessible. Call for more details about wheelchair accessibility. A Junior Ranger program is available.

ALSO IN THE AREA

Nearby, **French Creek State Park** offers outdoor family adventures such as hiking, fishing, swimming, and camping, as well as winter sports. You may wish to have lunch or do some shopping in **Victorian St. Peter's Village.**

Chester Springs

Where nature brought forth yellow water with medicinal properties, man has brought forth *The Blob*. Some would say Chester Springs's attractions have run "from the sublime to the ridiculous."

Historic Yellow Springs (ages 8 and up)

Art School Road; (610) 827-7414. Open for self-guided tours Mon through Fri 9 a.m. to 4 p.m., weekends by reservation. Closed major holidays. A donation is suggested.

For centuries, starting with indigenous peoples and, later, colonial settlers, presidents, and entertainers, people have come to Yellow Springs in hopes of finding a cure for their illnesses. In 1722 there was a health spa here. From 1916 to 1952 the Pennsylvania Academy of Fine Arts ran a landscape school on these beautiful grounds. And later still, Valley Forge Films made movies here, including the 1958 Steve McQueen classic, *The Blob*, and 4-D Man.

BLOBFEST!

Heading to Phoenixville in July? Grab your tinfoil hat—and prepare to run.

A handmade chapeau of aluminum, the sillier the better, is the preferred attire for those attending Blobfest, an annual salute to the cheesy '50s horror flick that put Chester County on the screen in 1959.

Starring a youthful Steve McQueen, *The Blob* staged one scene of a panicked crowd stampede at downtown's Colonial Theatre. Each year for the past decade, the theater (now run as a nonprofit corporation) has invited the public to reenact the scene on Friday night, kicking off three days of rock music, celebrity appearances, costume contests, and celebrations of all things blob-like. The foil hats? They protect against evil alien space rays.

Held the weekend after July 4. For details, visit www.thecolonialtheatre .com/blobfest.

At present this site is operated as Historic Yellow Springs, Inc. Visitors may take a self-guided tour of the grounds and eighteenth- and nineteenth-century buildings, but it's most fun to come during special events such as art shows, classes, and workshops or to attend annual events such as the Frolicks.

West Chester

American Helicopter Museum (ages 4 and up)

1220 American Blvd., West Chester (near Brandywine Airport); (610) 436-9600; www .helicoptermuseum.org. Open Wed through Sat 10 a.m. to 5 p.m. and Sun noon to 5 p.m. Admission: $.

The country's largest collection of helicopters is a terrific experience for kids, who are invited to climb into a whirlybird or walk through a V-22 Osprey. Most of the helicopters are displayed indoors; five of the largest are outside. Once a month, on Sunday, families can take off for real helicopter rides. A special kids' area helps children understand how helicopters fly and how they're used. There's even a party room for kids' birthday celebrations.

QVC Studio Tours (ages 6 and up)

1200 Wilson Dr.; (800) 600-9900; www.qvctours.com. Tours are conducted daily, every hour on the hour, 10 a.m. to 4 p.m. Reservations are not required. Not recommended for children under 6.

The QVC cable home-shopping channel conducts a tour of its large studio complex. If you're a fan of QVC, this tour is a must. If you're not a QVC shopper, the tour offers an interesting look behind the scenes of TV production. The guided tour follows the path of a QVC product from sourcing, testing, and TV presentation to home delivery. Overnight event packages are available.

Valley Forge

Valley Forge National Historical Park (all ages)

Visitor center at PA 23 and North Gulph Road; (610) 783-1077; www.nps.gov/vafo. Park buildings are open daily except Christmas from 9 a.m. until 5 p.m. Admission is $ for Washington's Headquarters. Children 16 and under are free. Park grounds are open to the public free.

After viewing the eighteen-minute introductory film and exhibits at the visitor center, you can get information about touring the park. The visitor center also displays various exhibits and artifacts that help you get more out of your visit.

Valley Forge National Historical Park offers bus tours three times per day from Memorial Day through Labor Day. To reserve a seat, call (610) 783-7503.

From June to Oct tour buses take a regular route, allowing visitors to get off when a particular site sparks their interest and then catch the next bus. A map allows families to take a self-guided driving tour accompanied by a narrated audiotape, if desired.

Trails are available for visitors who prefer to see the park by bike, on foot, or on horseback. Pick up a brochure at the visitor center for more information about the trails. There are fields perfect for kite flying and three different picnic areas.

Your kids will not want to miss the re-created encampment where Washington's troops spent the winter of 1777–78. Boys are especially interested in the Artillery Park, reconstructed fortifications, and the Grand Parade Grounds, where the troops trained for battle. General Washington set up his temporary headquarters in Isaac Potts's House (also known as Washington's Headquarters), now restored to look as it did during that famous winter. Costumed interpreters appear at the Muhlenberg Brigade daily from June through Aug, 10 a.m. to 4 p.m.; weekends year-round in good weather.

If the kids rebel at the thought of a forced march, offer them a bike ride instead. The park's paved bike trails, on 3,600 rolling acres, are ideal for pedaling. Bike rentals are available from the lower Welcome Center parking lot daily in summer and weekends from Labor Day to Halloween. Rates for two-hour rentals, $$; family rates for two adults and two children are also offered, along with buggies and tagalongs. For a short and easy expedition for school-age kids, try the ranger-led walking tours. The free forty-minute tours depart twice daily, at 11:50 a.m. and 1:50 p.m.

The American Revolution Center at Valley Forge is planned as a joint venture between the National Park Service and its private partner, the American Revolution Center. This partnership has already produced the new Encampment Gift Shop in the visitor center. The new center will be the first and only museum devoted to educating and inspiring people about the period of the American Revolution. It will be built into the

Amazing
Pennsylvania Facts

Battered by defeats throughout the fall of 1777, Gen. George Washington and his troops retreated to Valley Forge for the winter. By February 1778 he had lost nearly half his men to death, disease, and desertion.

quarry bluff at the far end of the main visitor parking lot adjacent to the current visitor center.

ALSO IN THE AREA

For another kind of family adventure in the Valley Forge area, contact **United States Hot Air Balloon Team,** Hopewell Road, P.O. Box 490, St. Peters 10470; (610) 469-0782 or (800) 763-5987; www.ushotairballoon.com.

The nation's second largest shopping mall, **the Plaza and Court of King of Prussia,** is only minutes from Valley Forge Park, on US 202.

Audubon

Although John James Audubon lived at Mill Grove for only three years, it was his first home in America (he arrived here in 1803) and the perfect place to inspire his career as a painter of birds.

Mill Grove (house, ages 6 and up; grounds, all ages)
Audubon and Pawlings Roads; (610) 666-5593; www.montcopa.org/historicsites. House open Tues through Sat 10 a.m. to 4 p.m.; Sun 1 to 4 p.m. Grounds open Tues through Sun 7 a.m. to dusk. Free.

One hundred and seventy-five acres of greenery, 175 species of birds, and 400 species of flowering plants surround the house, built in 1762. This is a lovely spot to stroll in the woods or enjoy a peaceful view of Perkiomen Creek. Inside the home you may tour eleven rooms filled with Audubon's collection of paintings, stuffed birds, and birds' eggs. The museum also owns a complete set of Audubon's greatest work, *The Birds of America,* with each bird painted in actual size. Call for a calendar of events and programs.

Paoli

What is it about the Philadelphia area that seems to breed unforgettable characters? Doylestown has Henry Mercer, Merion has Albert Barnes, and Paoli has Wharton Esherick.

Wharton Esherick Studio (ages 8 and up)

Horseshoe Trail Road. For directions and reservations call (610) 644-5822 or log onto www .levins.com/esherick.html. Reservations are required for one-hour tours of Esherick's home and studio. Tours are available Mar through Dec, Sat 10 a.m. to 5 p.m. and Sun 1 to 5 p.m. Admission is \$\$ for adults, \$ for children under 12.

Wharton Esherick started out as a painter, but after moving in 1913 to a stone farmhouse near Paoli, he became fascinated with wood. The Wharton Esherick Studio reflects this fascination. Everywhere you look, you discover some whimsical wooden object: wooden sculptures, wooden picture frames, wooden furniture.

Esherick was also entranced by what are now called "found objects." The handrail of his astounding double-spiral staircase is a real mastodon tusk! The artist created chairs out of hammer handles or wagon wheels.

Phoenixville

Water World (all ages)

On PA 724; (610) 935-1290; www.waterworldrec.com. Open daily May through Sept noon to 9 p.m. Admission is \$\$ per person. Access to waterslides is \$\$.

Water World is a relaxing place to cool off on a sticky summer day, with two waterslides, a rope swing, a large pool, and a wading pool for the little ones. There is a small snack bar and picnicking facilities.

Norristown

Elmwood Park Zoo (all ages)

1661 Harding Blvd.; (610) 277-DUCK; www.elmwoodparkzoo.org. Open daily 10 a.m. to 5 p.m. (gates close at 4:30 p.m.). Call for current admission rates.

Enter the aviary and you are surrounded by a naturalistic wetland environment filled with waterfowl, beaver, and two fun-loving river otters. The murky Bayou Building houses alligators, snakes, and armadillos. The Tom Kimmel Conservation Kingdom is an imaginative playground that teaches kids about conservation while they have fun. They can even crawl through a giant prairie dog tunnel at William's Prairie Dog Town. In all there are more than 200 animals representing forty species, including jaguars, cougars, timber wolves, and a peregrine falcon.

The youngest children still love feeding the ducks in the duck pond and petting the sheep and goats in the Petting Barn (open seasonally). There is also a snack shop, a gift shop, and pony rides. Wheelchair accessible, with diapering facilities in the restrooms.

Media

Media is the home of Ridley Creek State Park, where you can see the Colonial Pennsylvania Plantation.

Colonial Pennsylvania Plantation (ages 6 and up)

Located in Ridley Creek State Park; (610) 566-1725; www.colonialplantation.org. Open weekends Apr to Nov, 10 a.m. to 4 p.m.; 11 a.m. to 5 p.m. in Aug. Usually closed for rain.

On an eighteenth-century farm, animals were left to graze freely, not penned up as they are today. In the root cellar the farmer's family stored carrots, onions, and potatoes; in the springhouse, flowing water cooled milk and eggs. The clothing was made by hand, spun of natural fibers. All these details are meticulously re-created at Colonial Pennsylvania Plantation.

This is actually a working farm where 120 acres of crops are grown, using methods that date back more than 200 years. Also in the park, the adjacent Tyler Arboretum features a giant sequoia with a circumference of 9 feet and a unique fragrant garden designed specifically for the visually impaired. The arboretum is open daily 8 a.m. until dusk; admission is **free.** Call (610) 566-5431.

Linvilla Orchards (all ages)

137 W. Knowlton Rd.; (610) 876-7116; www.linvilla.com. Open daily year-round. Admission is free (separate fees for hayrides and special events).

One of the oldest farms in Delaware County, this is a 300-acre working farm with farm animals, fresh produce, baked goods, homemade candy, gourmet items, and play equipment. Its Pumpkinland Harvest Festival, held each fall, is a local family tradition. There are also concerts, fishing derbies, craft shows, and other events year-round.

Swarthmore

Scott Arboretum (all ages)

Swarthmore College campus; (610) 328-8025; www.scottarboretum.org. Open daily from dawn to dusk; free.

Amazing
Pennsylvania Facts

Although he founded Pennsylvania, William Penn lived here for only a total of four years.

Amazing
Pennsylvania Facts

In 1930 Dr. Albert Barnes commissioned the artist Henri Matisse to paint a mural for the Barnes Foundation in Merion. However, the measurements for the wall space were incorrectly translated from inches to centimeters, so when the mural arrived from France, it was 5 feet too short! Although he had spent more than a year on the first version, Matisse started all over again. The second version now decorates three arches above the main gallery in the Barnes Foundation.

One hundred and ten acres surrounding Swarthmore College constitute the college's Scott Arboretum. Come here for a quiet stroll through collections of flowering cherries, roses, conifers, daffodils, dogwoods, lilacs, hollies, rhododendrons, and more. Specialty gardens include the Theresa Long Garden of Fragrance, the Dean Bond Rose Garden, and the Winter Garden, which provides longed-for colors in the gray of winter.

Merion

The Barnes Foundation (ages 8 and up)
300 N. Latches Lane; (610) 667-0290; www.barnesfoundation.org. Open Thurs through Sun 9:30 a.m. to 5 p.m., Oct through Aug, by advance reservation only. In Sept, Fri through Sun. Admission: $$ per person. Audio tour: $$ per person.

The art lovers in our family have always been awestruck by the paintings at the Barnes Foundation, one of the nation's most amazing private collections of Impressionist and post-Impressionist art. Formerly a well-kept secret, the Barnes is scheduled to move to a downtown location on the Benjamin Franklin Parkway in 2012 .

Dr. Albert C. Barnes collected more than 180 Renoirs, 70 Cézannes, and many Matisses, including a mural specifically commissioned for the gallery. The wall ensembles explore light, line, color, and space in an amazing multicultural array that includes works by van Gogh, Picasso, El Greco, Soutine, and Glackens, as well as Greek, Roman, Egyptian, and Native American artists.

Barnes's idiosyncratic grouping of different artworks may be hard for young children to appreciate. Teens who know a bit of art history will be impressed by the collection.

Audio tour and gift shop available. Wheelchair accessible, with diapering facilities in the ladies' restroom. The Barnes is within fifteen minutes of Suburban Square, Ardmore, for shopping or a bite to eat at Ruby's Diner.

Wayne

Chanticleer (all ages)

786 Church Rd.; (610) 687-4163; www.chanticleergarden.org. Open 10 a.m. to 5 p.m. Wed through Sun, Apr through Oct. The garden is also open on Fri evenings until 8 p.m. from May through Aug. Adult admission $; under 16 **free.**

This whimsical garden looks like a hip children's picture book, with sculptures that add to fun. Sit on a stone sofa or find books made of rock on the floor of the "library." Bright colors, water features, and witty surprises will delight adults as well as children. Photographers and artists are welcome, but pets are not.

Glenside

Keswick Theater (ages 6 and up)

Easton Road and Keswick Avenue; (215) 572-7650; www.keswicktheater.com.

The Keswick Theater offers concerts, plays, and other productions year-round. Ticket prices vary.

Churchville

Churchville Nature Center (ages 6 and up)

501 Churchville Lane; (215) 357-4005; www.churchvillenaturecenter.org. The nature center is open Tues through Sun 10 a.m. to 5 p.m. The grounds are open dawn to dusk. Admission is **free.**

Trails at the Churchville Nature Center are open from sunup to sundown daily. Inside the nature center you can view dioramas depicting local wildlife. There are also children's programs, such as nature crafts, junior naturalist hikes, and activities centered on the Lenape Indians. The paths are wheelchair accessible, and wheelchairs are available.

Langhorne

Sesame Place (all ages)

100 Sesame Rd., US 1 to Oxford Valley exit; (215) 752-7070; www.sesameplace.com. Operating days and hours vary, with the park opening in May for weekends only; starting in mid-May, daily 10 a.m. to 5 p.m.; staying open later after Memorial Day and returning to weekend-only hours after Labor Day until mid-Oct, when it closes for the season.

Amazing
Pennsylvania Facts

Sesame Place has been included on the *New York Times*'s list of best water parks in the United States.

Single-day admission (ages 3 to 54) costs $$$$. Discounts are available for families of four or more or during late-afternoon hours. Holders of Passport tickets receive unlimited admission for the season, plus special benefits.

Just about any kid will have fun at Sesame Place. We've found that even kids too grown up for Cookie Monster can't help but enjoy many of the water rides and physical play environments.

You can walk down Sesame Street, a full-size replica of the thoroughfare seen on the popular TV show, and take pictures of your kids in front of Bert and Ernie's house. You'll love the Rock Around the Block parade and shows such as "Big Bird's Beach Party" starring *Sesame Street* characters. There are more than fifty kid-powered physical play elements, such as Nets and Climbs and Ernie's Bed Bounce.

The park has thirteen water attractions, and most will appeal to all members of your family. Rambling River is a winding, relaxing circular tube ride your kids can go around and around all afternoon. Even very young children have no fear on Teeny Tiny Tidal Waves and the Rubber Duckie Pond. Sky Splash is filled with giant-size water adventures, including an 8-foot-tall rubber duckie and huge tinker toys that spray water.

Sesame Place is located in Langhorne about thirty minutes from Philadelphia at exit 29A on I-95 North. Most areas are accessible to the disabled, and special events include some designed for disabled children. Bathing suits are required for all water attractions.

Morrisville

Pennsbury Manor (ages 6 and up)

400 Pennsbury Memorial Rd.; (215) 946-0400; www.pennsburymanor.org. Open Tues through Sat 9 a.m. to 5 p.m. and Sun noon to 5 p.m. Last tour begins 3:30 p.m. Admission is $$ for adults and $ for seniors and children 5 to 12; children under 5 enter free. Family rate $$$.

Pennsylvania was William Penn's "holy experiment," a colony founded on Quaker moral principles. Although he lived here for only a total of about four years, Pennsbury Manor was never far from his thoughts. Today his home has been restored, complete with icehouse, stable, smokehouse, garden, and livestock. The boathouse contains a replica of the vessel *Penn* used to commute to Philadelphia. The oven in the bake-and-brew house can bake up to thirty loaves of bread at a time.

On Sunday afternoons from Apr to Oct, Pennsbury Manor offers living history just for families. It has an activity room and a worker's cottage where kids can try seventeenth-century skills, such as writing with a quill pen. Geese, peacocks, sheep, and Red Devon cattle—authentic breeds wherever possible—populate the farm. In Dec, the farm is lit by glowing candles and roaring yule logs.

ALSO IN THE AREA

When William Penn was living at Pennsbury Manor, he attended Quaker Meeting at Falls Meeting in Fallsington, a town built around its meetinghouses. Guided tours start at the Gillingham Store and include several restored historic buildings: Moon–Williamson House, Burges–Lippincott House, and the Stagecoach Tavern. Fallsington is located on US 13 off I-95. For details contact Historic Fallsington, Inc., at (215) 295-6567; www.historicfallsington.org.

Washington Crossing

We picture "Washington's crossing" as in the famous painting by Emanuel Leutz, with George Washington standing heroically in the small boat as his troops row across the Delaware to surprise the Hessians on Christmas Day.

The German artist had never seen Washington Crossing when he painted it in the nineteenth century. It may not be safe to stand up in a small boat, but the image depicts an artist's impression of a historic event. In the Memorial Building at Washington Crossing National Historic Park, you can see a copy of the painting. It's larger than life in more ways than one—the painting is 20 feet long, 12 feet tall.

Washington Crossing National Historic Park and Bowman's Hill Tower (ages 8 and up)

PA 32 and PA 532, 3 miles north of I-95 exit 31; (215) 493-4076; www.spiritof76.net. The visitor center and historic buildings are open Mon through Sat 9 a.m. to 5 p.m. and on Sun noon to 5 p.m. There is a fee for the buildings ($). The park grounds, however, are open at no charge from 8 a.m. until sunset. Free.

A thirty-minute film at the visitor center describes the events of Dec 25, 1776, which led to a turning point of the Revolution. Washington planned his surprise attack from his headquarters in the Thompson–Neely House, and he ate dinner before the crossing at the Old Ferry Inn. In the Durham Boat House you can see the boats that were actually used for the crossing.

Every year on Christmas Day the park hosts a reenactment of Washington's crossing. Other special events here include Gingerbread Days, Tavern Nights, and special activities in honor of Washington's birthday. Gazebo Games, another special event, lets kids try out the games and toys enjoyed by eighteenth-century children.

Bowman's Hill Wildflower Preserve (ages 8 and up)

Located on the grounds of Washington Crossing Park but managed separately; (215) 862-2924; www.bhwp.org. Grounds open daily 8:30 a.m. to sunset; visitor center open daily 9 a.m. to 5 p.m. Admission $ for adults, seniors, and children. Members and children under 4 **free.** Closed major holidays.

Surrounding Bowman's Hill Tower but managed separately and with its own admission fee, Bowman's Hill Wildflower Preserve offers a breathtaking variety of wildflowers. Check the Web site for information, directions, and bloom lists. From mid-Mar through Oct guided walks are offered at 2 p.m. daily. At any other time, there are self-guided nature walks. The Wildflower Preserve also has a children's reading program, a weeklong summer day camp and many children's programs. The third Sat in July is Community Open House Day, a **free** event with guided tours offered all day, as well as music, nature crafts, and face-painting.

New Hope

In summer the streets of New Hope bustle with people drawn to the more than 200 art galleries, craft shops, restaurants, and history this town offers. But New Hope welcomes visitors any time of the year. You can get more information about bed-and-breakfasts in New Hope by stopping by the New Hope Information Center, 1 W. Mechanic St. For brochures about New Hope, call (215) 862-5880. To talk to a staff member about New Hope, call (215) 862-5030.

James A. Michener Art Museum—New Hope (all ages)

Located in Union Square complex on Bridge Street; (215) 862-7633; www.michenerart museum.org. Closed Mon and on major holidays; hours vary.

Doylestown's Michener Museum has opened a satellite location in the artistic community of New Hope. On permanent display here is Artists Among Us: Creative Bucks County: A Celebration of Art and Artists.

Coryell's Ferry Historic Boat Rides (all ages)

Ferries leave Coryell's Ferry at Gerenser's Exotic Ice Cream, 22 S. Main St.; (215) 862-2050; www.newhopepa.com/History/Coryells_Ferry/coryell_hist_2.htm. Apr through Oct starting at 11 a.m.

Coryell's Ferry began carrying passengers across the Delaware in canoes in 1733. Ferries still operate here for half-hour tours, but they now use more commodious paddleboats. The longest ride on the river, aboard a 65-foot Mississippi riverboat, leaves at 11 a.m. daily, May through Sept. On Wednesday kids get a discount.

Colonial New Hope Walking Tours (ages 6 and up)

Gerenser's Exotic Ice Cream, 22 S. Main St.; (215) 862-2050; www.spiritof76.net. Tours of New Hope are available Apr through Oct, starting at noon.

General Washington visited New Hope at least four times. To learn more about the history of this town, you can take a walking tour. Tickets and schedules for walking tours of New Hope are available here.

New Hope Mule Barges (all ages)

New Street; (215) 862-2842 or (800) 59-BARGE. Open Apr through Nov. Boat fares $$ for adults, $ for children.

You can take a ride on a mule barge, sailing past eighteenth-century homes, gardens, and workshops. Many barges are equipped with folk singers or historians. The Delaware Canal became operational in 1840, and, at its height, mules hauled thousands of barges carrying loads of coal and limestone. The canal includes 25 lift locks, 9 aqueducts, and 106 bridges.

Boat Rides at Wells Ferry (all ages)

At the end of Ferry Street on River; (215) 862-5965. Open May through Oct 11 a.m. to 6 p.m. Admission: adults $$, children $.

The *Star of New Hope* carries thirty-six passengers at a time on a guided tour. Tour guides offer a little history, as well as a glimpse at New Hope's varied architecture. Some tour guides play guitar music as well.

New Hope and Ivyland Railroad (all ages)

Station at Bridge and Stockton Streets; (215) 862-2332; www.newhoperailroad.com. Trains run daily Apr to Nov, weekends only Jan until Mar In Dec, special Santa Claus rides are offered. Tickets are $$$ for adults, $$ for seniors and kids 2 to 11, and $ for children under 2. The train operates seasonally.

The New Hope and Ivyland Railroad, built in 1889, eventually made the canal obsolete. If you take this train on its forty-five-minute narrated trip to Lahaska, you will notice a curved trestle bridge. If this bridge looks like something right out of *The Perils of Pauline*, that's because this actually was the bridge that was used in the 1914 movie series.

ALSO IN THE AREA

The **Bucks County Playhouse** offers a series of plays for children on Fri and Sat, at reasonable prices. Call (215) 862-2041 for a schedule, or check the Web site www.buckscountyplayhouse.com.

Lahaska

While in Peddler's Village, take a look at some of the unusual shops and restaurants.

Giggleberry Fair (all ages)

Peddler's Village, US 202 and PA 263; (215) 794-4047; www.peddlersvillage.com. Open Mon through Thurs 10 a.m. to 6 p.m., Fri and Sat 10 a.m. to 10 p.m., and Sun 10 a.m. to

7 p.m. Discovery Land/Giggleberry Mountain Combination Pass $$ per person. Individual tickets for specific attractions are also available.

Giggleberry Fair's goal is "to provide a wholesome, quality experience for children to be both educated and entertained." Comprising four children's attractions, Giggleberry Fair is 10,000 square feet of family fun.

Peddler's Village has recently restored its wonderful Grand Carousel, built in 1922 by the famous Philadelphia Toboggan Company. The carousel has been joined by Giggleberry Mountain, Discovery Land, and the Painted Pony Cafe to create Giggleberry Fair.

Giggleberry Mountain is the area's largest and most attractive indoor obstacle course, challenging for both children and adults. The colorful two-story, six-level structure is filled with tens of thousands of soft foam "berries." Kids fill tote bags with as many berries as they can grab and climb up through netting mazes to different levels where they can "blast" berries at their friends or reach the top of two different slides. Even adults get right in there with their kids. It's loud, but it's happy.

In Discovery Land, kids can explore a variety of calmer play environments. There's a pretend farm and orchard, a mini climbing wall, a rubber-duck waterway, and plenty of games. All games are rated "green"—suitable for all ages—by the Coin-Operated Video Game Parental Advisory System.

The Painted Pony Cafe offers pizza, hot dogs, a salad bar, and other kid-friendly choices.

Point Pleasant

The signers of the Declaration of Independence had to sweat it out in the notorious Philadelphia humidity, but you don't have to. Point Pleasant, north of Lahaska and New Hope, offers some great ways to cool off in its inviting, kid-friendly rapids. Bucks County River Country rents canoes, tubes, and rafts from April through October. To make reservations (which are required) or to find out about prices and special Pedal and Paddle trips, call Bucks County River Country at (215) 297-5000.

Bucks County River Country (ages 6 and up)

PA 32, Upper Black Eddy; (215) 297-5000; www.rivercountry.net. Call for days, hours, prices, and river conditions.

Our kids spent a carefree summer afternoon riding the current in tubes, occasionally dunking each other or taking time to see how deep the water was (not very). To protect your feet, remember to wear old sneakers that can get wet, and don't forget the sunscreen. Bucks County River Country also presents other events in the woods, such as the nation's largest haunted-woods hayride.

Doylestown

A wonderful choice for a day trip, Doylestown will charm you with its cast-iron lampposts, neat nineteenth-century houses, and unusual shops and galleries. You can walk to the Mercer Museum and James A. Michener Museum. Also within walking distance is the County Theater, showing art and vintage, as well as first-run, movies; the picturesque Doylestown Inn; as well as many other restaurants and shops. A short drive out of town, you may also wish to visit Fonthill and the Moravian Pottery and Tileworks. For information about Historic Doylestown, call (215) 345-9430.

Mercer Museum (ages 6 and up)

84 S. Pine St., near Ashland; (215) 345-0210; www.mercermuseum.org. Open Mon through Sat 10 a.m. to 5 p.m., Sun noon to 5 p.m. On Tues the museum closes at 9 p.m. Closed New Year's Day, Thanksgiving, and Christmas. Admission is $$ for adults, $ for ages 6 to 17; children under 6 enter free.

On Pine Street in the charming town of Doylestown stands what can only be described as a castle, not of stone but of poured concrete, brainchild of Henry Chapman Mercer (1856-1930).

In 1916 Mercer built what is now the Mercer Museum, with its turrets and parapets, to house his collection of more than 50,000 artifacts and tools of more than sixty different American trades. Entering the central court of the museum, you find yourself surrounded by odds and ends hanging over your head: a Conestoga wagon; a whaling skiff; wooden buckets. Then take the elevator up to the top floor and walk down, working your way through the implements left behind by shoemakers, bakers, candlemakers, milliners, and farmers of America's past.

Look for the "Go for the Green" tags that mark exhibits designed for kids to touch, to build things, to pull the reins, and more. Bright paw prints indicate clues on a family scavenger hunt around the collection, and the audio guides feature a channel just for kids. The museum also offers family events such as sleepovers, "Summer Boredom Busters," and "Under the Stars" movies.

Your kids may agree that the highlight of the collection is the vampire-killing kit. They can hunt for the footprints left in the concrete by Mercer's pet dog. The museum is unheated, so bring a sweater. There are special children's programs, as well as FolkFest in May.

James A. Michener Art Museum (all ages)

138 S. Pine St.; (215) 340-9800; www.michenerartmuseum.org. Open Tues through Fri 10 a.m. to 4:30 p.m.; Sat 10 a.m. to 5 p.m.; and Sun noon to 5 p.m. Open until 9 p.m. on Wed in summer only. Admission is $$ for adults, $ for students; children under 12 are free. Some exhibitions may require an additional fee.

The James A. Michener Art Museum, across the street from the Mercer Museum, offers the finest collection of Pennsylvania Impressionist paintings, as well as other important examples of regional contemporary and figurative art. Housed in a renovated historic site that served as the Bucks County Jail from 1884 to 1985, the museum features a permanent exhibit on James Michener and the Nakashima Reading Room, completely designed and furnished by wood artist George Nakashima. The family education center provides puzzles and discovery boxes for children to explore. Light snacks are available at the cafe. The Michener Museum has opened a satellite location in New Hope. (See listing for James A. Michener Art Museum—New Hope earlier in this chapter.)

Moravian Pottery and Tile Works (ages 8 and up)

E. Court St.; (215) 345-6722. Open daily, except major holidays, 10 a.m. to 4:45 p.m. Tours leave every thirty minutes, with the last tour departing at 4 p.m. Admission is $. The tile shop, open daily 10 a.m. to 4:45 p.m., can be entered without admission.

The Moravian Pottery and Tile Works is the legacy of Mercer's effort to preserve an American craft. You can purchase Moravian tiles here or take a tour to see how the tiles are made.

Fonthill (ages 8 and up)

East Court Street and PA 313; (215) 348-9461. Open Mon through Sat 10 a.m. to 5 p.m. and Sun noon to 5 p.m. Reservations are required. Admission for adults is $$, seniors and ages 6 to 17 $. Children under 6 are free.

Mercer's home, Fonthill, has forty-four rooms, eighteen fireplaces, and thirty-two staircases. Tours have been revamped to capture the interests of children. Be sure to check it out. Combination tickets are available for Mercer Museum and Fonthill.

ALSO IN THE AREA

Gardeners get a breath of fresh air at **Henry Schmieder Arboretum of Delaware Valley College** on US 202 (215-345-1500; www.delvalcol.edu/arboretum) and the nearby **Inn at Fordhook Farm** (a bed-and-breakfast; call 215-345-1766). The Burpee family (of Burpee Seeds) developed many well-known seed varieties in this area.

Chalfont

Byers' Choice Ltd. (ages 6 and up)

4355 County Line Rd.; (215) 822-0150; www.byerschoice.com. The factory is open at no charge Mon through Sat 10 a.m. to 5 p.m. and Sun noon to 5 p.m. Closed major holidays.

At Byers' Choice Ltd. the Byers family and their employees hand-sculpt thousands of delightful Caroler figurines every year, giving a percentage of their profits to charity. Doll-lovers' eyes grow wide when they see a gallery of tiny landscapes filled with figurines. There is also a gift shop and a short movie about the history of the company.

Amazing
Pennsylvania Facts

Bucks County's fertile soil has nourished Broadway luminaries like George S. Kaufman, Moss Hart, Oscar Hammerstein II; writers like James Michener and Pearl S. Buck; and artists such as George Nakashima and Edward Hicks.

Hilltown

Green Hills Farm (Pearl S. Buck House) (ages 10 and up)

520 Dublin Rd., 1 mile southwest of PA 313; (215) 249-0100, ext. 170, or (800) 220-BUCK; www.pearl-s-buck.org. Guided tours are available Mar through Dec, Tues through Sat at 11 a.m., 1 p.m., and 2 p.m. On Sun, tours leave at 1 and 2 p.m. only. Admission is $$ for adults, seniors, and students; free for children under 6.

Perhaps you or your kids have read *The Good Earth* or other books by Pearl S. Buck. The author settled in this farmhouse at Green Hills Farm. In her office here she wrote more than one hundred novels. Buck was not only a writer but also a humanitarian—an early supporter of human rights, civil rights, and women's rights. Her home still houses the offices of Pearl S. Buck International, "bringing hope to children worldwide."

The oldest section of the house was built in 1740, with sections added in 1825 and 1935. The furniture, artifacts, and contemporary artwork represent a true blending of East and West.

Worcester

Peter Wentz Farmstead (ages 6 and up)

Off PA 73 at Schearer Road; (610) 584-5104; www.montcopa.org/historicsites. Open year-round Tues to Sat 10 a.m. to 4 p.m. and Sun 1 to 4 p.m.; closed Mon and major holidays. Admission is free. Donations are accepted.

The historians at Peter Wentz Farmstead have done an exceptional job researching and restoring this farm to its appearance in 1777, when General Washington occupied the house before and after the Battle of Germantown.

If you thought colonial farms were painted in subdued tones, you'll be amazed at the paint colors and wild patterns on the walls: dots, zigzags, stripes, and more.

Special events are scheduled throughout the year, when you can watch costumed volunteers demonstrate colonial crafts and unusual arts such as *scherenschnitte,* the

German art of paper cutting. The kids especially like the farm animals. Annual events include a Market Day with Revolutionary War activities on the first Sat in June, the Colonial Craft Festival on the first Sat in Oct, and Candlelight House Tours on the first Sat in Dec.

ALSO IN THE AREA

Only a few blocks away, on Weikel Road, you can see the **Morgan Log House,** built in 1695 and more than 90 percent intact. The Morgans, who lived here, had ten children, one of whom grew up to become the mother of Daniel Boone. Open Apr to Nov, weekends only, noon to 5 p.m. or by appointment. Call (215) 368-2480.

Schwenksville

Pennypacker Mills (ages 8 and up)

PA 73 and Haldeman Road; (610) 287-9349; www.montcopa.org/historicsites. Open free of charge Tues through Sat 10 a.m. to 4 p.m. and on Sun 1 to 4 p.m. Last daily tour begins at 3:30 p.m. Closed Mon and major holidays.

Seven miles down Skippack Pike (PA 73) from the Peter Wentz Farmstead, you can see an excellent example of Colonial Revival architecture. Pennypacker Mills was owned by the Pennypacker family as early as 1747. In 1900 Samuel W. Pennypacker purchased it and added onto the home, making a turn-of-the-twentieth-century mansion. Pennypacker was governor of Pennsylvania from 1903 to 1907, as well as a respected historian, collector, and farmer. At present his home preserved by Montgomery County as a turn-of-the-twentieth-century country gentleman's estate.

Pennypacker Mills hosts special events for children, including a Halloween celebration with hayrides. Special children's events re-create the neighborhood parties once held by the Pennypacker daughters. There are also living-history events, including a Civil War reenactment and Christmas holiday celebrations.

ALSO IN THE AREA

The **Philadelphia Folk Festival,** which began in 1961, is one of the oldest and best folk festivals in the country. The folk festival brings music, crafts, dancing, and thousands of people to Old Pool farm in Schwenksville every Aug. For information call (800) 556-FOLK or check out the Web site at www.folkfest.org. Children twelve and under enter any concert **free!**

Alburtis

The anthracite iron industry played an important role in the development of this area, beginning in 1839.

Lock Ridge Furnace Museum (ages 6 and up)

Franklin Street; (610) 435-4664; www.lehighcountyhistoricalsociety.org. Open weekends May through Sept 10 a.m. to 4 p.m. Admission is free. Grounds open year-round.

Lock Ridge Furnace Museum operated as a furnace until 1914 and is now one of the sites administered by the Lehigh County Historical Society.

Allentown

On the waterfront in Allentown, long-quiet historic transportation and industrial buildings are being transformed into Lehigh Landing. The eleven-acre project will eventually include a visitor center for the region, playground, baseball field, riverfront walk, and more.

Lehigh Landing will be located immediately north of the Hamilton Street Bridge, a short walk east of downtown Allentown. Keep up to date on new developments by checking the Web site at www.americaonwheels.org.

America On Wheels (all ages)

718 Hamilton St.; (610) 432-4200; www.americaonwheels.org. Open Tues to Sat 10 a.m. to 5 p.m., Sun noon to 5 p.m. Admission: $ adults; children under 5 free.

America on Wheels explores the historical, economic, and social aspects of the development of over-the-road transportation in the Lehigh Valley and across America. The museum includes 23,000 square feet of exhibit space in its three main galleries, grand concourse, and lobby. Families can learn about carriages, wagons, bicycles, motorcycles, cars, and trucks through interactive stations focusing on the past, present, and future of transportation.

The Mack Truck Historical Museum (ages 6 and up)

997 Postal Rd.; (610) 266-6767; www.macktrucks.com. Regular hours Mon, Wed, and Fri 10 a.m. to 4 p.m. Hours subject to change. Please call ahead before you visit. Admission **free.**

The Mack Truck Museum has one of the original sightseeing buses built by Jack and Augustus Mack in the early twentieth century. You can also see a 1911 Mack Jr. that shared the streets with horse-drawn wagons as it delivered dry good and produce. The museum is home to antique Mack trucks, a UPS tractor, and many photos and memorabilia related to the truck that epitomizes endurance on the road. Kids are allowed to climb into the driver's seat of a few of the trucks, but others are for looking only. The museum is staffed by enthusiastic retired Mack employees.

Museum of Indian Culture and Lenni Lenape Historical Society (ages 5 and up)

2825 Fish Hatchery Rd.; (610) 797-2121; www.lenape.org. Open Fri through Sun noon to 4 p.m. Admission is $; special group rates are available. Wheelchair accessible.

If you can't understand another person until you've walked a mile in his moccasins, the Museum of Indian Culture and Lenni Lenape Historical Society has some that are the right size for kids. Hands-on exhibits illuminate Native American culture, as well as the exhibits of tools, baskets, and crafts. Three ceremonies are held annually: Corn Planting in May; Roasting Ears of Corn in Aug; and Time of Thanksgiving in Oct. There are also picnic facilities, two nature trails, and a fish hatchery.

Allentown Art Museum (all ages)

Fifth and Court Streets; (610) 432-4333; www.allentownartmuseum.org. Open Wed through Sat 11 a.m. to 5 p.m. and Sun noon until 5 p.m. Admission is $; **free** for kids under 12. Admission is also **free** on Sun.

Parents and kids can enjoy hands-on art activities themed to the current exhibition at Art Ways, the museum's interactive family gallery, included in your museum admission. On Sun from 1 to 4 p.m., museum educators host Sunday Artventures in the museum's Binney & Smith Learning Center. The museum also presents two family festivals per year, one in the fall and one in winter, themed to current museum exhibitions. Many programs are available for school and school groups, homeschoolers, and birthday parties. Please call (610) 432-4333, ext. 32, for information about group visits.

Haines Mill (ages 8 and up)

3600 Haines Mill Rd.; (610) 435-9601; www.lehighcountyhistoricalsociety.org. Open weekends from May until Sept, 1 to 4 p.m. Admission is **free.**

The mill was built in 1760 and operated until 1956, after having been renovated in 1909 with a water-turbine power source.

Lehigh Valley Heritage Center and Museum (ages 10 and up)

432 W. Walnut St.; (610) 435-1074; www.lchs.museum. The museum is open 10 a.m. to 4 p.m. Mon through Sat, 11 a.m. to 4 p.m. Sun. Library is closed Sun. $

This new home of the local historical society includes four spacious galleries. Permanent exhibits explore the county's history from the Native Americans through the rich heritage of the pioneering Pennsylvania German settlers, to the developments that made the county an industrial powerhouse, attracting immigrants from all over the world. The center also houses the historical society's library, an extensive collection of county, personal, business, and genealogical records.

The museum also includes the Scott Andrew Trexler II Memorial Library, an extensive collection of county and genealogical records.

Liberty Bell Shrine (ages 8 and up)

Zion Church at 622 Hamilton Mall; (610) 435-4664; www.libertybellmuseum.org/museum. Open May through Oct, Mon through Sat noon to 4 p.m. In Nov, Dec, Feb, Mar, and Apr, open Thurs through Sat noon to 4 p.m. Admission is free. Closed in Jan.

Did you know that during the Revolutionary War, when the British occupied Philadelphia, all the bells in the city were removed so that the British would not be able to melt them down for ammunition? From Sept 1777 to June 1778, the Liberty Bell was hidden under the floor of Allentown's Zion Church at 622 Hamilton Mall. At present the Liberty Bell Shrine includes an exact replica of the famous bell, as well as flags, maps, weapons, uniforms, and a 46-foot mural showing scenes from the Revolution.

Dorney Park and Wildwater Kingdom (all ages)

Near exit 16 on PA 309 South, at 3700 Hamilton Blvd.; (610) 395-3724; www.dorneypark .com. Hours for both parks vary according to season. Dorney Park is open weekends only in May and Sept, then daily from Memorial Day to Labor Day. Wildwater Kingdom is open mid-May to Labor Day and selected weekends in Sept. At the height of the season, tickets cost $$$$ for anyone 48 inches or taller, $$$ for anyone under 48 inches and seniors, and are free for children under 3. These prices include admission to both parks. There is a parking fee ($$).

According to ancient Greek legend, the hero Hercules defeated the nine-headed monster Hydra, but he was not able to kill all nine heads. There was one immortal head that could not be killed, so Hercules buried it under a huge boulder beside a lake.

But wait! What is that stirring by the edge of the lake? Hydra the Revenge!—a floorless coaster that includes seven inversions, a zero-gravity experience, several drops below ground level, and the jojo roll—the first-ever pre-lift inversion where riders twist upside down after exiting the launch station.

Hydra the Revenge joins Dorney Park's lineup of coasters: Dominator, Steel Force, Laser, Meteor Thunderhawk, and Talon.

Wildwater Kingdom has eleven waterslides. Younger children will love meeting the Berenstain Bears, playing in the TotSpot, and cooling off in two water park areas specifically for small-fry. Our kids could have spent the whole day in the giant wave pool.

In the fall, Dorney Park combines its rides with the frightening fun of Halloween to create Halloweekends.

ALSO IN THE AREA

The Lehigh County Historical Society administers a number of sites, including the Lehigh County Heritage Center and several historic homes. **Trout Hall** (414 Walnut St.; 610-435-9601) is Allentown's oldest home, built in 1770 by the son of the city's founder, William Allen. The **Troxell–Steckel House** in nearby Egypt (4229 Reliance St.; 610-435-9601) is an excellent example of a rural German-style farmhouse. Its barn contains a collection of old buggies and wagons. Trout Hall is open from 1 to 4 p.m. on Sat and Sun from May through Nov. From June through Aug, it is open the same hours on Thurs and Fri. The Troxell–Steckel House is open June through Oct, weekends only, from 1 to 4 p.m.

Frank Buchman, founder of the worldwide Moral Rearmament Movement, who was nominated for two Nobel prizes, lived at 117 North Eleventh St. in Allentown. The **Frank Buchman House** displays some of Buchman's souvenirs from an extraordinary life. The house is open for tours weekends only 1 to 4 p.m.

Schnecksville

Game Preserve, Lehigh Valley Zoo (all ages)

5150 Game Preserve Rd.; (610) 799-4171; www.lvzoo.org. Open Apr through Oct, 10 a.m. to 4 p.m. Admission: adults 13 to 64 $$; seniors 65 and older and children ages 2 to 12 $.

The Game Preserve is actually a zoo featuring a wide variety of wildlife in naturalistic habitats. There's a butterfly garden, pony rides, animal contact area, a birds of prey exhibit, and the zoo's newest residents: Arctic wolves. The Web site has fun animal puzzles for kids.

Claussville

Claussville One-Room Schoolhouse (ages 6 and up)

PA 100; (610) 435-9601; www.lehighcountyhistoricalsociety.org. Open on weekends from May through Sept 1 to 4 p.m. Admission is $ for adults; members and children free.

Children can picture what school must have been like in the Claussville One-Room Schoolhouse, in which children learned from 1893 until 1956. They can imagine kids sitting at these desks, reading the very books displayed there. The schoolhouse is one of the Lehigh County Historical Society sites.

Hellertown

If your kids are fascinated by crystal formations, rocks, minerals, and stalagmites and sta-lactites, don't miss Lost River Caverns, located in Hellertown.

Lost River Caverns (ages 6 and up)

726 Durham St., south of Bethlehem on PA 412, off I-78, exit 21; (610) 838-8767; fax (610) 838-2961; www.lostrivercaverns.com. Open year-round. From Memorial Day to Labor Day, 9 a.m. to 6 p.m.; the rest of the year, 9 a.m. to 5 p.m. Closed major holidays. Admission is $$ for adults and $ for children 3 to 12; children under 3 are free.

Yes, there is an actual lost river at Lost River Caverns. The clear water flows into the cavern from an unknown source, and then disappears just as mysteriously. Take an underground tour of a natural limestone cavern with crystal formations and a crystal chapel. There is also a museum, gift shop, and picnic grove.

Bethlehem

The Star of Bethlehem shines on Star Mountain every night of the year, watching over this city founded by Moravian settlers, who named Bethlehem on Christmas Eve 1741. You may wish to visit during Christkindlmarkt in December, when lanterns are lit, or in August, when Musikfest is held. But no matter when you visit, start out at the visitor center, where you can see a film and multimedia presentation about the city. You can pick up a schedule of events and walking-tour map, or you can schedule a guided tour. The visitor center is in the Historic District, off PA 378, at 52 W. Broad St. Call (610) 868-1513, (610) 867-0173, or (800) 360-8687.

Moravian Museum (all ages)

66 W. Church St.; (610) 867-0173. Open Fri through Sun 1 p.m. to 4 p.m. Closed in Jan. $$, free for children under 6.

A log cabin five stories tall, built entirely without nails, the Moravian Museum served as the Moravians' church when they first came to Bethlehem. It was also their sleeping quarters and workshop. Now it serves as a museum of Moravian history, exhibiting Moravian furniture, needlework, toys, and art.

Kemerer Museum of Decorative Arts (ages 8 and up)

427 N. New St.; (610) 868-6868; www.historicbethlehem.org. Open Fri through Sun noon to 4 p.m. Admission: $$ for adults, $ for children 6 to 12, and free for children under 6.

The Kemerer Museum features eighteenth- and nineteenth-century decorative arts such as furniture, folk art, textiles, paintings, and toys. Call for a schedule of changing exhibits.

Burnside Plantation (all ages)

1461 Schoernersville Rd., next to the Bethlehem Racquet Club; (610) 882-0450; www.historicbethlehem.org. Open for **free** self-guided tours Mon through Sun 8:30 a.m. to 5 p.m.

Seven acres of James Burnside's original farm have been developed as a living-history museum to interpret farming between 1748 and 1848. You can see the restored farmhouse, 1841 bank barn, summer kitchen, and kitchen garden. The new 2-mile walking trail, the Monocacy Way, actually starts at Illick's Mill Park, crosses Burnside Plantation, and continues through the Colonial Industrial Quarter. The plantation hosts an annual Blueberry Festival on the last weekend in July.

Da Vinci Science Center (ages 8 and up)

3145 Hamilton Blvd. Bypass; (484) 664-1002; www.davinci-center.org. Open 9:30 a.m. to 5 p.m. Mon through Sat and noon to 5 p.m. Sun. Admission: $$; children 3 and under **free.**

This successor to the Discovery Center of Science and Technology hosts more than 200 exhibits that stimulate kids' scientific curiosity. Six exhibit areas let them discover the answer to questions like "What's the Matter?" (about physics) or "What Hurts?" (about the human body). A 102-foot wind turbine outside generates clean power for the center, which is on the campus of Cedar Crest College.

Banana Factory (ages 5 and up)

25 W. Third St.; (610) 332-1300; www.bananafactory.org. Open Mon through Thurs 9:30 a.m. to 9 p.m., Fri 8:30 a.m. to 7 p.m., and Sun 9 a.m. to 5 p.m. Gallery hours subject to change. Admission is **free.**

The mission of the Banana Factory is "to kindle, support, and celebrate the artistic, cultural, and creative spirit of the Lehigh Valley." Located in a former warehouse for bananas, the Banana Factory offers classes for children and adults, as well as art exhibits. There are twenty-three artists' studios in the building, which is also home to the Pennsylvania Youth Theater and the Bethlehem Musikfest Association.

ALSO IN THE AREA

For ten days every August, the streets, plazas, and historic places of Bethlehem vibrate with music from all over the world. **Bethlehem's Musikfest** attracts hundreds of musicians and music lovers to performances at thirteen outdoor and six indoor venues. Specially for the children, clowns, jugglers, and magicians roam the streets. There is also an interactive theater for kids and parents. Hands-on crafts, an outdoor art studio called Muralplatz, and both regional and international foods, plus a fireworks display, complete the festivities.

Nazareth

Like Bethlehem, Nazareth was founded in the 1700s by Moravian settlers. At present Nazareth is also the home of Martin Guitars.

Martin Guitar Factory (ages 8 and up)

510 Sycamore St.; (610) 759-2837 or (800) 633-2060; www.martinguitar.com. Guided tours Mon through Fri at 1 p.m., except during holiday periods. For groups of ten or more, reservations are required and a per-person fee ($) is charged.

A small museum displays limited-edition guitars made for people like Gene Autry and Johnny Cash. The **free** tour takes about an hour and brings you close up to the craftspeople who create the instruments.

ALSO IN THE AREA

Other historical sites in Nazareth include **Moravian Historical Society** (214 E. Center St.; 610-759-5050; www.moravianhistoricalsociety.org), and **Whitefield** (pronounced *wit-field*) **House Museum** (214 E. Center St.; 610-759-5070).

Easton

Did you know that the average child in the United States will wear down 730 crayons by his tenth birthday? Your children won't want to miss out on the Crayola Factory at Two Rivers Landing, 30 Centre Sq.

Crayola Factory (all ages)

30 Centre Sq.; (610) 515-8000; www.crayola.com/factory. Open Tues through Sat 9:30 a.m. to 5 p.m., and Sun noon to 5 p.m. From Jan through May, weekday hours are 9:30 a.m. to 4 p.m.; from Memorial Day through Labor Day, also open on Mon and one hour earlier on Sun. Also open most national holidays. Closed New Year's Day, Easter, Thanksgiving, Christmas Eve, and Christmas. Admission price includes access to the Crayola Factory and the National Canal Museum. Admission $$ for adults and children. Children under two admitted **free.**

Spend some time with your family at this hands-on discovery center filled with creativity and fun for children and adults alike. You'll be sure to leave with a bag of your child's own original souvenirs. Make your own artwork with melted crayon wax at Crayola Meltdown, or use Crayola Model Magic to create three-dimensional art in Super Sculptures. Dance in Cool Moves and see your image projected onto a screen. Even the youngest visitors can explore Color Park.

Don't miss the Crayola crayon and marker demonstrations, where staff show how these products are made, or Crayola Chronology, where information abounds on the over one-hundred-year history of Binney & Smith, makers of Crayola products.

National Canal Museum (ages 8 and up)

30 Centre Sq.; (610) 559-6613; www.canals.org. Open Labor Day to Memorial Day Tues through Fri 9:30 a.m. to 3 p.m., Sat 9:30 a.m. to 5 p.m., and Sun noon to 5 p.m. From Memorial Day to Labor Day, open Mon through Sat 9:30 to 5 p.m. and Sun 11 a.m. to 5 p.m. Closed Mon except for the following holidays: Martin Luther King Jr. Day, Presidents' Day, Memorial Day, Labor Day, and Columbus Day. Admission to the National Canal Museum and the Crayola Factory is $$; children under age 2 are **free.**

Upstairs from the Crayola Factory is the National Canal Museum, whose interactive exhibits allow you to operate a lock model or pilot your boat through the lock. Whole families lived and worked on canal barges in Pennsylvania and elsewhere in the nineteenth century, and excellent exhibits explain this vanished way of life.

Josiah White II Canal Boat Rides and Hugh Moore Park (all ages)

Hugh Moore Park (look for Canal Boat signs); (610) 559-6613; www.canals.org. Rides available first Sat in May to mid-June: Tues through Fri 9:45 a.m. to 2:20 p.m.; Sat, Sun, and Memorial Day 1:30 to 4:30 p.m. From mid-June to Labor Day: Mon through Sat 10:30 a.m. to 5 p.m.; Sun 12:45 to 5 p.m. Weekends in Sept: Sat, Sun, and Labor Day 1:30 to 4 p.m. Fares: adults $$; children 3 to 15 $.

A costumed interpreter takes you on a forty-minute ride on a mule-drawn canal boat. Special evening rides with dinner and music are available, as are charter rides for groups.

While in Hugh Moore Park, you may wish to take advantage of the park's trails, pavilions, picnic areas, and playground. The Locktender's House Museum re-creates the life of a locktender and his family.

Upper Black Eddy

Ringing Rocks (all ages)

Ringing Rocks Road, west of Upper Black Eddy; (215) 757-0571; www.buckscounty.org.

This National Park includes an amazing three-and-one-half-acre field of boulders. If you (gently!) strike these rocks, they ring like bells! You might want to bring along some kind of hammer, but if you forget, you can even use smaller rocks to make the rocks ring.

Over the years legends grew up about the origins of Ringing Rocks. Maybe it was an Indian ceremonial site, some said, maybe a witches' meeting place, or a UFO landing site. In reality, Ringing Rocks is the result of millions of years of geologic activity. But magical nonetheless.

Sneakers or rubber-soled shoes recommended. Please be careful not to chip or harm the rocks.

Where to Eat

IN BUCKS COUNTY

Smokey Bones Barbeque & Grill, 2250 E. Lincoln Hwy., Langhorne; (215) 752-8305; www.smokeybones.com. Kids' menu. $$.

IN CHESTER COUNTY

Buca di Beppo, 300 Main St., Exton; (610) 524-9939; www.bucadibeppo.com. Dinner every day; weekends from noon. Giant portions of everyone's favorites at this popular chain.

Chester Springs Creamery at Milky Way Farm, 521 E. Uwchlan Ave. (PA 113), Chester Springs; (610) 363-8500. Ice-cream treats at a working farm. Seasonal hours vary in spring and summer; call ahead. $.

Hank's Place, US 1 and PA 100 (across from the Brandywine River Museum); (610) 388-7061. Breakfast, lunch, and dinner daily. Overlooking the Brandywine River, this little diner serves big breakfasts, burgers, and early dinners. $$.

IN MONTGOMERY COUNTY

Moon and Stars Cafe, 1617 The Fairway, Jenkintown; (215) 886-3130. Small, casual family restaurant with kids' menu, ice cream, and coffee bar. Open daily. $$.

Where to Stay

IN BUCKS COUNTY

Best Western New Hope Inn, 6426 Lower York Road, Doylestown; (215) 862-5221. Country setting, pool, restaurant.

Holiday Inn Select—Bucks County, 4700 Street Rd., PA Turnpike, exit 28, Trevose; (215) 364-2000 or (800) HOLIDAY. Indoor pool. Sesame Place packages available. Kids eat free.

IN MONTGOMERY COUNTY

Doubletree Guest Suites, Plymouth Meeting, 640 W. Germantown Pike, Plymouth Meeting; (610) 834-8300 or (800) 222-TREE; www.doubletreeplymouth.com. Suite accommodations, restaurant, indoor pool.

Holiday Inn Express, 260 N. Gulph Rd., King of Prussia; (610) 768-9500 or (800) HOLIDAY. Next to King of Prussia mall. Great rates for families.

The Inn at King of Prussia by Best Western, 127 S. Gulph Rd., King of Prussia; (610) 265-4500. Convenient to Valley Forge National Historic Park as well as King of Prussia shopping. Outdoor pool.

McIntosh Inn, 4 S. Middleton Rd., Media; (610) 565-5800. Convenient to Brandywine River Museum, Brandywine Battlefield, and Chadds Ford.

The Philadelphia Marriott West, 111 Crawford Ave., West Conshohocken; (610) 941-5600 or (800) 237-3639. Convenient to Valley Forge, Philadelphia, Main Line, and Manayunk.

For More Information

Bucks County, (800) 836-2825; www.bctc.org.

Bucks County Tourist Commission, Inc., (215) 345- 4552 or (800) 836-BUCKS; www.bctc.org.

Chester County Tourist Bureau, Inc., (610) 280-6145 or (800) 228-9933; www.brandywinevalley.com.

Delaware County Convention and Visitors Bureau, Inc., (610) 565-3679 or (800) 343-3983; www.brandywinecountry.org.

Lehigh Valley Convention and Visitors Bureau, Inc., (610) 882-9200 or (800) 747-0561; www.lehighvalleypa.org.

Montgomery County Historic Sites, www.montcopa.org.

Nazareth Area Visitor Center, 201 N. Main St., Nazareth 18064; (610) 759-9174.

Valley Forge Convention and Visitors Bureau, (610) 834-1550 or (800) 441-3549; www.valleyforge.org.

New Hope Visitors Center, 1 W. Mechanic St., New Hope 18938; (215) 862-5030; www.newhopevisitorscenter.org.

Hershey– Pennsylvania Dutch Country

Hershey–Pennsylvania Dutch Country beckons with amusement parks, historical sites, Pennsylvania Dutch arts and crafts, and lots of train rides. Lancaster's own minor league baseball team, the Lancaster Barnstormers, has played in a beautiful ballpark in downtown Lancaster. This is the Keystone State's classic countryside, with Amish farms and roadside markets. It was also the site of the Battle of Gettysburg, where more American lives were lost than in any other single battle in U.S. history.

Harrisburg, the state capital on the shores of the Susquehanna, is a great place to visit. City Island, once abandoned, has been transformed into a family-entertainment spot, with miniature golf, the Pride of the Susquehanna riverboat, Class AA baseball, a children's railroad, and more.

TopPicks in Hershey–Pennsylvania Dutch Country

- **Hersheypark,** Hershey
- **Strasburg Rail Road,** Strasburg
- **Railroad Museum of Pennsylvania,** Strasburg
- **Whitaker Center for Science and the Arts,** Harrisburg
- **Hershey Gardens,** Hershey
- *Pride of the Susquehanna* **riverboat,** Harrisburg
- **Fishing at Limestone Springs Preserve,** Richland
- **Herr Foods,** Inc., Nottingham
- **Gettysburg National Military Park,** Gettysburg
- **Capitol Building,** Harrisburg

HERSHEY–PENNSYLVANIA DUTCH COUNTRY

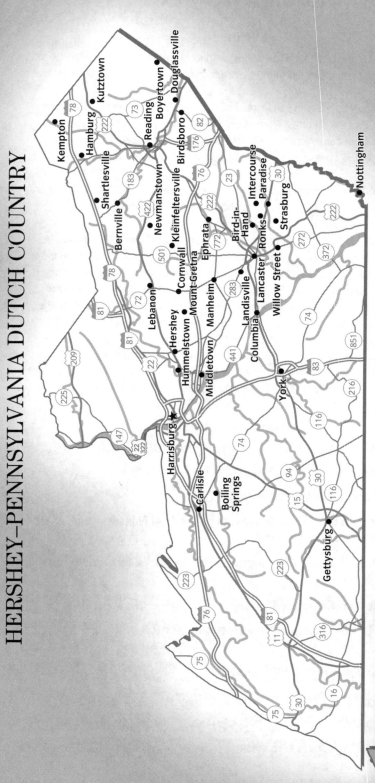

Kids delight in Hershey, ChocolateTown USA, with its streetlights shaped like chocolate kisses and its triple helping of kid-friendly attractions—Hersheypark, ZooAmerica, and Chocolate World.

Some 70,000 Plain People live in Lancaster County, members of communities such as the Amish, Brethren, and Mennonites. Plain People appreciate it when tourists respect their privacy and dislike of cameras. Visits to The People's Place, the Amish Farm, and "The Amish Experience" will present important opportunities to teach your children sensitivity.

Families who visit Pennsylvania Dutch Country often comment on the food: It's abundant and inexpensive. Family-style restaurants abound, with diners seated at large tables and delicious, simple food passed around in large bowls.

A reader asked about driving on country roads in Lancaster County. If you take PA 772 starting in Intercourse and continuing toward Columbia, this well-marked road loops through the county, past Amish and Mennonite farms. You can stop at a farm stand and buy vegetables or preserves from an Amish child. You'll poke through little towns like Lititz, stumble upon quilt and craft shops, and admire scenic overlooks. The staff at the Pennsylvania Dutch Convention and Visitors Bureau can help you map out your own route, taking into consideration your interests and the season.

The Pennsylvania Dutch area is a great place for a farm vacation. For more information on a vacation of any type in Pennsylvania Dutch Country, call the Pennsylvania Dutch Convention and Visitors Bureau at (717) 299-8901. To learn about farm vacations, write

TopEvents in Hershey–Pennsylvania Dutch Country

- **Pennsylvania Farm Show,** early Jan; (717) 787-5373.

- **Chambersburg Icefest,** Jan; (717) 264-7101.

- **Civil War Reenactments at Gettysburg National Military Park** (summer weekends); (717) 338-1525.

- **Kutztown Pennsylvania German Festival,** nine days surrounding July 4; (888) 674-6136.

- **Carlisle Summerfair,** July; (717) 240-7180.

- **Pennsylvania Renaissance Faire,** late summer to early fall; (717) 665-7021.

- **Fort Hunter Day,** Sept; (717) 599-5751.

- **Hersheypark Creatures of the Night,** Oct; (717) 534-3860.

- **Dickens of a Christmas,** Nov through Dec; (717) 665-7021.

- **Hersheypark Christmas Candylane,** Nov through Dec; (717) 534-3860.

to the Pennsylvania Farm Vacation Association, Pennsylvania Department of Agriculture, Marketing Department, 2301 N. Cameron St., Harrisburg 17110-9408. A list of farm B&Bs is included in this chapter.

Here are some useful contacts:

- **Gettysburg Convention and Visitors Bureau** (Adams County); (717) 334-6274 or (800) 337-5015; www.gettysburg.com.

- **Pennsylvania Dutch Convention and Visitors Bureau** (Lancaster County); (717) 299-8901 or (800) PA–DUTCH; www.padutchcountry.com.

- **Reading and Berks County Visitors Bureau;** (610) 375-4085 or (800) 443-6610; www.readingberkspa.com.

- **York County Convention and Visitors Bureau;** (717) 848-4000 or (888) 858-YORK; www.yorkpa.org.

- **The Pennsylvania Dutch Country Welcome Center;** www.800padutch.com.

Kempton

Hawk Mountain Sanctuary (ages 8 and up)
Five miles east of PA 61, north of Hamburg, off PA 895; (610) 756-6000; www.hawkmountain .org. The visitor center is open daily year-round 9 a.m. to 5 p.m.; extended hours in fall. Admission is $$ for adults, $ for seniors and children 6 to 12.

Every year about 75,000 visitors "flock" to Hawk Mountain nature-observation area to watch the many species of hawks and eagles that pass through the area on their annual migrations. During busy fall weekends, as many as a dozen very helpful interns, volunteers, and staff members are available to interpret the spectacle of migration for visitors.

Wind and weather conditions have a great impact on the birds, so plan your visit based on the weather. Before you go, be sure to check the Web site for weather conditions, directions, and specific information on which species you are likely to see that day. Bring binoculars (or rent them here), wear a jacket, and pack a lunch in a backpack—there's no snack bar. But remember that you'll be carrying home all your trash; there are no garbage cans at the lookout and you are responsible for any food wrappers, cans, or bottles you bring along. You might also want to bring along something soft to sit on.

Children should be reminded that noise may frighten the birds. Pets are not permitted. We recommend taking the kids on the rocky Escarpment Trail so that they can burn off some energy before arriving at North Lookout. The South Lookout is wheelchair accessible.

WK&S Railroad Line (all ages)
Take PA 143 North or PA 737 North into Kempton and follow signs to WK&S Railroad. For schedules and more information, call (610) 756-6469 or go to www.kemptontrain.com. The

steam train runs on Sun from May through Oct and on Sat during June, July, Aug, and Oct. The diesel train runs on Sat in June and Aug. Fares are $$ for adults, $ for children ages 3 to 11. Children under 3 ride **free.**

The train ride on the Wanamaker, Kempton, and Southern is about 6 miles round-trip and takes about forty minutes. Pack a picnic and have the train drop you off at a trackside grove. You can ride all day if you like. A Santa Claus Special rides the rails in Dec; in Oct, it's time for the Harvest Moon Special. Please note that although the train is sometimes known as the Hawk Mountain Line, it does not actually go to Hawk Mountain.

Kutztown

Crystal Cave (ages 8 and up)
Situated between Allentown and Reading off US 222 at Crystal Cave and Valley Roads. For information and the schedule of guided tours, call (610) 683-6765; www.crystalcavepa .com. Admission: $$ for adults, $ for children ages 4 to 11.

Crystal Cave, discovered in 1871, is the oldest operating cave in Pennsylvania. Just use your imagination and you can see the ice-cream cone, the crystal ballroom, the giant's tooth, and the prairie dogs inside the geological formations here. After your underground adventure, try some of the **free** activities such as the nature trail, picnic area, and Amish buggy display.

This cave is probably less strenuous than some others, with railings and walkways. No strollers are permitted in the cave, so put the baby in a backpack, if possible. The Main Inn has a large restroom and lounge but no changing table. Picnic tables are available, some covered. You can eat at the Pennsylvania Dutch Fast Food Restaurant, Sugar Shack, and ice-cream shop, open seasonally. Miniature golf is also available for a fee.

Reading

A day of AA baseball is even more fun for families and groups, with picnic tables, swimming, and cascading waterfalls. Water cannons erupt from the pool whenever the Phillies score a run. For details check www.readingphillies.com or call (610) 375-8469.

The Sovereign Center hosts many concerts and ice shows and is also home to the newly franchised Reading Royals Ice Hockey team. For information check www.sovereign center.com or www.royalshockey.com.

Reading Public Museum (ages 2 and up)
500 Museum Rd.; (610) 371-5850; www.readingpublicmuseum.org. Adults $$, children 4 to 17 $, children under 4, **free.** Open Tues through Sat 11 a.m. to 5 p.m.; Fri 11 a.m. to 8 p.m.; Sun noon to 5 p.m. Closed Mon and major holidays.

The Reading Public Museum boasts an impressive collection of both art and science exhibits, as well as an arboretum.

Hamburg

To describe Cabela's as an outdoorsman's superstore doesn't begin to tell the story. In the first year of operations in Pennsylvania, Cabela's attracted nearly four million visitors.

Cabela's

100 Cabela Dr., near the intersection of I-78 and PA 61; (610) 929-7000, www.cabelas.com. Open Mon through Sat, 8 a.m. to 9 p.m., Sun 10 a.m. to 8 p.m.

The largest of Cabela's retail stores and the only one in Pennsylvania, this 250,000-square-foot superstore has become a tourist destination in itself. Cabela's features a huge walk-through aquarium, an indoor mountain complete with waterfall, and more than 800 mounted wildlife specimens in museum-quality dioramas. It also has a shooting gallery, an archery range, and a restaurant.

Shartlesville

Roadside America (ages 4 and up)

109 Roadside Dr., near exit 23 off I-78/US 22; (610) 488-6241; www.roadsideamericainc .com. Summer (July through Labor Day): Open daily 9 a.m. to 6:00 p.m., weekends 9 a.m. to 7 p.m. Winter (Sept through June): Open daily 10 a.m. to 5 p.m., weekends 10 a.m. to 6 p.m. Admission is $. Children 5 and under enter **free.** Group rates available.

A fan wrote to suggest including a favorite destination of her family, Roadside America. This unique indoor miniature village is a wonderful piece of Americana. One man, Laurence Gieringer, created this scale model during more than sixty years of meticulous work. There are trains chugging through tunnels and over bridges, a gristmill, a trolley, and even a tiny fountain in the miniature zoo.

Young children may have to be lifted up to see some of the displays, but they'll love it anyhow.

Boyertown

Boyertown Museum of Historic Vehicles (all ages)

85 S. Walnut St.; (610) 367-2090; www.boyertownmuseum.org; e-mail: museum@enter.net. Open Tues through Sun 9:30 a.m. to 4 p.m. Closed major holidays. Admission is $. Children under 6 enter **free.** Reservations are required for groups.

During the early days of the automobile industry, dozens of manufacturers built cars, trucks, and motorcycles right here in southeastern Pennsylvania. More than fifty of these rare automobile products can be seen in the Boyertown Museum of Historic Vehicles, along with examples of the horse-powered vehicles they eventually made obsolete.

Every Labor Day weekend for the past forty years, the museum has celebrated all "wheeled classicalia" at its annual Duryea Day event.

Birdsboro

Daniel Boone Homestead (all ages)

400 Daniel Boone Rd.; (610) 582-4900. Open Tues through Sat 9 a.m. to 5 p.m., Sun noon to 5 p.m. year-round. Admission is $. Family rate $$$.

Daniel Boone was born in 1734 and grew up in a log cabin on this site. Only the foundation of the original cabin remains, but the oldest section of the log cabin that stands here now was built in 1750, around the time the Boones moved away. Here you can see a blacksmith's shop, smokehouse, bake oven, and sawmill. Children especially enjoy the horses and sheep. There are facilities available for picnicking and camping. The second floor of the house is not wheelchair accessible, but disabled visitors may view a video of it.

Bernville

Koziar's Christmas Village (all ages)

782 Christmas Village Rd., 7 miles past the Reading Airport, off PA 183; (610) 488-1110; www.koziarschristmasvillage.com. From Nov 1 to Thanksgiving, open Fri 6 to 9 p.m., Sat and Sun 5 to 10 p.m. From Thanksgiving to Jan 1, open Mon through Fri 6 to 9 p.m., Sat and Sun 5 to 9:30 p.m. Admission is $$ per person; children under 5 enter free.

Named "Best Outdoor Christmas Display in the World" by *Display World Magazine*, Koziar's Christmas Village is a holiday tradition—and every year it's new, improved, and all handmade. More than 500,000 lights sparkle on the lakeside house, along with its walkways, trees, and ten outbuildings including Santa's post office and toy shop. There are more than thirty buildings, about eight of which can be entered, but Koziar's is mostly an outdoor experience, so dress accordingly.

Kleinfeltersville

Middle Creek Wildlife Management Area (ages 8 and up)

Hopeland Road. Visitor center: (717) 733-1512; www.pgc.state.pa.us. Open Feb 1 to the day before Thanksgiving, Tues through Sun 8 a.m. to 4 p.m. and Sun noon to 5 p.m. Free.

Bundle up, bring your binoculars, and come to the Middle Creek Wildlife Management Area in Feb or Mar and you might see thousands of tundra swans and snow geese. In spring and fall there are many other species of migrating waterfowl. There are also 6,254 acres of state game land, with seven trails, plus fishing and hunting in designated areas only, including one trout stream that's accessible to the disabled. Picnic areas are available, but you must not feed the birds. Check the Web site to find out current migration patterns.

There are a number of annual events at Middle Creek. The first full weekend in Aug brings the annual art show. During the third full weekend in Sept, you can see an exhibit of wood-carving including decoys. Also in Sept is the annual Pennsylvania State Goose-Calling and Duck-Calling Championships.

Lebanon

The Daniel Weaver Company (ages 8 and up)

Located at the corner of Fifteenth and Weavertown Road, 0.5 mile off US 422 in Lebanon. For more information call (717) 274-6100 or (800) WEAVERS; www.lebanon-bologna.com. Open Mon through Fri 9 a.m. to 4 p.m.; free admission. Free tours also are available.

Lebanon is the one town where you can see how genuine Lebanon bologna is made. The Daniel Weaver Company, which produces both Weaver's famous Lebanon Bologna and Baum's Bologna, is the oldest commercial manufacturer of Lebanon bologna in the United States. Here you can see the outdoor smokehouses, visit exhibits, enjoy free samples, and visit their retail store.

Cornwall

Cornwall Iron Furnace (ages 10 and up)

Rexmont Road at Boyd Street, off PA 419; (717) 272-9711; www.cornwallironfurnace.org. Open daily Tues through Sat 9 a.m. to 5 p.m., Sun noon to 5 p.m. from June through Aug. From Sept through May, open Tues through Sat, 10 a.m. to 4 p.m., Sun noon to 4 p.m. Open Memorial Day, Independence Day, and Labor Day. Admission is $.

The massive stone furnace, steam-powered air-blast machinery, and several related buildings survive intact. Cornwall Iron Furnace operated from the 1740s until the 1880s. A guide takes you through the iron-making complex, the highlight of which is the 32-foot-tall furnace.

A handsomely updated museum helps children age ten and up understand the science and business of making iron, with clever interactive displays they can handle and explore. (Kids who are strong readers will gain the most from the exhibits.) They'll come away with an understanding of why so many towns in southeastern Pennsylvania have "Forge" or "Furnace" in their names: A seam of iron ore runs under most of this region.

Lebanon Valley Rail Trail (all ages)
Trailhead between PA 72 and Cornwall; www.lvrailtrail.com/project.htm. Free.

Cornwall is one of the trailheads (parking areas) for the Lebanon Valley Trail, which runs 12 miles south of the Lancaster County line. It's a quiet, peaceful crushed-gravel trail for bike riding or strolling (don't bring in-line skates, though). An extension north to the city of Lebanon is under way.

Mount Hope Estate, Pennsylvania Renaissance Faire (all ages)
Mount Hope Estate. Call (717) 665-7021 or check www.parenaissancefaire.com for details on schedules and admission.

On weekends from Aug through mid-Oct, join the raucous revelry of the Pennsylvania Renaissance Faire. Meet sixteenth-century knaves and wenches, jesters, pirates, princesses, and knights who will immerse your family in a spectacle of living theater. Events include jousting, human chess, children's games, crafts, short plays such as Robin Hood, and dancing. From the end of Oct through mid-Nov, you can be mystified at "Edgar Allan Poe Evermore." ("Edgar Allan Poe Evermore" is macabre and includes direct readings from Poe. It is recommended for older children, from thirteen up.) From Thanksgiving weekend until after Christmas, the estate is decked out quite differently for a festive "Dickens of a Christmas," recommended for all ages.

Mount Gretna

Another extension of the Lebanon Valley Rail Trail (see listing under Cornwall) is under way to Mount Gretna, off PA 72. This charming village, founded as a summer camp by the Methodists of the Pennsylvania Chautauqua Society in 1982, remains a favorite family destination in warm weather.

Kids love a day trip to Mount Gretna for two reasons. The first is Mount Gretna Lake; the second is the Jigger Shop ice-cream parlor. The village also offers the Gretna Theater (717-964-3627; http://mtgretna.com/theatre), a professional summer stock company; miniature golf; and a roller-skating rink. A Chautauqua program of lectures and concerts is offered each summer. Get the details at www.mtgretna.com.

Mount Gretna Lake (all ages)
130 Lakeview Dr. (off of PA 117 North; turn onto Timber Road at Mt. Gretna Country Store). Open daily Memorial Day through Labor Day, 11:30 a.m. to 6:30 p.m. $–$$, discount offered after 4:30 p.m.

Mount Gretna Lake has a sandy beach, picnic pavilion, swings, and an old-fashioned floating dock. (We loved grabbing the overhead swings from the dock and flying over, then into, the water.)

How to **Catch a Fish**

—by Trae Hoffner, age 9

If you like fishing, eastern Pennsylvania has some great trout to fish for, like brook and rainbow. You will see farms and big fields and maybe even a cow or two on your drive to get there. When you get there you can get your fishing supplies, like nets, poles, bait, and a basket to keep the trout that you have caught. The best kind of bait to use is colored marshmallows (my five-year-old brother always eats them). The trout like them the most. I cut the worm in half.

Here is a tip on fishing: The more you are relaxed, the better chance you have to catch a fish. Use a small hook to hide in the marshmallow or worm. The fish will not recognize it. You will be pulling them in once they eat it! You should reel it in slowly. You don't want to have too much tension on the line—it might break. You feel great when you catch a fish!

The Jigger Shop (all ages)

Gettysburg Avenue and PA 117; (717) 964-9686; www.jiggershop.com. Season ends Labor Day; call for hours in season. $$.

The Jigger Shop serves ice-cream drinks from a soda fountain with twirly stools inside and a shaded open deck outside. There's a sandwich menu and kid-friendly choices, too.

Richland

Limestone Springs Preserve (all ages)

930 Tulpehocken Rd.; (717) 866-2461; www.limestonespringspreserve.com. Open daily Apr through Oct. Admission $ (no Pennsylvania fishing license required). All fish caught are priced per pound.

Near Myerstown, a portion of the historic Union Canal is now a series of picturesque pools teaming with trout. These crystal waters produce over 750,000 pounds of fish a year! Families will enjoy this easy introduction to the sport. Bring a picnic or order a boxed lunch from nearby restaurants.

Ephrata

Ephrata is an interesting town where you may wish to browse in the art galleries and craft shops. Stop by at Artworks at Doneckers, 100 N. State St. (717-738-9503).

Ephrata Cloister (ages 10 and up)

632 W. Main St. (PA 272 and US 322); (717) 733-6600; www.ephratacloister.org. Open Mon to Sat 9 a.m. to 5 p.m. and Sun noon to 5 p.m. On Mon through Sat, tours leave at 10 and 11 a.m. and 1, 2, 3, and 4 p.m. Admission is $$ for adults and $ for ages 6 to 17. Children under 6 are free.

Older children may be interested in learning about a true alternative religious lifestyle at one time practiced in the eighteenth century at Ephrata Cloister. Here you can step into another reality in twelve restored buildings where hymns still seem to echo.

The guided tour starts with a film, *Anticipating Paradise*, and proceeds through three of the ten restored buildings. There are two cemeteries, a physician's house, a bakery, and more. Candlelight tours are offered in Dec. Most of the historic structures have some limits to wheelchair accessibility.

From Mar through Oct, on the second Sun of the month, the Cloister features a special "themed" day, with extra demonstrations and sometimes hands-on activities, at the regular admission price. Check the Web site for each month's theme.

Intercourse

Plain & Fancy Farm (all ages)

3121 Old Philadelphia Pike on PA 340 between Bird-in-Hand and Intercourse; (717) 768-4400; www.amishexperience.com. Open daily. Call ahead for hours.

Easily accessible to Mount Hope on the opposite side of PA 340 between Bird-in-Hand and Intercourse, you'll find Plain & Fancy Farm with its Pennsylvania Dutch crafts and food. There are a lot of things to do at Plain & Fancy, including buggy rides, "The Amish Experience," and Amish dining. Also at Plain & Fancy, you can visit the Amish Country Homestead (717-768-3600, ext. 10).

You can also take a guided bus tour of Amish country starting at Plain & Fancy Farm. Admission to each attraction may be purchased separately, or you may choose a combination ticket to the theater and homestead or a super-saver ticket that includes the theater, homestead, and guided bus tour. While here, pick up a copy of the *Amish Country News*.

Amish **Buggy Rides**

- **Abe's Buggy Rides;** (717) 392-1794; www.800padutch.com/abes.html.
- **Ed's Buggy Rides;** (717) 687-0360; www.edsbuggyrides.com.
- **Aaron and Jessica's Buggy Rides,** at Plain & Fancy Farm; (717) 768-4400; www.amishbuggyrides.com.

Where to Eat Amish-Style with Kids

- **Amish Barn Restaurant,** PA 340 between Bird-in-Hand and Intercourse; (717) 768-8886; www.amishbarnpa.com. Children's menu, petting zoo, gift shop; open seven days a week. Kids eat free.
- **Bird-in-Hand Family Restaurant,** Old Philadelphia Pike, 5 miles east of Lancaster on PA 340; (717) 768-1550; www.bird-in-hand.com/restaurant. Menustyle.
- **Harvest Drive Family Restaurant,** Intercourse; (717) 768-7186 or (800) 233-0176; www.harvestdrive.com. Great view. Full menu or family-style.
- **Plain & Fancy Farm,** 3121 Old Philadelphia Pike; (717) 768-4400.

Amish Country Tours ($$$) depart from the Amish Experience Theater, stopping at roadside stands, bakeshops, and craft shops along the scenic roads of the Amish farmlands. Children receive a worksheet and a small gift to make the tour more fun.

Lancaster County offers several opportunities to ride in a Pennsylvania Dutch buggy, but only one ride is owned and operated by an Amish family: Aaron and Jessica's Buggy Rides at Plain & Fancy Farm. The Web site offers a virtual tour and answers questions about the Amish and Mennonites.

Amish Country Homestead (all ages)

Plain & Fancy Farm, 3121 Old Philadelphia Pike; (717) 768-8400; www.amishnews.com. Hours subject to change seasonally. Admission to the homestead is $$ for adults, $ for children ages 4 to 11. Combination tickets available for homestead, theater, and bus tours.

This is the only Amish house open for guided tours that has received designation as a Lancaster County Heritage Site. The family depicted in the homestead is the Fisher family, also featured in Jacob's Choice, seen at The Amish Experience/FX Theater.

The Amish Experience/FX Theater (ages 7 and up)

Plain & Fancy Farm; (717) 768-8400 or (717) 768-3600; www.amishexperience.com. Hours subject to change seasonally. Admission to theater only is $$ for adults, $ for children 4 to 11. Combination tickets available to homestead, theater, and bus tour.

In a multimedia interactive "experiential theater" that defies labeling, a well-researched forty-minute program immerses the audience in the world of the Amish. The unique theater has five different image areas showing different pictures, and special effects. The show Jacob's Choice introduces a fictional Amish teenager and his family. Although younger kids will be entertained, children ages seven and up will get the point of what it means to be Amish.

Manheim

Kreider Farms (all ages)

PA 72 (ten minutes from PA 283) at 1461 Lancaster Rd.; (717) 665-4899; www.kreiderfarms
.com. Farm tour hours: Mon, Wed, and Fri 9:30 and 11:30 a.m. by reservation only.

"Mommy/Daddy, where does milk come from?" Here's a great way to answer this perennial question. At Kreider Farms, see cows milked on a carousel and learn how the milk
gets from the farm to the supermarket dairy case. Then top off your visit with lunch or
dinner at Kreider Farms restaurant, adjacent to the farm tour. (Kreider Farms also has restaurants at three other locations in the area.)

Bird-in-Hand

Americana Museum of Bird-in-Hand (ages 6 and up)

PA 340 East (2709 Old Philadelphia Pike); (717) 391-9780; www.bird-in-hand.com/americana
museum. Open Apr through Nov, Tues through Sat 10 a.m. to 5 p.m. (Last tour begins at
4:40 p.m.) Admission is $.

The Americana Museum focuses on American life from 1890 to 1930. Touring this indoor
complex with a self-guided tour pamphlet, you can stroll through a re-created town of the
period, including a fully stocked country general store and eight shops common to the
era. A children's activity sheet is available.

Weavertown One-Room Schoolhouse (all ages)

PA 340, east of Bird-in-Hand; (717) 768-3976 or (717) 291-1888; www.800padutch.com/wvr
town.html. Open Mar to Apr 11, Sat and Sun 10 a.m. to 5 p.m. From Apr 12 to Oct 24, open
daily 10 a.m. to 5 p.m. From Oct 25 to Nov 30, open Sat and Sun 10 a.m. to 4
p.m. Closed remainder of year. Admission is $.

Class is in session, with thirty animated figures of a teacher and pupils
in the Weavertown One-Room Schoolhouse. The building, desks, and
blackboard are original. The school was built in 1877 and held classes
for close to one hundred years.

Ronks

Cherry Crest Adventure Farm (ages 2 and up)

150 Cherry Hill Rd.; (717) 687-6843; www.cherrycrestfarm.com. Open seasonally; call or
check Web site for hours. Admission $$ (includes maze and farm activities); geocaching
only, $.

Cherry Crest is best known for its amazing five-acre corn maze, with a different theme each year. The Discovery Channel has named this "the World's Biggest Free-Standing Mind-Bender." In addition to exploring the maze by day, you can also try "flashlight tours" after dark. There are dozens of other activities, too, including pedal karts, slides, and even geocaching. In this high-tech treasure hunt game, participants use latitudes and longitudes entered into a GPS to explore the farm. This popular spot gets its biggest crowds in summer and early fall, and although it's usually closed on Mon, it makes exceptions for national holidays. Many people arrive to explore the maze by way of the Strasburg Rail Road.

The Outhouse (ages 4 and up)

The Village of Dutch Delights, Dienner's Restaurant Complex, 2853 Lincoln Highway East (US 30); (717) 687-9580. In winter open weekends only. During the rest of the year open Mon through Thurs 9 a.m. to 6 p.m.; Fri and Sat 9 a.m. to 7 p.m.

This combination store and funhouse features a "man-eating chicken" and "free foot of chocolate." A country store full of surprises and puns!

Strasburg

A reporter for the *New York Times* called the Strasburg area "command central for railroad buffs." Here in the town of Strasburg, transportation enthusiasts can learn about toy trains, real trains, classic cars, and more. It's the perfect place to take kids who are "into" vehicles.

Railroad Museum of Pennsylvania (all ages)

300 Gap Rd., on PA 741 East; (717) 687-8628; www.rrmuseumpa.org. Open Nov through Mar, Tues through Sat 9 a.m. to 5 p.m., Sun noon to 5 p.m. ; also open on Mon from Apr through Oct, Admission is $$ for adults and $ for children 6 to 12. A family rate is available.

The Railroad Museum of Pennsylvania will entrance your junior engineers. It's almost overwhelming to walk into the huge collection of locomotives and rolling stock at this museum, which specializes in railroad trains built or operated in Pennsylvania. Rolling Stock Hall is designed with a balcony and a pit so that you can see the forty-six locomotives and passenger cars from different angles. The new Stewart Junction Railway Education Center, located in a late-Victorian-era freight station, offers hands-on activities. Outdoors you can see some thirty-three more cars. The HO-scale layout and education center are open selected hours. There are changing tables in both the men's and women's restrooms. Wheelchair accessible.

Strasburg Rail Road (all ages)

PA 741 East; (717) 687-7522; www.strasburgrailroad.com. Hours vary seasonally. Coach fares are $$ for adults, $ for children 3 to 11. Fares for open-air cars and deluxe lounge cars are $$. Children under 3 ride free.

After you've seen the railroad museum, cross the street for a forty-five-minute ride on the Strasburg Rail Road. Food service is available. The East Strasburg Rail Road Station was built in 1882 and includes railroad gift shops and the Dining Car restaurant. The Strasburg Rail Road is the nation's oldest short-line railroad.

Choo Choo Barn—Traintown USA® (all ages)

PA 741 East; (717) 687-7911; www.choochoobarn.com. From Apr through Dec open 10 a.m. to 5 p.m. daily. Closed Jan 1 through Mar for annual renovations. Admission is $$ for adults, $ for children 5 to 12. Children under 5 enter free.

The Choo Choo Barn has twenty-two operating miniature trains that chug through 130 animated scenes. If your kids are like ours, you'll want to visit Thomas's Trackside Station, a shop devoted exclusively to Thomas the Tank Engine and his friends from the Island of Sodor. All displays and restrooms are wheelchair accessible, but not all the shops are. If you get hungry, there's a picnic area, candy shop, and Isaac's Restaurant and Deli.

National Toy Train Museum (all ages)

300 Paradise Lane; (717) 687-8976; www.traincollectors.org. Open Tues through Sun, May through Oct, 10 a.m. to 5 p.m. Open weekends only in Apr, Nov, and Dec. Admission is $.

This museum features metal electric trains and five operating layouts with buttons for the kids to push. And they let you blow the whistle! There is also a short video, plus display cases full of trains. The museum's theater shows cartoons and comedy films about trains. The gift shop offers a great selection of train-related toys.

Amish Village (all ages)

Two miles north of Strasburg on PA 896; (717) 687-8511; the Village of Dutch Delights, Dienner's Restaurant Complex. Hours vary seasonally. Admission is $$ for adults, $ for children 6 to 12.

Tours of the Old Order farmhouse at the Amish Village, which dates back to 1840, emphasize the culture of the Plain People. There's also a one-room school, a windmill, and a blacksmith shop. The smokehouse sells specialty foods like apple butter, candies, and cider. There is a wheelchair-accessible restroom with a changing table, but the second floor of the house is not accessible. In Dec, special house tours feature hot mulled cider.

Sight & Sound Theatre (ages 8 and up)

PA 896; reservations: (717) 687-7800; www.noahonstage.com. Tickets are $$$$ for adults and $$$ for children.

The specifically Christian shows at Sight & Sound's two huge theaters will remind you of something from the glory days of Radio City Music Hall. Recent spectacular productions have included Noah, In the Beginning, and The Miracle of Christmas. Noah, for example, featured a four-story ark, 56 actors, 100 live animals, and 125 animatronics (animated figures).

Paradise

Farmland Fun (ages 2 and up)

429 Strasburg Rd.; (717) 687-7353; www.farmlandfun.com. Open daily (no wagon tours or farmer's apprentice program on Sun). Tours $; farmer's apprentice program $$.

Play Old McDonald for a day at Verdant View Farm, where the Ranck family welcomes guests for tours. You can choose how much time you want to spend and the depth of skills you want to learn. On this 115-acre dairy and crop farm, activities can vary. Peek into the barn for morning milking, groom a baby calf, or feed goats their alfalfa by hand. The Rancks' unique farmer's apprentice program teaches you how to handle farmyard tasks and learn where our food comes from. The Rancks also operate a bed-and-breakfast on their farm, so you're welcome to spend the night. Reserve a room at www.verdantview .com and reserve tours at www.farmlandfun.com.

Nottingham

Herr Foods, Inc. (preschool and up)

At intersection of PA 272 and US 1. For details and reservations call (800) 284-7488 or (800) 63-SNACK; www.herrs.com. Tours are **free,** but reservations are requested. Open weekdays 8 a.m. to 5 p.m. Tours are conducted Mon through Thurs 9 a.m. to 3 p.m. and Fri 9 to 11 a.m.

You can see how Herr's snacks are made and then try some chips still warm from the fryer at Herr Foods, Inc. Cutting-edge tour technology uses DVD screens for close-up viewing in production areas. Chipper's Cafe offers hot dogs, chicken nuggets, PB&J, pizza, and cookies. Wheelchair accessible, with a changing table in the women's room.

Willow Street

Hans Herr House (ages 8 and up)

1849 Hans Herr Dr.; (717) 464-4438; www.hansherr.org. Open Apr through Nov 31, Mon through Sat 9 a.m. to 4 p.m. Closed Sun, Thanksgiving, and Dec 1 to Mar 31. Admission is $.

The date 1719 appears on the door lintel of the Hans Herr House. The Mennonite home is the oldest surviving home of European settlers in what is now Lancaster County. Andrew Wyeth, himself a relative of Hans Herr, created a well-known painting of the house.

Lancaster

Many of the nonprofit museums in the Lancaster area have cooperated in a joint ticketing program. Save your ticket stub from one museum, and when you go to another, you'll get a reduced rate. These museums include the Railroad Museum, Heritage Center Museum of Lancaster County, Ephrata Cloister, Wright's Ferry Mansion, National Association of Watch and Clock Collectors Museum, and many more.

Dutch Wonderland (ages 12 and under)

2249 US 30 East; (717) 291-1888 or (866) FUNATDW (866-386-2839); www.dutchwonder land.com. Open weekends in spring and fall and daily from Memorial Day to Labor Day. Admission includes everything but food and select activities and is $$$–$$$$. Wheelchair accessible.

Dutch Wonderland is still the family-oriented park you remember, only now it's had a $1.2 million makeover, and it has a new motto: A Kingdom for Kids! The new VR Voyager is a three-axis, computer-controlled motion simulator that creates a virtual-reality experience with more than fifteen different action videos to choose from.

A zero-depth water play area called Duke's Lagoon delights with bubbling geysers, tipping buckets, slides, and designated areas designed for toddlers, preschoolers, kids between five and eight years old, and kids nine to twelve years of age. You can meet the new Princess of Dutch Wonderland, who loves to read stories to kids in the park, and her sidekick, Duke the Dragon. High-dive shows continue the fantasy theme. Thomas Friends star in a train-themed singalong, one of several live stage shows. New kid-friendly rides include Duke's Dozers, Froghopper, Off-Road Rally, and The Wonder Whip.

Your six-year-old can drive an old-fashioned motorcar, your twelve-year-old can brave the Sky Princess roller coaster, your family can take a walk in the botanical gardens, and everyone can grab a burlap sack and race down the Giant slide. There are changing tables in both men's and women's rooms, and food offerings include chicken, pizza, and sandwiches.

Dutch Wonderland is within minutes of the Amish Farm and House, the Weaver-town One-Room School, the Old Mill Stream Camping Manor, and a great deal of outlet shopping.

North Museum of Natural History and Science (all ages)

400 College Ave.; (717) 291-3941; www.northmuseum.org. Open Tues through Sat 10 a.m. to 5 p.m., Sun noon to 5 p.m. Admission is $.

Amazing
Pennsylvania Facts

For exactly one day in 1777, Lancaster served as the U.S. capital.

The North Museum, on the campus of Franklin and Marshall College, offers collections of Native American artifacts, birds, fossils, minerals, and a planetarium. Children especially enjoy the Discovery Room's hands-on science and nature exhibits and the herpetarium with more than forty live reptiles.

Amish Farm and House (ages 6 and up)

2395 US 30 East, 0.5 mile east of Dutch Wonderland; (717) 394-6185. Open daily at 8:30 a.m., the site closes at 4 p.m. in winter, 5 p.m. in spring and fall, and 6 p.m. in summer. On selected dates in Sept and Oct, hours are extended for kerosene-lamp tours. Admission is $$ for adults and $ for children 5 to 11.

This is the only operating Amish farm open to the public. The farm itself dates from the 1700s, the house from 1805. Guided tours show the house and describe the history, culture, and clothing of Old Order Amish. You can take a guided tour of the farm, with its barns, carriage sheds, springhouse, and animals. Also on the grounds is an Early-Americana museum. A food pavilion is open seasonally, and there are changing tables in both men's and women's rooms. Sheep shearing days are in Apr, and there are kerosene-lamp tours in the fall.

Hands-On House, Children's Museum of Lancaster
(ages 2 through 10)

721 Landis Valley Rd.; (717) 569-KIDS; www.handsonhouse.org. Admission is $. Open Labor Day through Memorial Day, Mon through Thurs 10 a.m. to 5 p.m., Fri 10 a.m. to 8 p.m., Sat 10 a.m. to 5 p.m., Sun noon to 5 p.m. Memorial Day through Labor Day, open Mon through Thurs 10 a.m. to 5 p.m., Fri 10 a.m. to 8 p.m., Sat 10 a.m. to 5 p.m., Sun noon to 5 p.m.

The museum has eight interactive areas for children ages two through ten, including the exhibit "E-I-E-I-KNOW," which teaches kids about farming in Lancaster County through computer touch-screens, interactive games, and hands-on exhibits. The Hands-On House is on the grounds of the Landis Valley Museum, all on one level, completely wheelchair and stroller accessible.

Landis Valley Museum (all ages)

2451 Kissel Hill Rd.; (717) 569-0401; www.landisvalleymuseum.org. Open year-round, Mon through Sat 9 a.m. to 5 p.m., Sun noon to 5 p.m. Closed some major holidays. Admission is $$ for adults and children 6 to 12. Children under 6 enter free.

The Landis Valley Museum is a Pennsylvania German living-history museum with fifteen historic buildings, including a farmhouse, tavern, country store, and inn.

Downtown Lancaster

Downtown Lancaster is worth a visit, offering the Central Market, Lancaster Newspapers' "Newseum," Steinman Park, and more. A walking tour is available. Forinformation contact the Pennsylvania Dutch Convention and Visitors Bureau at (717) 299-8901 or (800) PA–DUTCH, ext. 4255.

Living the Experience (ages 8 and up)

Lancaster Bethel African Methodist Church, 512 E. Strawberry St.; (800) 510-5899, ext. 113, or (717) 538-0427; www.livingtheundergroundrailroad.com. Performances Feb through Dec, Sat 1 p.m. Additional performances for groups of thirty-five or more. For these groups, a meal is served after the performance.

This living-history performance intertwines storytelling and spirituals to reenact experiences of participants in the Underground Railroad in a vibrant and moving way.

Heritage Center of Lancaster County (all ages)

Penn Square; (717) 299-6440; www.lancasterheritage.com. The museum and hands-on room are open free year-round, Mon through Sat 9 a.m. to 6 p.m. and Sun 10 to 3 p.m. Additional hours on first Fridays and holidays. Donations accepted.

The Heritage Center comprises two museums: the Heritage Center Museum and the Lancaster Quilt and Textile Museum. In the Heritage Center, kids can pick up a children's guide designed for families and linked to a series of ten different interactive stations around the museum. In the midst of all the furniture, silver, paintings, needlework, folk art, and rifles, kids can try their hands at puzzles and games, paper cutting, and more. The Quilt and Textile Museum, a few steps away at 37 N. Market St., is a feast of color and pattern. Treats Creamery & Cafe is located inside.

Central Market (all ages)

West King Street on Penn Square; (717) 291-4739. Open Tues and Fri 6 a.m. to 4:30 p.m. and Sat 6 a.m. to 2 p.m.

Next to the Heritage Center, breathe in the delicious smells of Amish baked goods coming from the Central Market, which has been operating as a farmers' market since the 1730s. This a terrific spot to stock up for a picnic.

Lancaster Science Factory (all ages)

454 New Holland Ave.; (717) 509-6363; www.lancastersciencefactory.com. Open Tues through Sat (June through Aug, also open Mon) 10 a.m. to 5 p.m.; Sun noon to 5 p.m. Admission $.

Lancaster's newest museum is a hands-on hit. Each exhibit is a mini-lab in an aspect of science and engineering, with fun puzzles and brainteasers. Your kids can rebuild Stonehenge, create an electrical circuit, and learn about alternative sources of energy. With plenty of space in a renovated old factory (hence the name), the museum is just two minutes from the center of the city, with free parking across the street. All exhibits are handicapped accessible.

James Buchanan's Wheatland (ages 10 and up)

1120 Marietta Ave.; (717) 392-8721; www.wheatland.org. Open daily Apr through Oct, 10 a.m. to 4 p.m., and Fri through Mon in Nov. Also open selected days in Dec. Admission is $$ for adults and $ for seniors, students (up through college with ID), and children 6 to 11.

In spite of the pivotal role that Pennsylvania played in our history, the Keystone State produced only one U.S. president, James Buchanan. Located on the outskirts of downtown Lancaster, Wheatland, Buchanan's home, is well preserved. A video in the visitor center describes the life of our fifteenth president.

Lancaster Barnstormers (all ages)

650 N. Prince St.; (717) 509-4487; www.lancasterbarnstormers.com. Tickets $$.

The Barnstormers, the city's minor Atlantic League baseball team, have a new home at Clipper Magazine Stadium. For kids who need a seventh-inning stretch, the ballpark offers Bumper Boats in its Home Run Harbor (five-minute rides $$). It's the only water amusement of its kind in a U.S. ballpark. Power Alley, a picnic pavilion, offers an all-you-can-eat buffet and a chance to catch a home run ball.

Landisville

1852 Herr Family Homestead (ages 6 and up)

1756 Nissley Rd.; (717) 898-8822; www.herrhomestead.org. **Open Apr 1 through Oct 31, Sat and Sun 1 to 4 p.m.**

Although it is open only seasonally, the folks at the 1852 Herr Family Homestead do a nice job for children. There is a pleasant park nearby if you'd like to pack a picnic lunch.

Columbia

National Association of Watch and Clock Collectors Museum (ages 8 and up)

514 Poplar St., just off US 30; (717) 684-8261; www.nawcc.org. **Open Apr through Dec, Tues through Sat 10 a.m. to 5 p.m., Sun noon to 4 p.m. Closed Mon and major holidays. Jan through Mar, open Tues through Sat 10 a.m. to 4 p.m. Closed Sun, Mon, and major holidays. Admission is $.**

Now containing more than 12,000 items, this is the largest and most comprehensive horological collection in North America. And it's fun. Water clocks, candle clocks, sundials, musical clocks, grandfather clocks, wristwatches, pocket watches. . . . You've never seen so many kinds of timepieces as you'll find at the National Association of Watch and Clock Collectors Museum. Parents of school-morning slugabeds will get inspiration from the alarm-clock collection. For example, there's one alarm clock that gives the sleepyhead's big toe a yank. One tall musical clock runs seven days and plays seven different tunes.

Wright's Ferry Mansion (ages 10 and up)
Second and Cherry Streets; (717) 684-4325. Open May through Oct, Tues, Wed, Fri, and Sat 10 a.m. to 3 p.m. Last tour begins at 3 p.m. Admission is $$ for adults, $ for children ages 6 to 18.

Susanna Wright was known as the "bluestocking of the Susquehanna," but she was really more of a "Renaissance woman." (*Bluestocking* was a derogatory term for an intellectual woman.) At Wright's Ferry Mansion you can get acquainted with this colorful but little-known character in American history. Wright and her brother operated a ferry between their houses, on opposite banks of the Susquehanna. She also drew up legal documents, raised silkworms, practiced medicine, and corresponded with people like Benjamin Franklin. The house also served as a station on the Underground Railroad. Warning: With a collection of valuable eighteenth-century antiques and furniture, Wright's Ferry is a "don't touch" museum.

York

Harley-Davidson, Inc., Antique Motorcycle Museum (all ages)
1425 Eden Rd., just off US 30; (717) 848-1177; www.harley-davidson.com. Museum tours are offered at specified times Mon through Fri. Plant tours are offered Mon through Fri 9 a.m. to 2 p.m. and are open to people over 12. No cameras, no sandals allowed on factory tours. Visitors under 18 must be accompanied by an adult. Visitors over 18 must present two valid, government-issued photo IDs. Visitors will pass through a metal detector. Call ahead to check for times of museum-only tours or to make reservations for factory tours. **Free.**

A seven-year-old was disappointed to learn that kids under twelve are not allowed on the factory tours at Harley-Davidson, Inc. All ages are welcome, however, at the adjacent Harley-Davidson Museum, where antique motorcycles on display include police bikes, army bikes, and bikes owned by celebrities. Wheelchair accessible.

York County:
Factory Tour Capital of the World

York, Pennsylvania, is home to more than twenty of America's favorite products, including Harley-Davidson, Martin's Potato Chips, Pfaltzgraff, and Wolfgang Candy. These and many other companies invite visitors to get a behind-the-scenes look at how their products are made. To get a York County Visitors Guide or for more information, call (888) 858-YORK or visit www .yorkpa.org.

Hershey

If ever there were a town made for family enjoyment, it's Hershey, Pennsylvania. What child could resist the city that chocolate built, with Hersheypark as its main attraction. Even the streetlights are shaped like Hershey kisses! If you park your car at the Hersheypark entrance, you can get around town on foot. After you've enjoyed Hersheypark, ZooAmerica, and the other big attractions, if you're in the mood for something more low-key, there's a great playground on Cocoa Avenue near Chocolate Avenue.

Many of Hershey's attractions grew out of Milton Hershey's special interests. The rose collection at Hershey Gardens developed from his wife's passion for the flowers, ZooAmerica started out with the animals Hershey collected, and the Hershey Museum sprang from Hershey's original collection of artifacts.

Hershey's Chocolate World Visitors Center (all ages)

Hersheypark Drive; (717) 534-4900; www.hersheys.com/chocolateworld. Open year-round. Hours vary, but generally coincide with Hersheypark. Admission to the chocolate tour is free.

Hershey's Chocolate World, one of America's most popular attractions, hosts nearly three million visitors a year, and entrance is **free.** Learn about the chocolate production process "bean-to-bar" through a **free** chocolate-making tour ride. You can also view Hershey's *Really Big 3-D Show.*

At the new Hershey's Factory Works, visitors are invited to be part of an interactive, imaginative chocolate factory. Get your own employee ID and factory worker's hat. Stop by the Kiss Works machine and you can package Hershey Kisses as they stream by on a conveyor belt. Have lunch at the Kit Kat "Gimme a Break" Café, or enjoy desserts from Hershey's Bake Shoppe.

Hersheypark (all ages)

100 West Hersheypark Dr.; (717) 534-3090 or (800) HERSHEY; www.hersheypa.com. Hersheypark's season runs from mid-May through mid-Sept. The gates open at 10 a.m., and the rides open at 10:30 a.m. Closing times vary from 6 to 11 p.m. Admission plans range from regular (ages 9 to 54) at \$\$\$\$ to junior and senior, both at \$\$\$. Children 2 and under are free, and the sunset savings plan (after 5 p.m.) is \$\$\$. Admission includes all rides, all live performances, and a same-day visit to ZooAmerica (see next listing). There is a separate charge for paddleboats and miniature golf.

Hersheypark was built in 1907 by Milton S. Hershey, "the man behind the chocolate bar." Hershey planned the park as a picnic and pleasure grounds for his employees. Today Hersheypark has grown into a 110-acre world-class theme park with more than sixty rides and attractions.

The Carousel Circle has been renamed Founder's Circle, a gathering place with a sense of nostalgia. It reintroduces two classic Hershey family rides, Balloon Flite and Starship America. A new musical, *The Milkmen,* salutes one of the key ingredients in Hershey's chocolate: milk!

An O'Toole **Family Adventure**

All summer, James and Bill had looked forward to meeting their cousins at Hersheypark. But when the big day came, it was pouring. Oh well, we said sadly, we'll go on the Chocolate World tour. Not only did we enjoy riding through the plant and eating the free candy: When we came back outside, the sun was shining brightly, but the amusement park was empty. Without long lines to wait in, we rode our favorite roller coasters twice.

Hersheypark has ten other exhilarating coasters, including Storm Runner, the world's first hydraulic-launch coaster featuring inversions.

As you enter Hersheypark, have your kids stand next to the "measure-up" signs. Kids of a certain height are "Hershey Kisses" and can ride Hershey Kiss rides. Taller kids are "Reese's Peanut Butter Cups," "Hershey Milk Chocolate Bars," "Twizzlers," or "Nutra-geous." If your kids would like to get a bracelet that shows what candy-height they are, you can stop by the rides office in the operations building, located inside the park beside Swing Thing. (If you don't choose to get a bracelet, there are signs next to every ride.)

This manageable theme park is divided into small sections, which are centered around a different theme—and there's something for everyone. This way, your family can stay together and everyone can stay happy. For example, little ones can ride the Swing Thing, which is a kid-size version of Wave Swinger. The antique carousel will delight many visitors, whereas others flock to the Comet with its 95-foot drop. And don't stand anywhere near Tidal Force unless you don't mind getting wet! If you get hot and tired, a visit to the air-conditioned Music Box Theater may be just the ticket. If you decide to split up, the Kissing Tower makes a good meeting spot.

You may choose to ride the water rides in your clothes or bathing suits, but shoes are required, so we recommend wearing something waterproof like flip-flops or water shoes.

Traveling with an infant, we were delighted to find that Hersheypark offers facilities for nursing mothers and baby food at the first-aid station. Even some of the men's rooms have changing tables.

Besides its regular season, Hersheypark opens for two special family events: Creatures of the Night at Halloween and Hersheypark Christmas Candylane. At each of these events, the park is specially lighted and decorated, and most of the family-oriented rides are open.

ZooAmerica North American Wildlife Park (all ages)

Hersheypark Drive; (717) 534-3860; www.hersheypa.com. Open year-round. Hours vary seasonally; the zoo is open 10 a.m. to 8 p.m. whenever Hersheypark is open and 10 a.m. to 5 p.m. the rest of the year. Admission is $$. Children under 2 enter free**.**

You can enter ZooAmerica North American Wildlife Park directly through Hersheypark, and admission to the zoo is included in your Hersheypark ticket. The zoo is open year-round, not just seasonally, and a separate admission is also available. ZooAmerica focuses on plants and animals from different regions in North America.

Many of Hershey's attractions grew out of Milton Hershey's special interests. The rose garden at the Hotel Hershey developed from his own passion for the flowers, ZooAmerica started out with the animals Hershey collected, and the Hershey Museum sprang from Hershey's original collection of artifacts.

The Hershey Museum (all ages)

170 Hersheypark Dr.; (717) 534-3439; www.hersheymuseum.org. Open year-round. Admission to the museum is $$ for adults and $ for youth.

Administered by the Hershey Foundation, the Hershey Museum is located at the west end of Hersheypark Arena. Its permanent exhibits celebrate the history of Hershey—the town, its founder, and its industries. Younger children will enjoy the Discovery Room, which has hands-on activities on these themes.

Hershey Gardens (all ages)

170 Hotel Rd., Hershey; (717) 534-3492; www.hersheygardens.org. Open Apr through Dec; hours vary. Adult admission $$, children 3 to 12 $, children under 3 free.

The Children's Garden, one of 30 themed gardens here, allow children to become human sundials and discover directions in the Rose Compass Court. The outdoor Butterfly House, a kids' favorite, is open in warm weather.

ALSO IN THE AREA

You may want to check the schedule of events at **Hersheypark Stadium and Arena** (717-534-3911). Hershey also offers several golf courses, Milton Hershey School, and the Derry One-Room School.

Hummelstown

Indian Echo Caverns (ages 8 and up)

368 Middletown Rd.; (717) 566-8131; www.indianechocaverns.com. From Memorial Day to Labor Day open 9 a.m. to 6 p.m. Last tour enters cavern at 6 p.m. Labor Day to Memorial Day open 10 a.m. to 4 p.m., last tour at 4 p.m. Closed Thanksgiving, Christmas, and New Year's Day. Call for current admission prices.

Your young geologists can take a forty-five-minute tour of Indian Echo Caverns and hear the story of William Wilson, a hermit who lived in the caverns for nineteen years. You can also pan for gemstones at Gem Mill Junction (Memorial Day to early Oct). The cavern is open year-round, but the food cart is open only during the summer season. Strollers not permitted in cave.

Middletown

Middletown and Hummelstown Railroad (all ages)

136 Brown St.; (717) 944-4435; www.mhrailroad.com. Operates seasonally. Call for fares and schedule.

All ages seem to get a kick out of this folksy ride in a 1920 vintage railroad coach. You take a guided scenic ride 11 miles to Indian Echo Caverns. Your train will cross Swatara Creek on a 35-foot-high bridge. You can get off at the caverns, if you like, and take a forty-five-minute tour. On your return trip an accordionist leads a sing-along. The steam locomotive is used on Sat and Sun in summer only. Wheelchair accessible.

Harrisburg

Whitaker Center for Science and the Arts (ages 6 and up)

The Kunkel Building, 301 Market St.; (717) 221-8201; www.whitakercenter.org. Open Tues through Sat 9:30 a.m. to 5 p.m., Sun 11:30 a.m. to 5 p.m. IMAX theater shows begin at 5:30 p.m. A combination ticket to both the science center and the theater costs $$. Tickets to the theater only and to the science center only are $$. For tickets to the Sunoco Performance Theater, check the Web site or call (717) 214-ARTS. For all tickets, children under 3 enter free.

The Whitaker Center describes its theme as "science through the arts," making science fun through dance, film, music, and more. The center includes a state-of-the-art Select Medical IMAX 3-D movie theater, Hansco Science Center, and a Broadway-size Sunoco Performance theater, which hosts many concerts and performances. The Hansco Science Center includes nine permanent exhibits that explore physical science, natural science, life science, and technology. If you park at Strawberry Square, you can enter the Whitaker Center by way of an enclosed walkway.

State Capitol Building (ages 10 and up)

Third and State Streets; (717) 787-6810; www.legis.state.pa.us. Open to the public daily. Tours are given Mon through Fri, every half hour 8:30 a.m. to 4 p.m. Weekends and most holidays, tours are offered at 9 a.m., 11 a.m., 1 p.m., and 3 p.m. All tours are free. Reservations are strongly suggested and are required for groups of ten or more. Call (800) TOUR N PA for reservations. Wheelchair accessible.

On weekdays access is through any entrance, where you will be screened and provided with a visitor's pass. On weekends and holidays access is only through the front of the building, on Third Street at State Street.

The dome of the State Capitol Building is said to be the most impressive one of any state capitol in the country. Inside, huge murals depict scenes such as Penn's treaty with the Native Americans, the signing of the Declaration of Independence, and Washington's

Walking Tour of **Downtown Harrisburg**

Since 9/11, visitors cannot use the parking lot underneath the capitol building. But you can park at the Walnut Street parking garage at Fourth and Market Streets, next to Strawberry Square, a retail center with a pleasant food court and many shops. The Whitaker Center is across the street in the Kunkel Building.

Look up and you'll see the dome of the State Capitol Building. The circular building to the right as you leave the capitol is the State Museum of Pennsylvania.

If your feet aren't sore yet, you can walk over to the riverfront and cross Walnut Street Bridge, now exclusively for pedestrians. The bridge spans the Susquehanna River from Riverfront Park to City Island. (At night this bridge is illuminated, adding to the nighttime view of the city.)

troops at Valley Forge. The floors are made of tiles from the Moravian Pottery and Tile Works in Doylestown (see entry under Philadelphia Countryside). The main floor of the rotunda displays more than 350 flags formerly carried by regiments from Pennsylvania.

In the East Wing visit the eighteen interactive exhibits of the welcome center. This family-friendly introduction to the state includes a huge Rube Goldberg contraption that depicts how a bill becomes law, and it tells why the Great Dane is the state dog (because William Penn owned one).

State Museum of Pennsylvania (all ages)

Third and North Streets; (717) 787-4979; www.statemuseumpa.org. Open Tues through Sat 9 a.m. to 5 p.m. and Sun noon to 5 p.m. Closed holidays except for Memorial Day and Labor Day. Admission is free, but there is a small charge for Curiosity Connection and the planetarium show. Wheelchair accessible.

This museum strives to describe the entire history and prehistory of the state. You'll work your way through geology and go on through paleontology, archaeology, and the beginning of civilization. A new planetarium offers shows from the stars, like images from the Hubble Space Telescope.

Going down to the second floor, you can see a series of life-size dioramas that depict the life cycle of a Native American in this area. There are also displays about the Revolution and the Civil War, including a huge mural of the Battle of Gettysburg. One gallery recreates a typical early American Main Street.

Curiosity Connection, the State Museum's new kid-inspired exhibit for young children and families, encourages children seven and under to explore, discover, and imagine through the power of play. The adventure begins in a Magical Child's Bedroom and continues through secret portals leading to an entire miniature world of Curiosity. Other areas include The Living Forest, Industry and Transportation Zone, Farm Land,

Construction Zone, and Art Wall. There's even a special area for the very youngest visitors. Curiosity Connection is open Tues through Sat 10 a.m. to 4 p.m., Sun noon to 4 p.m. Admission for adults and children is $. Children under age one are admitted **free.**

On the first floor the museum displays a facsimile of its treasure, the original charter from the British crown that gave Pennsylvania to William Penn in 1681. This charter granted William Penn "rights, privileges and obligations" to Pennsylvania, as a payment of debts owed to Penn's father by King Charles II.

City Island Attractions　(all ages)

City Island sits in the middle of the Susquehanna, a spot of greenery amid the water. Its sixty-three acres of parkland now include Riverside Stadium, where the Senators play Class AA minor league baseball. You'll also find a steam train for children, a paddle-wheel riverboat, an arcade, miniature golf, jogging and skateboarding facilities, a **free** nautical-themed playground, Riverside Village Eatery, carriage rides, HarbourTown, and more. To get there from downtown, take the pedestrian-only Walnut Street Bridge. There's also parking on the island.

Pride of the Susquehanna **Riverboat**　(all ages)

City Island; (717) 234-6500; www.harrisburgriverboat.com. Boat sails on the hour in June, July, and Aug, Tues through Sun, and on a more limited schedule in May, Sept, and Oct. Call ahead to confirm, because schedule is subject to change, especially in May, Sept, and Oct. Fares are $. Children under 12 ride free.

From City Island take a ride on the *Pride of the Susquehanna* (operated by Harrisburg Area Riverboat Society, P.O. Box 910, Harrisburg 17108).

The riverboat tour gives an excellent view of this riverside city. Kids love looking up at the underside of the six bridges under which you'll pass, including the Walnut Street Bridge. Take your choice: You may sit indoors in air-conditioned comfort, where there is the Pride Galley for snacks and souvenirs, or on the lower or upper decks, where the wind blows through your hair.

From the riverboat you can see the wrought-iron railing around the grave of the city's founder, John Harris. You can visit his home, the John Harris/Simon Cameron Mansion, at 219 S. Front St. This historic home was built in 1766 and now houses the collection of the Historical Society of Dauphin County.

Amazing
Pennsylvania Facts

The State Museum of Pennsylvania in Harrisburg displays the original charter that gave Pennsylvania to William Penn. It's amusing to note that Penn was to pay the king two beaver furs and all the gold and silver found in the colony. Of course, there was no gold or silver found in Pennsylvania.

Farms of Lancaster County

There's a reason towns in Lancaster County have names like Eden and Paradise. This idyllic landscape is not only lush and green, but fertile as well. In fact, Lancaster County has the most fertile, nonirrigated farmland east of the Mississippi. According to Penn State University Agricultural Extension Office, every second the county produces ninety eggs, twenty-one pounds of corn, and thirteen pounds of hay.

Many Lancaster farms have been passed down from generation to generation. Since 1976, about 150 farms have been designated as Century Farms, or farms that have been in the same family for at least 150 years. For example, the sixty-acre Esbenshade Turkey Farm in Paradise is the oldest turkey farm in the United States.

You can experience this abundance at roadside produce stands and farmers' markets overflowing with whatever is in season: tomatoes, pumpkins, strawberries, cantaloupes, watermelons, and sweet corn.

Another way to get to experience Lancaster farmland is to plan a farm vacation. For a listing of farm vacations in Pennsylvania, go to www.pafarmstay .com. Milk a cow, feed the chickens, and experience farm living firsthand. You can get a list of working farms that offers lodging at www.padutchcountry.com/ lodging. You can make reservations online or by calling (800) PA–DUTCH (723-8824). Here are a few suggestions:

- **Country Vistas Bed & Breakfast,** Manheim; (717) 664-2931.

- **Country Gardens Farm Bed & Breakfast,** Mount Joy; (717) 426-3316.

- **Verdant View Bed & Breakfast,** Paradise; (717) 687-7353; www.verdant view.com.

Fort Hunter Mansion (ages 8 and up)

5300 N. Front St.; (717) 599-5751; www.forthunter.org. Open May through Dec, Tues through Sat 10 a.m. to 4:30 p.m. and Sun noon to 4:30 p.m. Admission is $.

Just outside Center City, on a bluff overlooking the Susquehanna River, stands Fort Hunter Mansion, surrounded by its outbuildings and park. The Federal-style mansion, built in 1814 by Archibald McAllister, is in remarkably good condition. While touring the house, open the closet doors to discover surprises such as sets of china or collections of fashionable clothing left behind by Helen Reily, last owner of the house. In the guest-room closet, you can peek at Mrs. Reily's bonnets (she had some one hundred), fans, hat pins, and other accessories. She also left a collection of dolls, toy soldiers, and even paper dolls. The dollhouse features a tiny hobby horse, a little dog curled up in a minute dog bed, and postcards glued to the walls for paintings. And don't miss the garden with its spicebush, smokebush, and boxwood. The Web site offers a downloadable walking tour.

In Dec, when the mansion is decorated for Christmas, it is open Tues through Sun from noon to 7 p.m. In Sept, Fort Hunter Day brings the whole park alive with bagpipe music (in honor of the McAllisters), arts and crafts, children's activities, food, and more. Programs for children and families are offered periodically.

Carlisle

The town of Carlisle has loads of history and a nice series of wayside markers to tell its tales. Perhaps more kid-friendly are attractions such as the Carlisle fairgrounds (depending on what's going on) and, for older children interested in history, the U.S. Army Heritage and Education Center. The Carlisle Summerfest is a real old-fashioned community event, with bike parades, baby races, an ice-cream social, and scavenger hunt.

U.S. Army Heritage and Education Center (ages 5 and up)

950 Soldiers Dr.; (717) 245-3971; www.usahec.org. Open Mon through Fri, 9 a.m. through 4:45 p.m.; open weekends from Apr to Oct, Sat 10 a.m. to 4 p.m., Sun noon to 4 p.m. Closed on federal holidays. Free admission.

This tribute to the fighting men and women of the U.S. Army has interesting displays inside, particularly of Civil War–era photography. But kids will like its outdoor museum best. The Heritage Trail is a 1-mile walking path with exhibits from U.S. conflicts. Little ones can explore a World War I trench, a D-day beachhead, and other displays. Look for the massive Huey helicopter at the edge of the trail, overlooking I-81.

Carlisle Fairgrounds (ages 8 and up)

1000 Bryn Mawr Rd. For a schedule of events contact Carlisle Productions at (717) 243-7855 or www.carsatcarlisle.com.

Maybe somebody in your family is nuts about cars or antiques. The eighty-two-acre Carlisle Fairgrounds hosts major collector events on many weekends throughout the year.

ALSO IN THE AREA

For hiking, cross-country skiing, hunting, and other outdoor activities, contact **King's Gap Environmental Center** on PA 174 West (500 Kings Gap Rd.) at (717) 486-5031; www.dcnr .state.pa.us/stateparks.

Boiling Springs

This lovely lakeside village is the home of the Allenberry Resort Inn and Playhouse. The Allenberry stretch of the Yellow Breeches River attracts many families to try their hands at fly fishing. Legend has it that the creek waters stained the uniforms of the British redcoats who had to wade through it—hence the name "yellow breeches." Here the rules are "catch and release" and "artificial lures only." It's a little different on the Letort Spring Run (pronounced *lee-tort),* which is considered more challenging and attracts devotees of *A River Runs Through It.*

Allenberry Resort Inn (all ages)

PA 174; (717) 258-3211; www.allenberry.com.

An eighteenth-century estate where you can enjoy professional theater, fishing, and special events. Call for a list of upcoming dinner theater productions.

Gettysburg

Every student in America should get a chance to visit Gettysburg. Before your visit, older kids and parents can prepare by watching either Ken Burns' PBS *Civil War* documentary or the 1993 movie *Gettysburg.* Placing the battle in context will enhance your visit.

You can also plan ahead by choosing a battlefield tour. To find the tour that best suits your needs, call the Gettysburg Travel Council at (717) 334-6274 or go to their Web site at www.gettysburg.com. You can also contact the Convention and Visitors Bureau at (717) 334-6274 or check www.gettysburg.travel.

If at all possible, avoid summer vacation season. The same smothering heat that enveloped the battlefield in July 1864 is liable to fell your little soldiers as well, and crowds are guaranteed. A spring or fall weekday is probably a better time to spend a day touring.

You may choose an individualized tour or a group tour. Group tours are available by bicycle, bus, or even on horseback.

- For a personalized tour with a licensed guide in your own vehicle, contact the Association of Licensed Battlefield Guides at (877) 438-8929. You can also sign up for one of these guides at the visitor center. This is one of the best ways to learn about the battlefield.

- Tours on CD are available at the American History Store, 461 Baltimore St. (717-338-0631).

- Bus tours on air-conditioned buses depart from the museum and visitor center at Gettysburg National Military Park (866-889-1243; www.gettysburgfoundation.org).

- Tours on horseback, called "Ride into History," are available through National Riding Stables (717-334-1288). Reservations six to eight weeks in advance are highly recommended. Tours are $$$$. Inexperienced riders welcome.

- Tours on bikes are offered by GettysBike Tours (717-752-7752; www.gettysbike.com).

The Gettysburg Convention and Visitors Bureau asks that drivers be aware of all the other visitors crossing the streets at peak times, especially after dark when "ghost tours" are out. The speed limit in town is 25 miles per hour, and state law requires that you stop for pedestrians.

Gettysburg's **Ghosts**

—by Cara Nardone, age 13

Gettysburg is a real-life ghost town. Every time I've visited there, I'm half expecting to see an airy figure of a man or woman. On my eighth-grade class trip, our guide led us up into the cliffs of Devil's Den, where soldiers long ago must have crouched and hid in all the crevices under rocks and sprung out like mountain lions at gunfire. There on the top of a rock, people claim have seen a Civil War soldier in blood-stained clothes. He supposedly points to the woods below and says, "That is the best place to take a picture," but when the person looks back at him, he's gone.

On my Thanksgiving trip to Gettysburg, I do believe I saw a real ghost, but a harmless one. On my family's walk down from Pickett's Charge to the little cabin that was General Meade's headquarters, my little brother Will ran ahead and called "Cara, come here!" I rushed down to him. There in the field was a skinny little black cat with pale blue eyes. He walked into the grass—and vanished.

If your kids are a bit rusty on the history of the battle, give them a quick movie refresher. Put them in the center of Pickett's Charge at *Fields of Freedom,* which plays every half hour at Gateway Gettysburg in the new, bigger-than-IMAX theater off US 15 near the National Military Park at 20 Presidential Circle. Tickets: $$. Call (717) 334-5575.

The Gettysburg Travel Council recommends a minimum visit of three days to see all that Gettysburg has to offer. To prevent an overdose of history, plan for breaks and vary your activities. Here are some highlights.

Gettysburg National Military Park (ages 8 and up)

Steinwehr Avenue (Business US 15 South); (717) 334-1124; www.nps.gov/gett. The Gettysburg Museum and Visitor Center at 1195 Baltimore Pike is open daily at 8 a.m., except major holidays; hours vary seasonally. Park roads open at 6 a.m,; closing time varies seasonally. Hikers, bikers, and horses welcome. Although admission to the park and visitor center are free, the museum, film, Cyclorama, and bus tours are ticketed. The least expensive ticket is $ for adults; combination packages for several choices or several days are available. Children under 6 are free.

A visit to this ghostly battlefield can be a truly moving experience. Gettysburg National Military Park brings to life the story of three days in July 1863. About 400 artillery guns stand along the Union and Confederate battle lines, and more than 1,300 monuments help visitors picture what happened here.

The park has a spacious new museum and visitor center, operated by the Gettysburg Foundation. It provides a wonderful overview of the causes and effects of the Civil War and the battle of Gettysburg. Exhibits and a film narrated by Morgan Freeman provide a good introduction to the battle. Upstairs, the famous Cyclorama, a 360-degree painting of the battle by Paul Phillippoteaux, has been beautifully restored, with lighting and sound to bring it vividly to life.

Licensed battlefield guides who are experts on every facet of the battle and the war narrate the bus tours that depart from the visitor center. (Allow two and a half hours for the tour). They are also available to accompany you for private tours in your car, if you book at least three days in advance. The fee is $$$$ per car.

Gettysburg National Military Park offers a Junior Ranger program. Go to the information desk to pick up a **free** Junior Ranger booklet.

From mid-June to mid-Aug, the park offers a **free** kids' program called "Join the Army." This hour-long program takes place daily at 11 a.m. (You must preregister.) You'll learn how to march and drill, get to try out the job of captain or drummer, and even get to charge.

When children have prepared by studying the battle before their trip, many are able to imagine themselves as soldiers on the field. They'll want to reenact Pickett's Charge and then realize how hard it would be if they were carrying rifles and surrounded by cannon smoke.

Walking Tour of **Downtown Gettysburg**

After you've toured Gettysburg National Military Park and, optionally, Eisenhower National Historic Park, you may think you've "done" Gettysburg. Well, think again, because you've only just begun! Downtown Gettysburg offers an array of museums, shops, and attractions.

Start at the town's official information center, located at 35 Carlisle St., across Lincoln Square from the center of town.

Cross Lincoln Square and turn left down Baltimore Street, where most of the museums and sights are.

Going down Baltimore Street away from Lincoln Square, you can stop at points of interest such as Schriver House, Farnsworth House, and the **free** Rupp House History Center.

Baltimore Street then forks. The left fork is the continuation of Baltimore Street, where you'll find such sites as the Confederate States Armory Museum, Jennie Wade House and Olde Town, Soldiers National Museum, and Hall of Presidents and First Ladies.

The right fork is Steinwehr Avenue, where you'll find the National Civil War Museum and the Lincoln Train Museum.

Eisenhower National Historic Park (ages 10 and up)

Located on Business US 15 South, adjacent to the battlefield; (717) 338-9114, ext. 10; www .nps.gov/eise. The farm is open daily from Apr through Oct. It is closed Mon and Tues from Nov through Mar. Admission: Adults $$, children ages 6 to 16 $, under 6 free.

Adjacent to the battlefield is the Eisenhower National Historic Site, the 189-acre retirement home and farm of President and Mrs. Dwight Eisenhower. If you wish to tour the home, pick up tickets at the Gettysburg National Park Visitor Center, and then take a shuttle bus to the Eisenhower farm.

To liven up the visit for children ages five to thirteen, there's a Junior Secret Service Agent program. Pick up a free booklet at the information desk. Kids get a chance to use a park radio, look through binoculars, learn how the president is protected, and earn a Junior Secret Service Agent badge at the end.

Pace yourself, because you've only just begun. You may wish to take a walking tour of downtown Gettysburg to get yourself oriented before visiting some of the many sites in town. The town's official information center is located at 35 Carlisle St., across from Lincoln Square in the center of town.

David Wills House (ages 5 and up)

8 Lincoln Sq.; (717) 334-2499; www.davidwillshouse.org. Open year-round, including most federal holidays; hours vary seasonally. Admission $; children 5 and under free.

Opened in 2009, this modest museum was the home of wealthy civic leader David Wills. He and his family hosted Abraham Lincoln on Nov 18, 1863. That night, Lincoln finished his Gettysburg Address in an upstairs bedroom. Exhibits explore why the famous speech continues to echo in our history.

Gettysburg Train Station (ages 5 and up)

35 Carlisle Street; (717) 337-8233. Open daily 10 a.m. to 4 p.m. Free admission.

Lincoln arrived at this station on his famous 1863 visit. Modest exhibits show how trains evacuated hundreds of wounded soldiers after the battle.

Schriver House Museum (ages 5 and up)

309 Baltimore St.; (717) 337-2800; www.schriverhouse.org. Guided tours every half hour Apr through Nov, Mon through Sat 10 a.m. to 5 p.m., Sun noon to 5 p.m. Closed Jan except for special appointments.

The Battle of Gettysburg didn't just take place on the battlefield; it also took place in the streets of the town. At the time of the battle, there were less than 3,000 permanent residents of the town of Gettysburg. When the battle was over, about 22,000 wounded were left behind for the residents to care for. This award-winning museum is dedicated to the civilian experience during and following the battle. Schriver House has been restored to its 1860s appearance. Guides in period costume lead tours through all four floors of the house, including the attic, where Confederate sharpshooters set up their nest.

Rupp House History Center (all ages)
451 Baltimore St.; (717) 334-7292; www.friendsofgettysburg.org. Open Mar through Dec, Fri noon to 8 p.m., Sat 11 a.m. to 8 p.m., and Sun 11 to 5 p.m. **Free.**

The house currently on this site was built shortly after the battle, but there was a house that stood here earlier in July 1863. The History Center, right in the center of town and within walking distance of the park, offers visitors a hands-on, interactive experience of the sights, sounds, touch, and even the smell of nineteenth-century Gettysburg. And it's **free!**

Jennie Wade House (ages 8 and up)
758 Baltimore St.; (717) 334-4100. Admission is $$ for adults, $ for children. The Jennie Wade House and Olde Town are open daily. In summer hours are 9 a.m. to 7 p.m. Off-season hours are 9 a.m. to 5 p.m.

In addition to the thousands of men who died at Gettysburg, there was one woman. Twenty-year-old Jennie Wade was baking bread for the Union soldiers when she was hit by a stray bullet. You can see the bullet hole. A clever holographic display tells Jennie's story. Jennie Wade's house is adjacent to Olde Town, where the streets of Gettysburg of 1863 are re-created.

Hall of Presidents and First Ladies (ages 8 and up)
789 Baltimore St.; (717) 334-5717. Open daily 9 a.m. to 5 p.m. Admission $$ adults, $ students.

You can hear U.S. presidents "speak" at the Hall of Presidents and First Ladies. A series of life-size wax figures and taped messages can help kids learn the difference between Andrew Jackson and Andrew Johnson. The First Ladies appear in reproductions of their inaugural gowns.

American Civil War Museum (ages 8 and up)
297 Steinwehr Ave.; (717) 334-6245; www.gettysburgmuseum.com. Hours vary seasonally but are usually 9 a.m. to 5 p.m. daily. Admission: $; children 5 and under **free.**

The American Civil War Museum has organized its more than 200 life-size figures into an audiovisual presentation including thirty different scenes. You can see animated figures reenact the Battle of Gettysburg and an animated Lincoln deliver the Gettysburg Address. On weekends from May until Labor Day, special events include living reenactments.

Lincoln Train Museum (ages 8 and up)
425 Steinwehr Ave.; (717) 334-5678. Open in summer 9 a.m. to 9 p.m. and in spring and fall 9 a.m. to 5 p.m. Closed during the winter months. Admission is $$ for adults, $ for children.

You can join Lincoln for the train ride to Gettysburg on a twelve-minute simulated trip at the Lincoln Train Museum. The museum also exhibits a toy train collection, including a model-railroad layout that represents the Civil War.

Lighter Attractions in Gettysburg

Okay, so your younger ones have had enough history. Now's the perfect time for some lighter fare. For something spookily different, hear stories by candlelight at **Farnsworth House Mourning Theater and Ghost Walks** at 401 Baltimore St. In season, stories are given Tues through Fri at 9:30 p.m. and Sat at 8 and 9:30 p.m. Hours vary seasonally. Call (717) 334-8838 for details and the current schedule. Tickets are $$ for adults; children under six are **free.** Not recommended for children who are afraid of the dark or for very young children.

In season you can enjoy **Mulligan MacDuffer Adventure Golf.** Adjacent to the battlefield, it offers miniature golf and ice cream. Call (717) 337-1518; www.mulliganmacduffer.com.

Land of Little Horses is outside Gettysburg at 125 Glenwood Dr. The smallest Falabella horses may weigh seventy pounds and stand less than 20 inches high. Kids less than eighty pounds can climb up on their backs (for an additional fee). The horses perform tricks three times a day from Memorial Day through Labor Day. There's also a carousel, train tram, nature area, gift shop, and snack bar. The Land of Little Horses is open 10 a.m. to 5 p.m. daily, Apr through Oct. Call (717) 334-7259; www.landoflittlehorses.com. Admission is $$ for adults, $ for children two to twelve. "Herd" rates are available. Wheelchair accessible.

Another fun stop—but one that could get expensive—is **Boyd's Bear Country** (866-367-8338; www.BoydsBearCountry.com), off Business US 15 (Steinwehr Avenue) at 75 Cunningham Rd. Here you can see and, of course, purchase the popular collectible stuffed toys.

Soldiers National Museum (ages 10 and up)

777 Baltimore St.; (717) 334-4890. Hours vary seasonally. Admission $$ adults, $ children.

Ten Civil War dioramas are housed in the building that was General Howard's headquarters during the battle and later the Soldiers' National Orphanage. The museum features artifacts and memorabilia from the Civil War as well as other major American conflicts.

General Lee's Headquarters (ages 10 and up)

US 30 West, 8 blocks west of Lincoln Square; (717) 334-3141; www.civilwarheadquarters .com. Open daily 9 a.m. to 6 p.m. mid-Mar through Nov. Extended hours in summer. Admission is $.

In this house General Lee and his staff made plans for the battle. Now the building houses a collection of Civil War relics.

Chambersburg

Chambersburg has a historic square that is the setting for the annual Ice Fest, a great excuse to get out of the house and enjoy food, ice sculptures, and entertainment.

Chambersburg Heritage Center (all ages)

100 Lincoln Way East; (717) 264-7101; www.chambersburg.org. Open 8 a.m. to 5 p.m. Mon through Fri. From Apr to Dec, also open Sat 10 a.m. to 3 p.m. Free admission.

In a grand old building on the town square, Chambersburg recounts three hundred years of history. In the 1700s, early white settlers and Indians fought here. During the Civil War, the town, at a major railroad crossing, was invaded several times by the Confederate Army. A thoughtfully designed children's corner at the center offers games and dress-ups. Pick up brochures for excellent driving tours themed to different historical eras.

Olympia Candy Kitchen (all ages)

43 S. Main St.; (717) 263-3282; www.olympiacandy.net. Open Mon through Sat 10 a.m. to 5 p.m. (open unti 6 p.m. Fri).

The wonderful scent of the homemade candies at this century-old, family-owned store will make everyone in your family hungry. In addition to chocolates and other treats, there's a nice selection of gift items.

Where to Eat

IN READING/BERKS COUNTY

These non–fast food restaurants offer kid-friendly dining:

Antique Airplane Restaurant, Best Western Dutch Colony Inn, 4635 Perkiomen Ave., US 422, East Reading; (610) 779-2345. An authentic 1927 airplane hangs from the ceiling, and aviation memorabilia hang from the walls.

Peanut Bar and Restaurant, 332 Penn St., Reading; (610) 376-8500; www.peanutbar .com. Lunch through late night, it's one of the few places where parents can enjoy gourmet selections while youngsters eat more kid-friendly choices. Besides, where else can you tell the kids, "go ahead, throw the peanut shells on the floor"?

IN THE LEBANON AREA

The Blue Bird Inn, 2387 Cornwall Rd.; (717) 273-3000; www.bluebirdinn.com. Casual pub grub in the country, with outdoor dining on the deck.

IN GETTYSBURG

These restaurants in Gettysburg offer children's menus:

Dobbin House Tavern, 89 Steinwehr Ave.; (717) 334-2100; www.dobbinhouse.com. A historic building with country store, bakery, and underground slave hideout. Children's menu available.

Farnsworth House Inn, 401 Baltimore St., (717) 334-8838; www.farnsworthhousedining .com. A historic building with one hundred bullet holes. Gettysburg's only Civil War dining. The Travel Channel has named the inn one of "America's Ten Most Haunted Inns".

Where to Stay

IN LANCASTER AND PENNSYLVANIA DUTCH COUNTRY

Bird-in-Hand Family Inn, 2740 Old Philadelphia Pike, Bird-in-Hand; (717) 768-8271. Indoor/outdoor pools, free bus tour, restaurant, bakery.

Fairfield by Marriott—Lancaster, 150 Granite Run Dr., Lancaster; (717) 581-1800. Indoor pool.

Outdoor World: Pennsylvania Dutch Country, 185 Lebanon Rd., Manheim; (717) 665-2500 or (800) 588-2222 (for reservations); www.campoutdoorworld.com. One of the Outdoor World camping resorts.

Quality Inn & Suites, 2363 Oregon Pike, Lancaster; (717) 569-0477. Restaurant, outdoor pool.

Red Caboose Motel, P.O. Box 303, Strasburg 17579; (717) 687-5000 or (888) 687-5005. Sleep in authentic cabooses and dine in authentic dining car. Seasonal buggy rides, petting zoo, flea market, country music.

IN THE LEBANON AREA

Cornwall Inn, 50 Burd Coleman Rd., Cornwall; (866) 605-6563; www.cornwallinnpa.com. Historic old company store is now a B&B with several family-friendly suites. Steps from the bike trail and Cornwall Iron Furnace.

IN THE HERSHEY AREA

Chocolatetown Motel, 1806 E. Chocolate Ave., Hershey; (717) 533-2330. Good location.

Cocoa Nights Motel, 1518 E. Chocolate Ave., Hershey; (717) 533-2384.

Hershey Highmeadow Campground, 1200 Matlack Rd., Hummelstown; (717) 534-8999 or (800) 533-3131. Cabins, campsites, pool, playground equipment, showers, and free shuttle buses to Hersheypark.

The Hershey Lodge, West Chocolate Avenue and University Drive, Hershey; (717) 533-3311 or (800) 533-3131. Casual resort with indoor/outdoor pool, a playground, children's pool, and free shuttle buses to Hersheypark.

The Hotel Hershey, Hotel Road, Hershey; (717) 533-2171 or (800) 533-3131; www.hersheypa.com/accommodations. Luxurious resort hotel with indoor/outdoor pool, children's pool, and free shuttle buses to Hersheypark. Has two restaurants to suit different tastes. Choose the Fountain Cafe if you're traveling with young children.

IN HARRISBURG

Ramada Inn on Market Square, 23 S. Second St.; (717) 234-5021 or (800) 2-RAMADA. Restaurant, indoor pool. Minutes from Hershey, Lancaster, Gettysburg.

For More Information

While surfing the Web, you may wish to check out the Web site of the **Dutch Country Roads region of VisitPennsylvania** at **www.dutchcountryroads.com,** or any of the Web sites given in this chapter.

Laurel Highlands Region

The beauty of the Laurel Highlands area of Pennsylvania will take your breath away. One hundred miles of countryside, mountains, and valleys; two mountain ridges; and thirteen state parks and forests provide the setting for golfing, skiing, fishing, and hiking. The Youghiogheny River (the "Yock") means white-water rafting, and Raystown Lake offers calmer boating, swimming, and more.

In this area the Rails-to-Trails Conservancy is converting old railroad paths to hiking and biking trails. (For a $$ guidebook, call Rails-to-Trails of Pennsylvania at 717-238-1717 or go to www.traillink.com.)

TopPicks in the Laurel Highlands Region

- **Idlewild Park**, Ligonier
- **Family float trip on Youghiogheny River**, Ohiopyle
- **Laurel Caverns**, Uniontown
- **Lincoln Caverns**, Huntington
- **Raystown Lake**, Hesston
- **Gravity Hill**, New Paris
- **Bat hike in Canoe Creek State Park**, Hollidaysburg
- **The Pike to Bike Trail**, Breezewood–McConnellsburg
- **Horseshoe Curve**, Altoona
- **Johnstown Inclined Plane**, Johnstown

LAUREL HIGHLANDS REGION

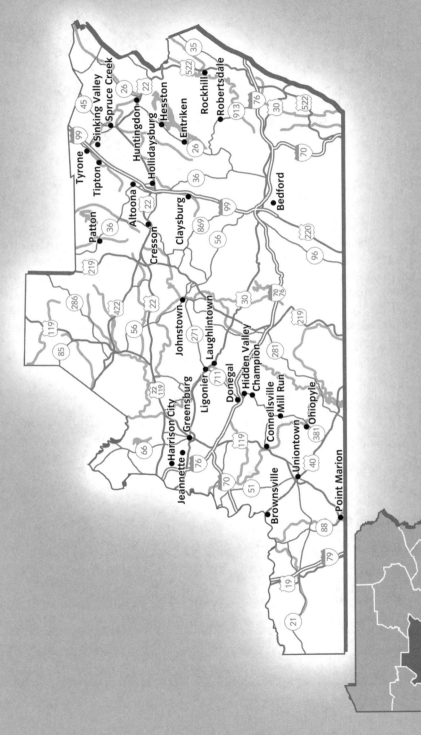

Here you'll find a masterpiece of modern architecture, Frank Lloyd Wright's Fallingwater. Old Bedford Village re-creates our history, and Idlewild Park takes us to the Land of Make-Believe.

The Laurel Highlands is rich in history, especially sites associated with the French and Indian War, a conflict that helped pave the way for the American Revolution—sites such as Fort Necessity and the authentically restored Fort Ligonier.

In 1806 the National Road was built to link the East with what was then the western frontier. This road is now US 40, where every May wagoners with teams of horses commemorate the opening of the nation's first turnpike (the National Road Festival; www .nationalroadpa.org). Two old tollhouses still exist along US 40, which is also a great foliage route in October.

This area saw remarkable industrial development: coal mining, the steel industry, the growth of railroading, and the building of canals. Many families enjoy driving the 500-mile Path of Progress Heritage Route, which takes them past many of the sites described in this chapter. (For further information about the Path of Progress, call 814-696-9569 or check the Web site at www.nps.gov/papr.)

If you're looking for something completely different, a visit to Gravity Hill should give you something to talk about. In Bedford County, near the town of Schellsburg, is an area where gravity appears to go backwards. It may be an optical illusion, but in this area, cars seem to roll uphill and water flow the wrong way. For very clear directions go to www .gravityhill.com or call (800) 765-3331.

TopEvents in the Laurel Highlands Region

- **Hidden Valley Resort Spring Carnival,** Mar; (814) 443-8000.

- **Seven Springs Resort Spring Festival,** Mar; (800) 452-2223.

- **National Road Festival,** May; (724) 437-9877.

- **Children's Living History weekend** at Compass Inn, Laughlintown, June; (724) 238-4983.

- **Christmas in July at Idlewild Park,** July; (724) 238-3666.

- **July 3 Memorial at Fort Necessity,** July; (724) 329-5805.

- **Ligonier Scottish Highland Games,** Idlewild Park, Sept; (412) 238-3666.

- **Flood City Music Festival,** Johnstown, Sept; (888) 222-1889.

- **Pumpkin Fest,** Confluence, Oct; (800) 333-5661.

- **Fort Ligonier Days,** Oct; (724) 238-4200.

Point Marion

Friendship Hill National Historic Site (ages 10 and up)
**Off US 119; (724) 725-9190; www.nps.gov/frhi. Open daily year-round 9 a.m. to 5 p.m.
Closed major holidays. Free.**

Friendship Hill is the home of Swiss-born patriot Albert Gallatin, who was elected to the
U.S. Senate and the House of Representatives, played an important role in the Whiskey
Rebellion, and was Secretary of the Treasury, a member of the team that negotiated
the end of the War of 1812, minister to France, and sometimes called the "father" of the
National Road.

   There are 8 miles of trails and a picnic area. You can take a pleasant walk to the grave
of Gallatin's first wife, Sophia Allegre. The site overlooks the Monongahela River, but
watch out for the steep banks. Also, be aware that there may be potential dangers in old
buildings and mine works that have not yet been restored. Since the house is sometimes
closed, it's wise to call ahead.

Uniontown

In the Uniontown area, you can visit Searight Toll House, Fort Necessity National Battlefield, and Laurel Caverns.

Searight Toll House (ages 8 and up)
**US 40 West; (724) 439-4422. Open Tues through Sat 10 a.m. to 4 p.m. and, from mid-May
to mid-Oct, Sun 2 to 6 p.m. Admission is $ for adults; children enter free. Group tours
arranged by appointment.**

The U.S. government authorized construction of the National Road in 1806 to connect
the East and the West. One of the National Road's tollhouses, Searight Toll House is open
to the public and is administered by Fayette County Historical Society. Built in 1835 and
recently restored, the octagonally shaped tollhouse includes the toll keeper's office,
kitchen, living room, and living quarters.

Fort Necessity National Battlefield National Park (ages 9 and up)
**On US 40 (the National Road), 11 miles east of Uniontown; (724) 329-5512; www.nps
.gov. The fort building is open daily from dawn to dusk. The visitor center is open 9
a.m. to 5 p.m. Closed all federal holidays except Memorial Day, July 4th, Labor Day, and
Columbus Day.**

At Jumonville Glen, 5 miles from here, the 22-year-old George Washington met with his
first experience of battle in 1754, during the French and Indian War. Washington's forces
won the first encounter. The fort was built afterward in expectation that the French would

Amazing
Pennsylvania Facts

The banana split was invented by Dr. David Strickler at his drug store fountain on Ligonier Street in Latrobe in 1904.

return, which they did, but this time Washington was forced into the only surrender of his career. Here you can also visit the grave of General Braddock.

The visitor center offers a gripping twenty-minute film about the young George Washington (then working for the British), the fort, and the creation of the National Road. Its rich interactive exhibits include Indian culture and artifacts unearthed during the construction project. The center's playground introduces kids to heroes of the fort's history. You'll probably be surprised when you see the size of the reconstructed fort. The circular stockade is 53 feet in diameter. The gate is only 3.5 feet wide.

While you're in the neighborhood, you may wish to visit the Mount Washington Tavern, built in the 1820s on land once owned by George Washington himself. The tavern has been restored to look as it might have in the period when it was constructed to serve travelers along the new National Road, which was built in 1818.

Laurel Caverns (all ages)

Located 5 miles east of US 40, at the crest of Summit Mountain; (800) 515-4150; www.laurel caverns.com. Open daily from May to Oct 9 a.m. to 5 p.m.; weekends only in Mar, Apr, and Nov. Family guided tours leave every twenty minutes. Tours: $$; preschoolers are free. Group rates are available with advance notice. Indoor miniature golf course: $$ per person, $ group rate.

Located on a mountainside, Pennsylvania's largest cave offers not only the underground caves but also a breathtaking view. Although the adventurous may choose the challenging Caving Adventure, the easy guided family tour is recommended for families with children under twelve and the physically challenged. Watch your step in the narrow passageways.

At the end of the tour, don't miss the sound-and-light show, sort of an underground Fantasia. There's even "Kavern Putt," a wheelchair-accessible miniature golf course housed in a huge man-made cave.

Bring a jacket and a flashlight: The caverns are 50 degrees year-round. Rappelling and climbing sessions are available to groups inside the caverns, as are fossil-hunting excursions. Restrooms in the visitor center are wheelchair accessible and include changing tables. There is a picnic shelter, or stop a tenth of a mile up US 40 for home cooking at Glisan's Restaurant. Dozens of flavors of pies are baked fresh here daily.

Brownsville

Nemacolin Castle (ages 8 and up)

Front Street; (724) 785-6882; www.nemacolincastle.org. Open weekends only 11 a.m. to 5 p.m. mid-Mar through mid-Oct. In June, July, and Aug, it's also open Tues through Fri 11 a.m. to 5 p.m. Admission: adults $$, children 12 and under $.

Despite its name, Nemacolin Castle is not a castle but the home of Jacob Bowman, who opened a trading post in Brownsville in 1786. It looks a little like a castle with its turreted tower and battlements. You can take a guided tour of more than twenty furnished rooms. Around the holidays, Christmas candlelight tours are offered.

Connellsville

Crawford Cabin (ages 6 and up)

North Seventh Street at the Youghiogheny River; (724) 628-5640; www.fay-west.com. Open by appointment only. Free.

The Connellsville Area Historical Society (275 S. Pittsburgh St.; 724-628-5640) administers Crawford Cabin. George Washington visited his lifelong friend Col. William Crawford in this humble log cabin, 14 by 16 feet, built in 1765. Colonel Crawford and his men served Washington at the crossing of the Delaware and the battles of Trenton, Princeton, Brandywine, and Germantown.

Ohiopyle

Ohiopyle State Park's Youghiogheny River (affectionately nicknamed the "Yough," pronounced *Yock*) offers a wide range of river adventures. From March into October thousands of vacationers challenge the Yough. Find the guided or unguided trip that suits your family's taste and ages.

An O'Toole **Family Adventure**

On a weekend along the Youghiogheny River, we pedaled between Ohiopyle and Confluence on the Great Allegheny Passage, and floated in a huge rubber raft down the gentle stream. But when night fell, James and Bill were disappointed that our B&B didn't have television. But I'd planned ahead: I'd brought two copies of the latest Harry Potter book. The result: a magical evening all around.

The most beautiful stretch of the Great Allegheny Passage, a long-distance recreational trail, runs through the state park. This easy, level rails-to-trails path is an ideal family bike outing (but in-line skates won't roll on the crushed gravel surface). Ride along the shady bank of the rushing Yough to Confluence, a charming village 10 miles upstream. Lunch at a casual spot like the Sisters Cafe or the River's Edge, then pedal back. Families with older children might enjoy ending the day at The Slides, a slick water ride over submerged boulders in a stream (careful!). For a trail map, go to www.gaptrail.org.

Rafting on the Youghiogheny
(ages 4 and up for the Middle Yough only)

For novices or families with younger children, the **Middle Yough** is the best choice, with its gentler Class I and II rapids and relaxing scenery. Laurel Highlands River Tours offers a guided trip on the Middle Yough, which they call their Family Float Trip, for families with children ages four and up. (Many seniors also enjoy this trip.) Both Wilderness Voyageurs and White Water Adventures offer similar relaxing float trips. Wilderness Voyageurs rents easily maneuverable rafts for unguided rafting. (See below for information on these establishments.)

The **Lower Yough's** Class III and IV rapids are a little wilder. The minimum age for this 7.5-mile stretch of the river is twelve. Mountain Streams offers a minitrip on the Lower Yough that lasts about two hours. Many of these organizations also provide bike rentals, kayaks, or "duckies." A duckie is sort of an inflatable kayak, used with a double-ended paddle, available with one or two seats. Most outfitters recommend duckies rather than canoes. A Thrillseeker, also used with a double-ended paddle, is made of a harder plastic.

Teenagers and adults with a taste for adventure can take on the **Upper Yough.** This 11-mile stretch of the river in Maryland includes Class IV and V rapids and is recommended for experienced paddlers only. The minimum age is sixteen.

Ohiopyle State Park (all ages)

Park office, located on Dinnerbell Road; (729) 329-8591. Open dawn to dusk.

Ohiopyle is also the starting point for the Laurel Highlands Hiking Trail. You can hike 70 miles here from Ohiopyle to an area near Johnstown. Eight overnight sites have been set up along the trail, which is designed for serious hikers.

There are flush toilets and shower facilities in Ohiopyle State Park, and Fox's Pizza is not far away. The park offers campsites, cabins, and yurts. Nearby, the community center offers a licensed day-care center for children under the minimum rafting age of four; call (724) 329-1444.

Kentuck Knob (ages 9 and up)

Kentuck Road, Chalk Hill; (724) 329-1901; www.kentuckknob.com. Open Tues through Sun and Mon holidays. Regular tours depart from 10 a.m. to 4 p.m. Reservations are recommended. Tours are $$$. Longer, in-depth tours are $$$$ and depart at 8:30 a.m. or by reservation.

If you are a Frank Lloyd Wright fan, you won't want to miss this example of one of Wright's late designs, built in 1953. Children nine and up are welcome to join the regular tour. There are no day-care facilities for younger ones.

Mill Run

Fallingwater (ages 9 and up except for children's tours for ages 5 to 9)   (m)
PA 381; (724) 329-8501; www.fallingwater.org. Open for guided tours Apr to mid-Nov, Tues through Sun and Mon holidays 10 a.m. to 4 p.m. In Dec tours are offered weekends only 11 a.m. to 3 p.m. Closed Jan and Feb. On weekends tours are $$$; on weekdays tours are $$. Children under 9 are not permitted on the regular tour. Special tours for children ages 5 to 9; call for schedules and admission prices.

The story goes that Frank Lloyd Wright told Edgar Kaufmann, "I want you to live with the waterfall, not just look at it." Because of the technology of cantilevers, Wright was able to do just that.

In a beautiful wooded setting, Wright placed Fallingwater, one of his most significant architectural achievements. It seems as if it has always been here, with the waterfall cascading from it. Inside the house, walls of windows look out into the woods. The American Institute of Architects has called Fallingwater "the best all-time work of American architecture."

The regular tour takes about forty-five minutes to an hour, but if you like, you may make a reservation for a longer tour, which is very detailed and can take up to two hours. (These in-depth tours are available at 8:30 a.m. and carry a fee of at least $$$$ per person.) Tours do require a fair amount of walking. Only the first floor is wheelchair accessible.

Please note that children under six are not permitted to take the regular one-hour tour of the house. If you wish to see it yourself, however, you may take advantage of child care provided here ($ per child per hour). There's also an in-depth two-hour tour. Children must be nine to attend this tour. Reservations are strongly recommended for both regular and in-depth tours. Lunch is available in Fallingwater's restaurant.

If you would like to see more of Wright's work, visit Kentuck Knob, described earlier in the Ohiopyle section.

ALSO IN THE AREA

Fallingwater is operated by the Western Pennsylvania Conservancy, which also runs **Bear Run Nature Preserve,** 0.5 mile away. It is very convenient to Ohiopyle.

The family can camp at **Yogi Bear's Jellystone Park,** but even if you're not camping here, you can take advantage of the waterslides, playground, and other recreational activities. For information and pricing schedule, call (800) 439-4644 or go to www.jelly stonemillrun.com.

Champion

Seven Springs Mountain Resort (all ages)

Located between exits 9 and 10 on the PA Turnpike; (800) 452-2223; www.7springs.com.

Ski magazine has rated Seven Springs Mountain Resort the number-one ski resort in the mid-Atlantic. New features include two chairlifts and a "magic carpet" conveyor lift. This large facility offers lodging for more than 5,000 people in hotel rooms, condos, and chalets. Besides ski and snowboard rentals and ski lessons, the resort offers snow-tubing (eight chutes), swimming, bowling, concerts, snowmobile tours, snowcat rides, indoor miniature golf, and game rooms. The sleigh rides are picture-perfect. And in summer there's an alpine slide, chairlift rides, hayrides, horseback rides, fly fishing, mountain biking, and more.

Donegal

Caddie Shak Family Fun Park (all ages)

Located 1.5 miles east on PA 31 off exit 9 of the PA Turnpike; (724) 593-7400 or (877) 416-7400; www.caddieshak.com. Open daily Mar through Oct. Admission and parking are **free.**

You can't drive past Caddie Shak Family Fun Park without a reaction from your kids. ("Their tongues hang out," says one parent.) Convenient to the turnpike, Caddie Shak has three go-kart tracks, miniature golf, batting cages, games, and food. Other attractions include bumper cars with water cannons, a petting zoo, paintball, and horseback riding. A nice way to break up the trip. The rides and attractions are moderately priced, and family discounts are available. Wheelchair accessible.

Living Treasures Animal Park (all ages)

PA 711, south of PA 31; (724) 593-8300; www.ltanimalpark.com. Open Memorial Day through Labor Day 10 a.m. to 8 p.m. In Apr, May, Sept, and Oct, open daily 10 a.m. to 6 p.m. Admission is $$ for adults and $ for children 3 to 11; children 2 and under are **free.** Please note that there are two "Living Treasures" locations. The other, also listed in this guide, is in Moraine.

Get up close to more than one hundred species of friendly animals from all over the world at Living Treasures Animal Park.

Hidden Valley

Hidden Valley Four Seasons Resort (all ages)

4 Craighead Dr.; (814) 443-8000; www.hiddenvalleyresort.com.

The instructors at Hidden Valley Ski want you to learn to ski with them. One of the mid-Atlantic's most popular family ski resorts, Hidden Valley has twenty-five ski slopes and trails, more than 30 miles of cross-country ski trails, and a half-pipe for snowboarders. There's also a kids' camp, indoor and outdoor pools, boating, fishing, tennis, ecotouring, and more.

In spring and summer there's still a lot to do, such as golfing, mountain biking, and swimming. The many restaurants cater to a variety of tastes, and all are kid-friendly with the possible exception of the Snow Shoe Lounge (kids may be served with parents, but it is a lounge). Mountain Munchkins Child Care offers babysitting for children eighteen months to eight years. There are changing tables in both men's and women's restrooms.

Greensburg

In addition to Hanna's Town (below) you may want to check out the cozy Kid Space and kid "scavenger hunts" at the **Westmoreland Museum of American Art** (221 N. Main St.; 724-837-1500; www.wmuseumaa.org) or catch a play or pop concert at the historic Palace Theatre (724-836-8000).

Hanna's Town (ages 8 and up)

951 Old Salem Rd.; (724) 836-1800; www.starofthewest.org. Open Memorial Day through Labor Day, Wed through Sat 10 a.m. to 4 p.m.; Sun 1 to 4 p.m. Open weekends only in May, Sept, and Oct 1 to 4 p.m.

Archaeological research in Greensburg has unearthed nearly one million artifacts at Hanna's Town, which was founded in 1773.

A stockade fort, the home of Robert Hanna, the town jail, and a wagon shed are reconstructed. Klingensmith House has been moved here. You can visit the field museum and see archaeological artifacts unearthed here.

Jeannette

Depending on how you look at it, Bushy Run Battlefield is in either Jeannette or Harrison City. Either way, it's about 11 miles northwest of Greensburg, and it's an interesting place to visit.

Bushy Run Battlefield (ages 8 and up)

PA 993; (724) 527-5584; www.bushyrunbattlefield.com. Visitor center: Apr through Oct, Wed to Sat 9 a.m. to 5 p.m. and Sun noon to 5 p.m. Battlefield: Wed to Sun 9 a.m. to 5 p.m. year-round. From Nov to Mar the museum is closed. Admission is $.

Here's an opportunity to acquaint your family with a lesser-known conflict: Pontiac's War. In 1763 Native American forces, under the command of war chief Pontiac, struggled against the British, eventually laying seige to Fort Pitt. At the Bushy Run Battlefield, the British turned the tide against this rebellion and saved Fort Pitt.

At the visitor center a fiber-optic map helps you get your bearings. Take some time to observe the interactive exhibits, maps, flags, and weapons and learn about this episode in our history. In the Kids' Corner you can try on a reproduction uniform. Then you can take a guided tour of the battlefield. There are 3 miles of historic hiking trails, education programs, and special events. On the Edge Hill Trail, each stop represents one aspect of the Battle of Bushy Run, including the Flour Bag Entrenchment in which flour bags were used to protect the British wounded. There is also a gift shop. Wheelchair accessible.

Another trail, the Flour Sack Discovery Trail, focuses on how humans have used things from the forest. For example, the black walnut tree provided food, dye, insect repellent, gunstocks, and furniture.

The Iroquois Nature Trail was designed by the Boy Scouts to demonstrate the changes in the environment between the nineteenth and twenty-first centuries. There are thirteen stations, such as Beauty in Nature Through Adaptation, where you can see how nature has healed itself in what was once a stone quarry.

Ligonier

Idlewild and SoakZone (all ages)

US 30 West; (724) 238-3666; www.idlewild.com. Operating season runs from late May through Labor Day. Open daily from mid-June through late Aug. The gates and Story Book Forest open at 13 a.m., many rides and attractions open at 11:30 a.m. Closing times vary. Fun-Day passes include all rides and attractions. Season passes also available. Children 2 and under enter free.

Idlewild and SoakZone, once named "America's Most Beautiful Theme Park," is the home of Mister Rogers' Neighborhood of Make-Believe, complete with the Neighborhood Trolley your preschoolers have always wanted to see up close. The late Fred Rogers himself served as creative consultant for this charming replica with the castle, King Friday, Queen Sarah Saturday, and all the details you'll recognize right away. In July, characters such as Mr. McFeeley may appear in person.

Located about 50 miles east of Pittsburgh and a sister park to Kennywood and Sandcastle, Idlewild and SoakZone began as a picnic area in 1878. This relaxing and manageable park, nestled in the woods, is perfect for children twelve and under, but it also has rides for older kids such as the Wild Mouse steel coaster and Rollo Coaster, a classic wooden coaster built in 1938. At present the three-row carousel, built by the Philadelphia Toboggan Company in the 1930s, still entrances children of all ages. The entire family can cool off on Paul Bunyan's Loggin Toboggan—a wet and wild water ride.

The beloved Story Book Forest was added in 1956, with its more than forty scenes and live characters from fairy tales and nursery rhymes. You'll literally step through the pages of a storybook to visit the homes of The Old Woman Who Lived in a Shoe, Snow White and the Seven Dwarfs, and The Three Little Pigs, among others. It takes about an hour to explore Story Book Forest.

Jumpin' Jungle gets families climbing, crawling, and, well, jumping! Climb up the netting or jump in a ball pit. SoakZone is a giant water attraction for all ages. Pirate wannabes will love its newest attraction, Captain Kidd's Adventure Galley, with six new waterslides and interactive spray features. It has Hydro Racers, Pipeline Plunge, Tipping Bucket, and a huge swimming pool, plus Little Squirts—wet fun for younger ones. Bring your bathing suit if you plan to go on any of the waterslides or swim in the pool.

Fort Ligonier (ages 8 and up)

Intersection of US 30 and PA 711; (724) 238-9701; www.fortligonier.org. The fort is open daily Apr to Oct, Mon through Sat 10 a.m. to 4:30 p.m. and Sun noon to 4:30 p.m. Admission is $$ for adults, $ for children 6 to 14 years old.

Fort Ligonier was built by the British during the French and Indian War. The entire fort, except for its foundation, was destroyed by 1800, but it has been carefully reconstructed. It has gun batteries and a retrenchment. The visitor center offers a comprehensive exhibit on the Seven Years' War, called the first world war because it involved many nations and several continents. Several artifacts from George Washington's military career are displayed here. You can visit several restored buildings such as a quartermaster's storehouse, magazine, hospital, and commissary.

Every Oct, on the anniversary of its most famous battle, the fort celebrates Fort Ligonier Days.

Powdermill Nature Reserve (ages 5 and up)

Rector (3 miles south of Ligonier on PA 381); www.powdermill.org. Summer camps for children age 5 to 12; special programs for families year-round.

Powdermill is a research station of the Carnegie Museum of Natural History in Pittsburgh. It is known worldwide for the bird-banding program at its Avian Research Center, which

Amazing
Pennsylvania Facts

At 3,213 feet, Mount Davis in Somerset County is the highest peak in Pennsylvania.

tracks the migrations of hundreds of species of songbirds that rest and feed here. Families can participate in annual events like the July butterfly count. The 1,600-acre preserve includes several walking trails and a nature center with interpretive programs.

Laughlintown

Compass Inn Museum (ages 8 and up)

Three miles east of Ligonier, on US 30 East; (724) 238-4983; www.compassinn.com. Open mid-Apr through Oct, Tues through Sat 11 a.m. to 4 p.m. and Sun 1 to 5 p.m. Admission is $$ for adults, $ for students, free for children under 5.

If you want to get a picture of what it was like in a typical roadside inn of the eighteenth and nineteenth centuries, visit the Compass Inn Museum. The log part was built in 1799 and the stone addition in 1820. The Ligonier Valley Historical Society has restored the building, and the kitchen, blacksmith's shop, and barn have been reconstructed on their original sites.

You can find out where terms like "upper crust" and "toasting" came from. You can see how travelers spent the night crammed into beds with other guests. You can visit the family's quarters, as well as the barn, where old horse- and ox-drawn vehicles still remain and sometimes a blacksmith is on duty, demonstrating the craft. You can also see tools of the period.

During summer, living-history days are held on the third weekend of each month. In Nov and Dec candlelight tours are offered on weekends only.

Johnstown

The town of Johnstown will always be remembered as the site of the tragic flood that occurred on May 31, 1889. The stress of a storm proved too much for the town's neglected dam, which broke, sending a wall of water down the mountain and through the town, killing more than 2,000 people.

But Johnstown is not just a place of tragedy; it is a town full of life. In late June Johnstown hosts "Thunder in the Valley," an unusually family-oriented motorcycle rally. In Aug, the Cambria County Ag-Tour offers a day in the country with free refreshments at several area farms. The Log House Arts Festival, during Labor Day weekend, has many activities for children. That weekend also hosts the popular annual Johnstown Flood City Music Festival, and shuttle buses run between the two events (see "Also in the Area"). Also, the Pasquerilla Performing Arts Center has "Sydney's Series" of plays for children. Besides these annual events, Johnstown has the Bottle Works Ethnic Arts Center.

Johnstown Flood National Memorial (ages 8 and up)

Located in Saint Michael, 10 miles northeast of Johnstown; (814) 495-4643; www.nps.gov/ jofl. Open Memorial Day to Labor Day 9 a.m. to 5 p.m. Closed on Veterans Day, Martin

Luther King Jr. Day, Presidents' Day, Thanksgiving, Christmas, and New Year's Day. Admission $; children 16 and under enter **free.** Call for details. Take US 219 to the Saint Michael/Sidman exit. Head east on PA 869, and turn left onto Lake Road at the sign.

The Johnstown Flood began on the site in Saint Michael, where you can see the Johnstown Flood National Memorial, administered by the National Park Service. You can see what little is left of the South Fork Dam from here. A weakness in this dam is suspected of having made the flood so disastrous.

An award-winning documentary, *Black Friday,* brings the events to life. The thirty-five-minute film puts you inside the terror of the flood. In fact, it is so effective parents are warned that it may be too frightening for young children.

In summer you can see reenactments of some of the events surrounding the flood. You can also take a tour around the dam. The flood happened on Memorial Day, so every year during that holiday weekend, the abutments of the dam glow with the light of thousands of luminaries. Special presentations are offered, including *Tales of the Great Flood,* a theater event in which costumed interpreters read from eyewitness accounts of the flood.

Johnstown Inclined Plane (all ages)

711 Edgehill Dr.; easily accessible to PA 56, PA 403, and PA 271; (814) 536-1816; www .inclinedplane.com. Seasonal hours. Call ahead or check the Web site. **Free** parking is available at both the top and the bottom.

After visiting the memorial, you'll want to complete the story with a tour of the Johnstown Flood Museum. But first you might want to break up the seriousness with an exhilarating ride on the Johnstown Inclined Plane. You'll travel up on an amazing 71.9 percent grade, the steepest vehicular inclined plane in the world. Your car can ride the incline with you, if you desire, so that you can drive around the borough of Westmont.

In Westmont you can see Luzerne Street, noted in the Guinness Book of World Records as the longest street with elm trees. Historic Grandview Cemetery is just a ten-minute walk from the Incline.

After the Johnstown Flood, the frightened residents of the area wanted to live at the top of the hill, but they needed a way to commute to and from the city, so this incline was built. An "incline" is an unusual kind of cable railway found in Johnstown and Pittsburgh. During Johnstown's two subsequent floods (1936 and 1977), the incline became the

Amazing
Pennsylvania Facts

The Laurel Highlands get more than 100 inches of real snow per year, plus another 60 to 80 inches from man-made snow machines.

people's escape route. At night, when both the tracks and the cars are lit up, the incline is a spectacular sight.

At the top of the incline, 634 feet above the city, there is an observation deck, visitor center, and the City View Bar and Grill Restaurant, open daily (call 814-534-0190). The view of the Conemaugh Valley is spectacular, as seen from the glass-walled Plane Visitor Center. From this vantage point you can see the largest free-flying American flags in the country.

The Johnstown Flood Museum (ages 6 and up)

304 Washington St. (P.O. Box 1889, Johnstown 15907); (814) 539-1889; www.jaha.org. Open seven days a week year-round, 10 a.m. to 5 p.m. From Memorial Day through Labor Day, hours are extended to 10 a.m. to 7 p.m. on Fri and Sat. Tickets are $ and are good for admission to both the Johnstown Flood Museum and the Heritage Discovery Center.

The museum, located in a former Carnegie Library, tells the story of the Johnstown flood disaster. Photos show how the town looked before the waters came, and after. An animated map with light and sound effects shows how the water swept through Johnstown, destroying thousands of homes and businesses.

First see the documentary film *The Johnstown Flood,* which won the Academy Award for Best Documentary Short Subject in 1989. This twenty-five-minute movie is shown hourly and was made using black-and-white still photos taken after the flood. A longer version of this movie has been shown on PBS's *The American Experience.*

Then visit the two floors of permanent exhibits, artifacts, and a 3-D multimedia presentation. The museum store offers a large selection of books and gifts.

Johnstown Heritage Discovery Center (ages 8 and up)

PA 56, Broad Street and Seventh Avenue; (814) 539-1889. www.jaha.org. Open daily 10 a.m. to 5 p.m., with extended hours in the summer months. Admission is $$ for adults, $ for seniors and students, and tickets are good for both the Heritage Discovery Center and the Johnstown Flood Museum.

The Heritage Discovery Center is housed in the former Germania Brewery Company building, built in 1907. The Frank and Sylvia Pasquerilla Heritage Discovery Center immerses the visitor in turn-of-the-twentieth-century Johnstown as experienced by immigrants from Eastern and Southern Europe who came to Johnstown from 1870 to 1914 to work in the mills and mines.

As you enter the museum, you'll receive a card with a photo of one of eight immigrant characters. As you move through the exhibits, you can plug your card into different interactive stations that demonstrate the immigrant's experience. The permanent exhibit, America Through Immigrant Eyes, allows you to experience the sights, sounds, and even the smells of immigrants' daily lives.

The Children's Discovery Museum features more hands-on activities to teach about the new Americans' experience.

Bottle Works Ethnic Arts Center (ages 6 and up)

411 Third Ave.; (814) 536-5399; www.bottleworks.org. Open Tues through Fri 10 a.m. to 4 p.m. and Sat 11 a.m. to 3 p.m. Admission is free. Some special events have additional fees.

In 1994 the old Tulip Bottling Company building was converted into the Bottle Works, whose mission is "to educate, preserve, and celebrate the ethnic heritage of the people of the Johnstown region." The Tulip Bottling Company was founded by a family of Russian and Hungarian Jews. In just a few years, the Bottle Works has become well known in the area for its Celebrations of Heritages through visual, performing, and folk arts. Summertime offers ethnic camps for children and ethnic arts and crafts at the FolkFest.

ALSO IN THE AREA

Every Sept, the Johnstown Area Heritage Association hosts the **Flood City Music Festival** (formerly the Johnstown Folk Festival) a three-day outdoor music festival with four stages providing more than seventy hours of entertainment. For information call (888) 222-1889, or check the Web sites www.jaha.org and www.floodcitymusic.com.

The Johnstown Area Heritage Association also administers the **Wagner–Ritter House,** which re-creates the domestic lives of the thousands who toiled "in the shadow of the mills." For information check the Web at www.jaha.org.

Stackhouse Park offers many special programs for children in its 277 acres of wooded land.

Claysburg

Blue Knob All Seasons Resort (all ages)

US North (from PA Turnpike, exit 11). For details call in-state (814) 239-5111; out-of-state call (800) 458-3403; www.blueknob.com.

One of the top ski resorts in the area, Blue Knob offers a KinderSki program, a ski school, an outdoor ice rink, tubing park, and cross-country skiing. In the warmer months there's golf, hiking, biking, tennis, and swimming.

Cresson

Allegheny Portage Railroad National Historic Site (ages 8 and up)

Twelve miles west of Altoona and 10 miles east of Ebensburg on US 22, off the Gallitzin exit; (814) 886-6150; www.nps.gov/alpo. Open daily 9 a.m. to 5 p.m. Closed some holidays and in inclement weather. Admission is $; children under 17 enter free.

In the middle of the nineteenth century, when Philadelphia was being linked to Pittsburgh by rail and canal, this portion of the Allegheny Mountains between Hollidaysburg and

Johnstown seemed impassable. So someone came up with a "portage railroad." A series of inclines carried the freight and passengers up the hills.

The visitor center has exhibits, a twenty-minute movie, and well-informed rangers. The Engine House Interpretive Building features full-scale models and hands-on exhibits. The railroad no longer exists, but you can walk along a portion of its route and see one section of restored track. As you enjoy the view from the overlook, be sure to note Skew Arch Bridge, which is actually twisted so that a wagon road could pass over the track. Rangers can direct you to the Staple Bend Tunnel, located 2.5 miles from Allegheny Portage Railroad in another section of the park. Costumed presentations and ranger-led hikes are available during the summer months.

Hollidaysburg

Trough Creek State Park (all ages)

PA 994. For information and pricing schedule, call (814) 658-3847; www.dcnr.state.pa.us. Twenty-four-hour access. Free.

The 554-acre Trough Creek State Park is a scenic gorge created by Trough Creek as it cuts through Terrace Mountain and empties into Raystown Lake. If you want to stay in comfort in a beautiful forested setting, Trough Creek Lodge, at Trough Creek State Park, is available for rental year-round. It is a two-story home built in the 1800s as an ironmaster's house. Now completely renovated, it offers a modern eat-in kitchen, four bedrooms, a bathroom, and central heat. The lodge is fully accessible for people with disabilities.

Canoe Creek State Park (all ages)

On US 22, about 13 miles east of Altoona and about 7 miles east of Hollidaysburg or 11 miles west of Water Street; (814) 695-6807; www.dcnr.state.pa.us. The day-use side is open 8 a.m. to sunset. The cabin area and east side have twenty-four-hour access. Admission is free.

You can reserve either a rustic or modern cabin and enjoy a wide variety of nature education programs at Canoe Creek State Park, one of a few parks that offer bat hikes, a favorite with our boys. At Canoe Creek you can join in on a bat hike to look in on Pennsylvania's largest bat nursery colony (females and young) in the attic of an old church. As night falls, they emerge from their home—about 10,000 of them! Children under twelve must be accompanied by an adult. Bring a flashlight. Other programs teach about bluebirds, birds' nests, frogs and toads, and wildflowers. Persons with disabilities may call (814) 695-6807 if assistance will be needed to participate in the program.

Paton

Seldom Seen Tourist Coal Mine (ages 8 and up)

Located on PA 36, 4 miles north of Patton, 7 miles from Prince Gallitzin State Park; mine phone, in season only, (814) 247-6305 or (800) 237-8590; www.seldomseenmine.com. Open Memorial Day, July Fourth, and Labor Day, plus weekends throughout June, as well as Thurs and Fri in July and Aug. Haunted Mine Tours offered during the last three weekends in Oct. Hour-long tours are conducted daily from noon to 6 p.m. Admission: adults $$; children under 12 $. Group rates available.

Many of the coal mines in southwestern Pennsylvania were small, family-run mines like this one. This nonprofit educational attraction is one of the region's most popular sites. Many of the tour guides are former miners and descendants of immigrant miners. Somehow, once your kids have imagined themselves hand-digging and hand-loading coal for 25 cents a ton, taking out the garbage doesn't seem so bad.

Altoona

Altoona has a lot to offer, including its new minor-league baseball team, the Altoona Curve.

Railroaders Memorial Museum (all ages)

1300 Ninth Ave.; (888) 4-Altoona; www.railroadcity.com. From Apr to the end of Oct, open Mon through Sat 10 a.m. to 5 p.m. and Sun 11 a.m. to 5 p.m. In Nov and Dec, open Fri, Sat, and Mon, 10 a.m. to 5 p.m., Sun 11 a.m. to 5 p.m. Closed Jan through Mar, except for group tours (by appointment) and special events. Admission is $$; children under 5 are free.

There are many museums devoted to the technology of railroading, but the Railroaders Memorial Museum tells the story of the men and women of the Pennsylvania Railroad (PRR). Here you'll experience Altoona at the height of industrial America. Located in the former Pennsylvania Railroad Master Mechanics building, this high-tech interpretive facility guides visitors through a firsthand experience of life in a booming railroad town. A film about the men and women of the PRR is also featured and included in the admission price. The Railroaders Memorial Museum displays the state's official steam locomotive, the K–4 1361, the last working model of its kind.

The museum is across from the Amtrak station, so real fanatics can come by train, see the trains, and go home by train. After your visit, stop by the adjacent Boyer Candy and browse through the specialty shops in the historic downtown business district.

Horseshoe Curve National Historic Landmark (all ages)

Located 6 miles west of Altoona; (814) 946-0834 or (888) 4-ALTOONA; www.railroadcity .com. Open Apr through the end of Oct, Mon through Sat 10 a.m. to 6 p.m., Sun 11 to 6 p.m. During Nov and Decr the visitor center and funicular incline are closed weekdays but open Sat and Sun noon to 6 p.m. Admission is $; a yearly pass is $$. Children under 5 are free.

At the Railroaders Memorial Museum, you can see a film that describes how the Horseshoe Curve was built by some 450 immigrants with picks and shovels and opened in 1854. Then you can ride uphill to watch the trains at Horseshoe Curve National Historic Landmark. Administered by the Railroaders Memorial Museum, this incredible engineering feat revolutionized rail travel, cleared the way for the westward expansion of the railroad, and made the Allegheny Portage Railroad obsolete (see previous entry under Cresson).

The story of Horseshoe Curve is told at a modern interpretive center. Visitors can ride to track elevation onboard the single-track funicular or walk the 194 evenly spaced stairs. At track elevation, more than fifty trains can be viewed every day along the Norfolk Southern mainline. One round-trip funicular ride is included in the admission.

There is a food concession open seasonally, and all restrooms have changing tables. Thomas the Tank Engine play-days include activities and movies.

Quaint Corner Children's Museum (ages 3 to 10)

On PA 36, at 2000 Union Ave., only a few blocks from the Railroaders Memorial Museum; (814) 944-6830. Open Thurs through Sun from 1 to 5 p.m. Admission is $.

Kids love exploring closets and attics, and they're welcome to snoop around in the fourteen rooms of the Quaint Corner Children's Museum. Peek in the International Closet or the Amish Closet, the Medical Room, or Pirate Treasure Closet.

The Quaint Corner Children's Museum was designed as a place for families to explore together, promoting creative hands-on learning and an appreciation for art, history, and science. The house itself is charming with its stained-glass windows and fine woodwork. Children love the craft room, dress-up clothes, and the sandbox in the basement. There's even a player piano in the gift shop. The bathroom, like the house, is old, with no changing or wheelchair facilities. The annual Quaint Corner Children's Fair comes in mid-Aug with puppet shows, games, and food.

Benzel's Pretzel Bakery (all ages)

5200 Sixth Avenue (PA 764); (814) 942-5062; www.benzels.com. Open Mon through Fri 10 a.m. to 5 p.m. and Sat 10 a.m. to 1 p.m.

You can walk to Benzel's from the Quaint Corner Children's Museum. Operated by a third generation of the Benzel family, Benzel's Pretzel Bakery makes about five million pretzels every day. At one time the pretzels were shaped by hand, but at present the dough goes through an extruder. There is a changing table in the wheelchair-accessible restroom.

Lakemont Park (all ages)

700 Park Ave.; (814) 949-PARK; www.lakemontparkfun.com. Open early May through mid-Sept, plus selected weekends in Oct, Nov, and Dec. Several different passes are available, with the most expensive All Day Ride & Slide Pass costing $$ per person.

In 2000 Lakemont Park reopened its treasured historic Leap the Dips roller coaster, the world's oldest roller coaster and the last remaining example of the side friction figure-eight design. In 2001 the Tin Lizzy Antique Auto ride opened. In all, there are more than thirty rides and attractions, including the Island Waterpark, two roller coasters, two go-kart tracks, an arcade, food, and more.

Every year from Thanksgiving through the Sunday after New Year's, Lakemont hosts its "Holiday Lights on the Lake."

Altoona Curve (all ages)

1000 Park Ave.; (814) 943-5400; www.altoonacurve.com. Admission $$–$$$. Seasonal.

Altoona's popular minor league baseball team plays at Blair County Park, a cozy 7,200-seat stadium next to Lakemont Park. There's plenty of room for the family to roam and plenty of good vantage points so you kids can watch a professional game up close. Best of all, there's a real roller coaster right in the park: Ride the Skyline before, after, or during the game.

Sinking Valley

Fort Roberdeau Historic Site and Natural Area (ages 8 and up)

Off PA 433 north of the Bellwood exit of I-99; (814) 946-0048; www.fortroberdeau.org. Fort and visitor center open May 15 through Sept 30, Tues to Sat 11 a.m. to 5 p.m. and Sun and Mon 1 to 5 p.m. Trails open year-round daily 8 a.m. to sunset.

Sinking Valley, which is between Altoona and Tyrone, is the site of Fort Roberdeau. This 1778 stockade has been reconstructed, and it now offers living-history reenactments, forty-five acres of field and forest, nature trails, tours, and a picnic area.

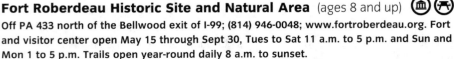

Going **Batty**

For a tenth birthday, we took about twelve pals on a bat hike. The guide told us that July was a good time for a bat hike because the bats would recently have had young, and the colony would be at its largest.

As the sun set we waited outside the dilapidated barn that was the bats' home. The kids were all impatient to see the bats fly out to feed on the millions of insects that congregated over the nearby field.

Our guide had brought a device that amplified the bats' sonar sounds. He explained how to distinguish the sounds the bats made as they located and devoured their prey.

As darkness fell, first one bat emerged from a crack in the roof of the barn. Then another. Then another, then more and more until we counted more than 200, then lost count. The sky over the field was dark with bats.

Tipton

Del Grosso's Park (all ages)

Twelve miles north of Altoona on old US 220, off I-99 exit 41 or 46 ; (814) 684-3538; www .delgrossos.com. Open seasonally. All-day Waterworks and rides: $$.

Del Grosso's Park features more than thirty rides, an extensive water park, an interactive children's park, an eighteen-hole minigolf course with five waterfalls and two lakes, go-karts, and miniature train rides.

Tyrone

Gardners Candies (all ages)

2600 Adams Ave.; (814) 684-0857 for information or to schedule a tour; www.gardners candies.com. Open Mon through Sat 9:30 a.m. to 9 p.m. and Sun 1 to 9 p.m. Admission is **free.**

A sweet taste of nostalgia for children of all ages, Gardners Candies has been making candies for more than a century. Here you can see first-hand how chocolates are made; this is not a simulated tour. Inside its History of Candyland Museum, you can see antique candy-making equipment, a 10-cent Coke machine, and other nostalgic artifacts.

Spruce Creek

Indian Caverns (all ages)

Eleven miles east of Tyrone on PA 45, between Water Street and State College in Hunting-ton County; (814) 632-7578; www.indiancaverns.com. Open daily Memorial Day through Labor Day 10 a.m. to 6 p.m. I. Tours offered on the hour 11 a.m. to 4 p.m. Call for admission prices.

One reason for Indian Caverns' popularity is the real cave paintings on the walls. Here you can see ancient paintings of a turtle, a tepee, and a Mohawk chief.

More than 400 years ago, Native Americans used these caverns as a winter shelter, council chamber, and burial ground. Adjacent to Indian Caverns is a second cavern, Giant's Hall, where you can view the Grotto of the Wah Wah Taysee, a cave that glows, and the Frozen Niagara, which is more than two stories tall. Kids enjoy the sounds made by a musical rock.

The wide concrete walkways and Native American artifacts make this an excellent cavern if your family includes a wide range of ages, attention spans, and energy levels.

Huntington

Greenwood Furnace State Park (all ages)

On PA 305; 5 miles west of Belleville; park office: (814) 667-1800; visitor center: (814) 667-1805; www.dcnr.state.pa.us. The visitor center is open 8 a.m. to 4 p.m. Wed through Sun during summer and 9 a.m. to 5 p.m. on weekends only in spring and fall.

Less than thirty minutes from Huntingdon, Lewistown, or State College is a green park area on the site of the Greenwood iron furnaces and the "village built around an inferno." You can take a one-hour self-guided walking tour of a portion of the historic district and see parts of the town such as the tramway, historic roads, charcoal hearths, a stone mansion, stone church, and stables. History and nature programs are presented every weekend during the summer. The park's most popular event is Old Home Days, during the first full weekend of Aug, when living-history interpreters offer historical demonstrations such as soap making, brew making, and bonnet making. Campsites are available.

Lincoln Caverns and Whisper Rocks (all ages)

On US 22, 3 miles west of Huntingdon; (814) 643-0268; www.lincolncaverns.com. Tour hours vary seasonally. Admission is $$ and free for children 3 and under. A single admission fee gets you into Lincoln Caverns and Whisper Rocks.

These two caverns are a bit more challenging than some other nearby caverns. The walkways are often damp, but the minerals in the water droplets keep this a living cave. In fact, exploration for new caverns continues. The rock formations are spectacular: flowstones, stalactites, calcite, and crystals.

Many educational programs are available, including geology and speleology workshops, as well as programs focused on debunking common misconceptions about bats. Bring a sweater. Special offerings include a kids cave camp in June, Ghosts and Goblins tours in Oct, and Ultimate Underground Birthday Parties with pizza.

The Swigart Museum (all ages)

US 22 East, 4 miles east of Huntingdon; (814) 643-0885; www.swigartmuseum.com. Open daily Memorial Day through Oct, 9 a.m. to 5 p.m. Admission is $; children under 6 enter free.

This museum is the oldest automobile museum in America, established by the late W. Emmert Swigart in 1920. William E. Swigart Jr. continued the collection upon his father's death in 1949. The Swigart collection emphasizes the era when America was first becoming a mobile society. Featured cars include its newest acquisition, a 1909 Overland; a 1900 Winton; a 1904 Rambler; and the only remaining Carroll. Other highlights include two Tuckers and Herbie, the "Love Bug." About thirty-five cars from the collection of 200 are on display at any given time. Supporting these is an outstanding collection of license plates and name plates. Children will enjoy seeing the exhibits of antique toys, trains, and bicycles. In Aug, the museum and the local chapter of the Antique Automobile Club of America sponsor the Swigart Museum Meet.

Amazing
Pennsylvania Facts

The Lincoln Highway Pump Parade makes for a fun car game on road trips. As you drive along US 30 through the Laurel Highlands, put the kids on the lookout for vintage-looking gas pumps, created by artists to honor the nation's first interstate. Visit Vincent Van Gas at Mountain View Inn, Greensburg, or stop at the Saturday Evening Pump near the Arnold Palmer Regional Airport in Latrobe. Other pumps stand near Idlewild Park and the Mountain Playhouse. Traveling east to Bedford, Fulton, Franklin, and Adams Counties, you can see the entire collection of twenty-three pumps. Other interpretive displays created by the Lincoln Highway Heritage Corridor pop up at town centers all along the route.

Hesston

Area residents believe that Raystown Lake doesn't get the attention it deserves. This huge man-made lake is located in Huntington County, surrounded by two state forests, trout-stocked streams, museums, historic sites, campgrounds, and lots of family recreation. Call (800) RAYSTOWN.

Seven Points Marina (all ages)
Raystown Lake, off PA 26; (814) 658-3074 for departure times and details; www.7points marina.com. The boats operate for both private charter and for the public, Apr through Oct. Public cruises depart up to three times a day at the height of the summer season and cost $$ for adults and $ for children under 12.

Seven Points Marina, Pennsylvania's largest marina, offers a variety of ways to enjoy the lake and its countryside, including houseboat rentals and daily boat rentals. The 75-foot lake cruiser *Princess* is available for public cruises, dinner cruises, and private charters. Seven Points Restaurant, with both indoor and outdoor tables, overlooks the inner harbor. Kids enjoy feeding the hundreds of carp at the Fish Feeding Station.

Entriken

Lake Raystown Resort and Lodge
100 Chipmunk Crossing, Raystown Lake; (814) 658-3500; www.raystownresort.com.

Raystown Resort is a great spot for recreation. The resort includes twenty-five lakeside vacation cabins, 122 campsites, several different kinds of cabins (some with hot tubs), luxury houseboats for rent, and a lodge. The list of activities for families goes on and on: the WildRiver Water Park (with a totally dark waterslide called the Atomic Blaster), Caddy's Revenge miniature golf, bank-shot basketball court, and a full-service marina featuring boat rentals, Jet Skis, etc. From Memorial Day to Labor Day, there are daily organized activities for children.

Rockhill

East Broad Top Railroad and the Rockhill Trolley Museum jointly host a Fall Spectacular during Columbus Day weekend. On the first Saturday in December, Santa's Trolley runs with decorations, an outdoor train display, and hot cocoa.

East Broad Top Railroad (all ages)

PA 994, 1 mile west of Orbisonia in Rockhill; (814) 447-3011; www.ebtrr.com. Open from June through Oct, Sat and Sun, with three train trips daily. Trains depart at 11 a.m., 1 p.m., and 3 p.m. Fares are $$; children under 2 ride free. Group rates available for groups of twenty or more.

Now a National Historic Landmark, East Broad Top Railroad once carried coal and other raw materials. At present it is the most complete and authentic rail site in North America.

Board the train at Orbisonia Station for a ride on the only narrow-gauge railroad in the East still running at its original site. The narrated train ride takes about fifty minutes and carries you past countryside that is virtually unchanged since the days when East Broad Top Railroad transported coal along these tracks. If you like, bring along a picnic lunch. You can get off at Colgate Grove, picnic, and go back on a later train. There are no restrooms or concessions on the train. Riders using wheelchairs are encouraged to call ahead so arrangements can be made.

Every year during Columbus Day weekend, railroad buffs come from all over the United States to East Broad Top's Fall Spectacular. For this event all four locomotives operate at once, and scheduled shop tours are available.

Rockhill Trolley Museum (all ages)

Meadow Street (PA 994); (814) 447-9576; www.rockhilltrolley.org. Open weekends only Memorial Day through Oct, 11 a.m. to 4 p.m., plus some holidays. Fares are $; children under 2 ride free. For more information write to Railways to Yesterday, Inc., P.O. Box 1601, Allentown 18105.

Adjacent to East Broad Top Railroad, the Rockhill Trolley Museum has twenty-six trolleys and streetcars, including cars from Philadelphia, Johnstown, Harrisburg, Scranton, and York. Nine trolleys are currently operational, including open cars, closed cars, an interurban car, a snowplow, a sweeper, and a Philadelphia PCC. You can take a more-than-3-mile ride on a restored trolley, passing the Rockhill Iron Furnace.

Like the National Trolley Museum near Pittsburgh, the Rockhill Trolley Museum is staffed by volunteers who love what they're doing. Volunteers here are members of Railways to Yesterday, Inc. Your trolley ticket is good for unlimited rides on the date

A Living **Hell?**

We'd chosen a sunny late-August day for a paddle along the Juniata River— a scenic, normally waist-deep stream. But after weeks without rain, it was so shallow that our plastic kayaks occasionally scraped bottom. After being grounded several times, twelve-year-old James was ready to scream—and did. "This is a living hell!" he exclaimed furiously. Lesson learned: The water's deeper earlier in summer or the day after some rain.

purchased. Most days, you can try out two or three different cars. If you time it right, you can meet the returning East Broad Top Railroad train, passing just a few feet away.

Robertsdale

Broad Top Area Coal Miners Museum
and Entertainment Center (ages 8 and up)

Reality Theater, Main Street; (814) 635-3807, or (814) 635-3220. Open year-round Fri and Sat 10 a.m. to 5 p.m. and Sun 1 to 5 p.m. Admission is $. On show nights, tickets are $$ for adults, $ for children.

This museum offers exhibits about coal mining and railroading in the area.

Bedford

If you like the tradition of stealing a kiss on a kissing bridge, you'll love Bedford County. It has fourteen covered bridges, and you can cuddle your toddlers and embarrass your older kids on every one of them. Bedford's history dates back to 1758, and its downtown has a number of eighteenth-century buildings. You can take a pleasant walking tour of Historic Downtown Bedford and stop at several historic houses and the Fort Bedford Museum. The town's annual fall festival is a popular event, because of the colorful trees on the surrounding mountains. Don't miss the famous three-story Coffee Pot, a roadside attraction by the county fairgrounds on US 30.

For information call the Visitors Bureau at (800) 765-3331 or go to www.bedford county.net. You can also find ideas for scenic bicycle tours and driving tours on this Web site.

Bedford offers plenty of water sports and fishing for trout and smallmouth bass in these streams. The Raystown Branch of the Juniata River, which flows through Bedford, is not deep enough for motorboating, but it's an official Pennsylvania water trail. Adventure Marine outfitters will rent you kayaks and canoes, even for overnight expeditions. Call (814) 623-1821. In Shawnee State Park the lake is stocked for fishing, and its sandy

An O'Toole **Family Adventure**

On silent SR 4016 near New Paris, there's a country road that's downright spooky: Gravity Hill. It's fun, it's **free,** and it thrilled James, age 12, and Bill, age 10. "Stay calm," read my husband Jim from the directions in our county-issued brochure. "Keep cool. Put your car in neutral and take your foot off the brake." We did. And then the car began moving. Backwards. Up the hill. On cue, we screamed.

Whatever its explanation, Gravity Hill is one of those certifiably off-the-beaten-path attractions that you can't miss. And once you get there, you'll find a second Gravity Hill three-tenths of a mile past the first. Get the very specific directions from the Bedford County Visitors Bureau.

public beach is guarded for family swims. Modern bathhouses offer showers and changing facilities. There's a paved lakeshore trail for biking and dozens of miles of hiking trails.

Old Bedford Village (all ages)
Business US 220, 0.5 mile south of PA Turnpike, exit 11, also reachable from US 30; (814) 623-1156; www.oldbedfordvillage.com. Spring and summer hours: Memorial Day weekend through Labor Day weekend, open 9 a.m. to 5 p.m. daily except Wed. Fall hours: Thurs through Sat 9 a.m. to 5 p.m., Sun 10 a.m. to 4 p.m. Admission is $$ for adults and $ for students and children 6 and over.

Drive over the Claycomb Covered Bridge to Old Bedford Village. This village of more than forty reproduction and authentic log, stone, and frame structures is beautifully laid out to re-create a typical village of about 1750 to 1900, with homes, schools, a church, and shops. Interpreters in period costumes bake cookies and make brooms, and much more. About fourteen indigenous crafts are represented. The kids will love stopping for ice cream or doughnuts as you tour the town.

Meals are available at Pendergrass Tavern in the village. Dress comfortably and wear walking shoes. Wheelchair accessible. The Village Craft and Gift Shop offers many unusual crafts made in the village, as well as souvenirs. Almost every summer weekend features a military re-enactment, concert, or other event.

Fort Bedford Museum (ages 8 and up)
Fort Bedford Drive; (814) 623-889; www.bedfordcounty.net. Open daily May through Oct, except Tues in May, Sept, and Oct, 10 a.m. to 5 p.m. Admission is $; children under 6 are free. Family rate $$.

Old Fort Bedford was a British stockade built in 1758 during the French and Indian War. Later it was used as a British outpost on the frontier until the early 1770s. Fort Bedford is gone, but you can learn about its past by touring the Fort Bedford Museum. The little museum includes a large scale model of the fort, some Native American artifacts, weapons, uniforms, a Conestoga wagon, and children's toys of the period. Wheelchair accessible.

ALSO IN THE AREA

One of the state's most unusual recreational trails runs through **Buchanan State Forest.** It's the **Pike to Bike Trail,** which runs along an abandoned stretch of the Pennsylvania Turnpike. With two dark and spooky tunnels, the remote 8.5-mile trail is a fun adventure. The access routes at the trailheads in Saluvia and Breezewood are being rebuilt, so check before you ride. Call (814) 784-5000 or visit www.piketobike.org. And don't forget the flashlights.

Where to Eat

Coney Island Lunch, 127 Clinton St., Johnstown; (814) 535-2885. This casual place serves hot dogs, hamburgers, etc. Children always welcome.

Falls City Restaurant and Pub, 112 Garrett St., Ohiopyle; (724) 329-3000. Casual indoor and outdoor dining; salads, sandwiches, and burgers. Lunch served on weekends only; dinner daily year-round. Kids' menu.

Johnnie's Restaurant and Lounge, 415 Main St., Johnstown; (814) 536-9309. Greek-style food including Greek salads and gyros, but also spaghetti and rigatoni. Children always welcome.

River's Edge Cafe, 203 Yough St., Confluence; (814) 395-5059. Sandwiches and entrees served in a Victorian-era home overlooking the Youghiogheny River, 0.5 mile from the Great Allegheny Passage trail. Kids can explore the riverbank while parents watch from a table on the porch.

Where to Stay

IN THE OHIOPYLE AREA

Historic Summit Inn, 101 Skyline Dr. (US 40 East), Farmington; (724) 438-8594. This mountaintop landmark, on the National Register of Historic Places, has a grand old porch, pools, and activities; dining room offers a children's menu. Open May through Oct.

Ohiopyle State Park Kentuck Campground; (729) 329-8592 call (888) PA–PARKS to reserve.

Yough Plaza Motel; (800) 992-7238; www .youghplaza.com. Within walking distance of the river.

IN THE JOHNSTOWN AREA

Comfort Inn Ebensburg, US 22 West, Ebensburg; (814) 472-6100 or (800) 221-2222. Suites available, indoor pool, free continental breakfast.

Comfort Inn Johnstown, 455 Theatre Dr., Johnstown; (814) 266-3678 or (800) 228-5150. Centrally located near all major attractions.

Holiday Inn, downtown, 250 Market St., Johnstown; (814) 535-7777. Indoor pool, Harrigan's restaurant, sidewalk cafe.

IN BEDFORD

Oralee's Golden Eagle Inn, 131 E. Pitt St.; (814) 624-0800; www.bedfordgoldeneagle .com. An authentic eighteenth-century tavern, restored as a hotel and charming restaurant.

Omni Bedford Springs Resort, 2138 Business Route 220; (814) 623-8100; www.bedfordspringsresort.com. This luxury resort, with a spa and golf course, offers day care and children's programs.

IN THE RAYSTOWN LAKE AREA

Lake Raystown Resort & Lodge, 100 Chipmunk CrossingPA 994, Entriken; (814) 658-3500. Wild River Waterpark, miniature golf, hiking, fishing, picnic areas, camping, and restaurants all nearby.

Seven Points Marina/Houseboat Rental, Seven Points Marina, off PA 26; (814) 658-3074. Fully equipped houseboats for rent. Cruises aboard the Raystown Bell and Queen.

For More Information

Allegheny Mountains Convention and Visitors Bureau; (800) 842-5866; www.alleghenymountains.org.

Bedford County Visitors Bureau; (814) 623-1771 or (800) 765-3331; www.bedfordcounty.net.

Fulton County Tourist Promotion Agency; (717) 485-4064; www.fultoncountypa.com.

Greater Johnstown/Cambria County Convention and Visitors Bureau; (800) 237-8590; www.visitjohnstownpa.com.

Greene County Tourist Promotion Agency; (724) 852-5399 or (888) 852-5399; www.co.greene.pa.us.

Huntington Country Visitors Bureau; (888) RAYSTOWN; www.raystown.org.

Indiana County Tourist Bureau; (724) 463-7505; www.visitindianacountypa.org.

Laurel Highlands Visitors Bureau; (724) 238-5661 or (800) 925-7669; www.laurelhighlands.org.

Pittsburgh and Environs

Whether you see it spread out below you from the dizzying height of one of its inclines or from the Gateway Clipper, rising from the merging waters of the Monongahela, Allegheny, and Ohio Rivers, Pittsburgh is a sight filled with surprises!

The expanded Children's Museum of Pittsburgh is filled with delightful interactive sculptures and new exhibits. It's been honored as one of the best of its kind in the country.

The Senator John Heinz Regional History Center's latest addition is a wing that hosts traveling Smithsonian exhibitions, as well as the Western Pennsylvania Sports Museum, where you can see a few classic artifacts such as Satchel Paige's baseball glove and the shoes Franco Harris was wearing when he caught the "Immaculate Reception."

The Phipps Conservatory has opened its $36.6 million expansion, offering a tropical forest conservatory, new state-of-the-art greenhouses, and a new welcome center.

The Carnegie Museum of Natural History, named by the Discovery Channel and Forbes as one of the best places in the world to see dinosaurs, has revamped its famous fossil collection in a soaring exhibit called Dinosaurs in Their Time. Its sister museum, the Carnegie Science Center, goes high-tech with the world's largest robotics show. Thanks to Andrew Carnegie and the museums he helped to create, your trip to Pittsburgh can include not only dinosaur bones but also paintings, sculpture, history, and more.

The **August Wilson Center for African American Culture,** in downtown Pittsburgh, features galleries, classrooms, a theater with 400-plus seats, a gift shop, a cafe, and many multipurpose spaces for visual and performing art and expression.

Pittsburgh is also home to Kennywood, America's favorite traditional amusement park, and Sandcastle, an outstanding waterpark. If you're looking for a decidedly different way to tour Pittsburgh, there are several options. **Kayak Pittsburgh** rents both kayaks and bikes, so you can paddle or pedal around downtown (under the Clemente Bridge next to PNC Park; 412-969-9090; www.kayakpittsburgh.org). On land, riders over age eight can tour across bridges on Segway scooter tours (724-625-3521; www.segwayinparadise

PITTSBURGH AND ENVIRONS

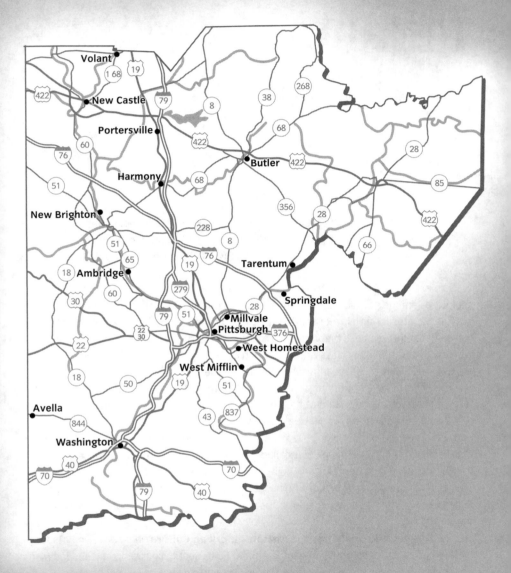

.com). Or combine river and shore in Just Ducky Tours, guided tours on a World War II military amphibious vehicle. Call (412) 928-2489; www.justduckytours.com.

When planning your visit, you may want to check out the Greater Pittsburgh Convention and Visitors Bureau Web site, www.visitpittsburgh.com, or any of the Web sites of the museums and attractions listed in this chapter.

Downtown Pittsburgh

Start your adventure with a stop at the visitor center on Liberty Avenue near Stanwix Street, a handy place to pick up maps and brochures.

Point State Park (all ages)

Point State Park is the tip of Pittsburgh's Golden Triangle, where the Allegheny and Monongahela Rivers join to form the Ohio River. The thirty-six-acre state park is accessible from I-376. (www.dcnr.state.pa.us/stateparks/parks/point.aspx). Free.

Point State Park is the traditional heart of Pittsburgh, where its rivers meet. It was the site of the original Fort Pitt, which succeeded Fort Duquesne in 1758. The park has a paved promenade to the 100-foot, geyserlike fountain where you can enjoy the view of the confluence. Old-fashioned stern-wheelers, Jet Skis, and kayaks zip around the point in warm weather, and the park is a popular site for outdoor concerts. Performance space and

TopEvents in Pittsburgh and Environs

- **Pittsburgh International Children's Theater Festival,** May; (412) 456-6666.

- **Three Rivers Arts Festival,** first two weeks of June; (412) 471-6070.

- **Mattress Factory Community Garden Party,** June; (412) 231-3169.

- **"Fireworks Capital of the World,"** July, July Fourth Celebration in New Castle; (724) 654-5593.

- **Greater Pittsburgh Renaissance Festival** (last three weeks of Aug through Sept on Sat, Sun, and Labor Day; (724) 872-1670.

- **"Pumpkin Patch Trolley,"** Pennsylvania Trolley Museum, Oct; (412) 228-9256.

- **Pittsburgh Light-Up Night,** Nov; (412) 281-7711.

- **Ice skating at PPG Ice Rink,** Nov through Feb; (412) 394-3641.

- **Holidays at the Carnegie,** Nov through Dec; (412) 622-3131.

- **First Night Pittsburgh,** Dec; 412-456-6666.

outdoor cafes keep the park lively. You can even go fishing (there are fifty varieties of fish in the newly clean rivers).

Fort Pitt Museum (ages 8 and up)

Point State Park; (412) 281-9284. Fort Pitt recently came under new directorship. Please call ahead for information.

The British occupied Fort Pitt until 1772, when the Americans took over. In the Fort Pitt Blockhouse and Fort Pitt Museum, you can view exhibits that describe the city when it was America's western frontier.

North Shore and North Side

Cross any of three identical bridges—named for famous residents Roberto Clemente, Andy Warhol, and Rachel Carson—from downtown to some of the city's most kid-friendly museums.

Children's Museum of Pittsburgh (ages 14 and under)

10 Children's Way, Allegheny Square–North Side; (412) 322-5058; www.pittsburghkids .org. Open Mon through Sat 10 a.m. to 5 p.m., Sun noon to 5 p.m. Admission $$ for adults, seniors, and children. Children under 2 are free.

The Children's Museum of Pittsburgh connects two grand historic buildings with a contemporary glass "lantern." The three-story structure has a facade screened by a shimmering wind sculpture. With four times more space, the museum presents programs, exhibits, and performances to nurture children's innate joy, creativity, and curiosity.

Kids interact with Real Stuff exhibits, where they can explore a Mini Cooper to learn about mechanics in the Garage; create and sail a boat down a 53-foot waterway in Waterplay; climb into the Attic, where gravity and common sense take a holiday; create a silkscreen, make paper, emboss and sculpt in the Studio, visit King Friday's palace, drive the trolley and sing familiar songs in a life-size re-creation of the original Mister Rogers' Neighborhood television set, and much, much more. There's even a special space designed for toddlers.

Carnegie Science Center (all ages)

One Allegheny Avenue; (412) 237-3400; www.carnegiesciencecenter.org. Open Sun through Fri 10 a.m. to 5 p.m., Sat 10 a.m. to 7 p.m. $$$, additional charge for IMAX.

Carnegie Science Center connects science and technology to everyday life in a fun way. With a four-story Omnimax Theater, an interactive Planetarium, a real World War II submarine, the world's best model railroad display, three live demonstration theaters, and a building full of 400 hands-on exhibits, the Science Center brings the world of science alive for visitors of all ages.

A smiling, talking robot named Andy (get it?) greets visitors to the center's roboworld. The nation's largest and most comprehensive permanent robotics exhibition features more than 30 hands-on interactive stations in three areas: robotic sensing, thinking, and acting.

The Carnegie Science Center has also launched an expanded version of its popular SportsWorks. Kids and adults will still be able to measure the speed of their fastballs, climb a rock wall, or bounce on a trampoline. They can also explore three different exhibit areas focusing on the physics of sports, health, and sports nutrition. Exhibits include You-Yo, where visitors can learn about the transfer of energy, and Chomp!, a multi-player video game where they will chase down a healthy diet.

National Aviary (all ages)

Allegheny Commons West; (412) 323-7235; www.aviary.org. Open daily 10 a.m. to 5 p.m. Closed Christmas. Admission: $$ for adults, $ for seniors and for children 2 to 12. Children under 2 enter free.

Visit over 600 exotic and endangered birds rain or shine at the National Aviary, a Victorian glass palace that's pleasant no matter what the weather. Get up-close and personal with beautiful flamingos, talk with colorful parrots, and take photos of majestic bald eagles. Stroll through a free-flight indoor rain forest, a 210,000-cubic-foot atrium featuring over 100 amazing birds. Guided tours require reservations. Limited free parking. ADA accessible.

The Andy Warhol Museum (all ages)

117 Sandusky St., on Pittsburgh's North Side near the cultural district, and across the Warhol (Seventh Street) Bridge from downtown; (412) 237-8300; www.warhol.org. Open Tues, Wed, Thur, Sat, and Sun 10 a.m. to 5 p.m. and Fri 10 a.m. to 10 p.m. Closed Mon. Admission is $$ for adults, $ for children (3 and over) and students.

Artist and pop icon Andy Warhol was born in Pittsburgh and the Museum bearing his name for the famed artist is the most comprehensive single-artist museum in the United States. Housed in a funky historic industrial warehouse are 3,000 original works of art, including paintings, drawings, prints, films, and a lot more. Public parking lots with attendants are located under the North Shore Expressway, 1 block north of the museum off Sandusky Street. There is additional parking across the street from the museum.

At the Warhol museum children are especially drawn to the Silver Clouds gallery on the fifth floor, where silver, pillow-shaped balloons float around you. Not every exhibit at the museum is suitable for children, but hands-on activities are offered in the Weekend Factory on Sat and Sun noon to 4 p.m.

Mattress Factory (all ages)

500 Sampsonia Way; (412) 231-3169; www.mattress.org. Open Tues to Sat 10 a.m. to 5 p.m., Sun 1 to 5 p.m. Admission: Adults $$, students and seniors $. Children under 12 enter free. Free parking is available at 505 Jacksonia St. Wheelchair accessible.

The Mattress Factory is a museum of contemporary installation art that presents "art you can get into" created by in-residence artists. Located on Pittsburgh's North Side since 1977, the Mattress Factory is one of few museums of its kind anywhere. Visitors of all

Amazing
Pennsylvania Facts

With seven floors and more than 3,000 original works of art, the Andy Warhol Museum is the most comprehensive single-artist museum in the United States.

ages examine the unique nature of site-specific art and explore a range of nontraditional media and environments—from recorded sound and running water to mirrored rooms and projected light. The museum's multisensory permanent collection includes works by Yayoi Kusama, Rolf Julius, Winifred Lutz, and more.

The Mattress Factory offers a variety of Family Fun Activities. During ARTLab, families can participate in thematic art-making projects that illuminate the creative process. ARTlab activities are offered on the first and third Sat of every month, noon to 3 p.m., **free** with suggested admission. Children must be accompanied by an adult. Check the Web site for listings of exhibitions and events, including youth art classes, family days, and public forums.

The "Strip District"

Pittsburgh's "Strip District" has nothing to do with exotic dancing. This is the nickname given to Pittsburgh's open-air marketplace. It's fun to take in the atmosphere on this 0.5-mile strip along Penn Avenue and Smallman Street, starting at Eleventh Street. Enjoy the colorful produce, the smells of ethnic food, bakeries, restaurants, and other shops.

Near the Strip District give your children a really extraordinary experience by participating in a children's workshop at the Society for Contemporary Craft.

Society for Contemporary Craft (ages 4 to 12)
2100 Smallman St.; (412) 261-7003; www.contemporarycraft.org. Open Tue through Sat 10 a.m. to 5 p.m. The Exhibition Gallery and Drop-In Studio are free and open during public hours. Guided group tours of exhibitions are $ per person. Tour with artist-led craft activity is $$ per person. Please schedule group tours in advance.

The Society for Contemporary Craft (SCC) provides an unusual chance to make art a part of your life. SCC includes an exhibition gallery, an education center, The Studio, and The Store, featuring one-of-a-kind handmade works for all ages.

The gallery stages four craft exhibitions per year. Each exhibition is accompanied by a related artist-designed project that invites families to create art together in the Drop-In Studio. Past visitors have made object jewelry and cereal box–cardboard quilts. Come as you are, and stay until your masterpiece is complete.

More in-depth art experiences are available through studio classes in book arts, fiber, metal, and wood for adults, children, and families. SCC also hosts special family events throughout the year. Both the building and the restrooms are accessible to all visitors.

The Senator John Heinz Pittsburgh Regional History Center (all ages)

1212 Smallman Street; (412) 454-6000; www.pghhistory.org. Open daily 10 a.m. to 5 p.m. Admission: $$ for adults, $ for children ages 6 to 18, seniors (ages 65 and older), and students with ID.

The Senator John Heinz Pittsburgh Regional History Center is Pennsylvania's largest museum dedicated to history. The first floor of the newest wing serves as the Smithsonian's "home in Pennsylvania," hosting world-class traveling exhibitions from the Washington museums.

"Pittsburgh: A Tradition of Innovation" is the museum's new flagship exhibit, showcasing the many inventions that were produced here, like the world's first Ferris wheel and the first radio station. The center also features permanent exhibits spotlighting life in western Pennsylvania from 1750 to the present. In the Great Hall children immediately notice a 1949 restored trolley, a Conestoga wagon, and the Pittsburgh city fire bell, cast after the great fire of 1845. "Kidsburgh" invites kids to zip down a spiral slide.

The Western Pennsylvania Sports Museum here contains over 300 artifacts in seventy hands-on interactive exhibits. Here you can see Satchel Paige's baseball glove, Billy Conn's gloves and light-heavyweight championship belt, Arnold Palmer's golf bag and trademark sweater, and the shoes Franco Harris was wearing when he caught the "Immaculate Reception."

The building is wheelchair accessible, and there are baby-care facilities on the first and third floors. There is also a cafe and a museum shop.

Southside

On the South Side of Pittsburgh, you'll have an excellent opportunity to see the city from the water or from one of two inclines.

Board the Gateway Clipper at Station Square, a five-minute stroll across the Smithfield Street Bridge from downtown Pittsburgh. Two contiguous railroad buildings have been beautifully restored to create Station Square, which includes a Hard Rock Cafe, Joe's Crab Shack, and an observation tower.

Just Ducky Tours, Inc. (all ages)

Station Square Dock; call (412) 928-2489 for information and reservations; www.justducky tours.com.

There's a unique way to tour the city of Pittsburgh—by DUCK! Not the kind of duck with feathers, but a World War II military amphibious vehicle, a bright green bus-boat that carries passengers on a tour of Pittsburgh, on land and water. The only requirement for passengers is that they quack. Hour-long tours depart from Station Square on Pittsburgh's South Side.

The Gateway Clipper Fleet (all ages)
9 Station Sq. Dock; call (412) 355-7980 for information and a schedule of cruises; www .gatewayclipper.com.

The Gateway Clipper Fleet has a schedule of day and night cruises year-round, ranging from narrated sightseeing trips to elegant dinner cruises with entertainment. Family Fun cruises are aimed at children twelve and under; these include the Goodship Lollipop Ride and seasonal cruises like Santa Family Fun, Halloween Monster Fun, and Bunny Fun. All the riverboats are climate controlled. The different vessels vary in facilities, but all have plenty of restrooms, some with changing tables, others with wide counters. Some also have snack bars, and certain cruises include boxed lunches or pizza. Goodship Lollipop cruises feature Lolli the clown.

Monongahela Incline (all ages)
Across the street from Station Square; (412) 442-2000. It runs Mon through Sat 5:30 a.m. to midnight. On Sun and holidays it is open 8:45 a.m. to midnight. The fare is $ each way.

The Incline (pronounced *IN-cline* here) is a thrill ride that everyone in the family will enjoy—going up or down. The "Mon," the first passenger incline in the United States, is 635 feet long and rises to an elevation of about 368 feet at a 35-degree angle. It is operated by the Port Authority.

Inclined Planes of Pittsburgh

Two of Pittsburgh's famous inclines are located near Station Square: the Monongahela Incline and the Duquesne Incline.

So what is an "incline" anyway? It's a cable railway designed to carry passengers or freight up Pittsburgh's steep hills. Inclines were invented before electric streetcars and before automobiles. At one time the city had seventeen of these steam-driven engineering marvels. At present two survive, although now they are driven by electricity. Thousands of commuters use the inclines every day. (Both stations and inclines are now wheelchair accessible.)

What's the difference between the two? Well, the Duquesne has red cars, and the tracks are lit with red lights. The Monongahela has green and yellow lights on the tracks, and the cars are ivory with black trim. Both have overlooks from Mount Washington, with a great view of the city. Both have historical information in their upper stations.

Duquesne Incline (all ages)

Located on Carson Street, directly across the river from Heinz Field. Call (412) 381-1665 for information. The Duquesne operates Mon through Sat 5:30 a.m. to 12:20 a.m., Sun 7 a.m. to 12:20 a.m. The fare is $ each way. Free parking is available at the lower station.

Currently operated by the Society for the Preservation of the Duquesne Heights Incline, this cable car has been in operation since 1877. The interiors are made of hand-carved cherry panels, with oak and bird's-eye maple trim and amber glass transoms. You can rise up 400 feet at a thirty-degree angle to the observation deck at the upper station on Grandview Avenue and take in the spectacular vista.

Pittsburgh's East End

Three miles east of downtown, you'll discover Pittsburgh's Oakland cultural district, where you can see the University of Pittsburgh, Carnegie-Mellon University, the Carnegie Museums of Art and Natural History, Schenley Park, and the Phipps Conservatory. Also in this area you can visit Kennywood, Sandcastle Waterpark, and the Pittsburgh Zoo and Aquarium. (Technically, Kennywood is in West Mifflin and Sandcastle is in West Homestead, both of which are east of the city, so it gets a little confusing. In this guide we have listed them under West Mifflin and West Homestead respectively.)

Carnegie Museums of Art and Natural History (all ages)

Located side by side on Forbes Avenue; (412) 622-3131; www.carnegiemuseums.org. Both museums open Tues through Sat 10 a.m. 5 p.m. Open Sun noon to 5 p.m. Closed on Mon. A combination admission to both museums is $$. Wheelchair accessible.

The Carnegie Museum of Natural History has one of the world's finest dinosaur collections, a hall of gems and minerals, Egyptian artifacts (including mummies), and Polar World.

Dinosaurs in Their Time showcases the most recent research about these fascinating fossils, and the bones have been reassembled to show them in both the proper era and the proper position (heads down, tails up). The Hillman Hall of Minerals and Gems includes some of the finest specimens of their kinds, plus a dazzling display of fluorescent minerals. Polar World explores the culture of the Inuit, including their keenly observed carvings. There are also Egyptian artifacts; African and North American wildlife; colorful displays of insects, butterflies, birds; and so much more.

The Discovery Room, for all ages, is open selected hours. There are also special programs for children, including Camp Earth, a summer-camp program.

Founded in 1895 by Andrew Carnegie, the Carnegie Museum of Art was planned as a collection of "the old masters of tomorrow." At that time, that meant artists like Winslow Homer, James McNeill Whistler, and Camille Pisarro. Today the museum is known for its collections of American, French Impressionist, and post-Impressionist works. It also includes European and American decorative arts, Asian and African art, and the Hall of Architecture, housing a collection of plaster casts of architectural monuments, considered one of the world's finest collections of this type.

Schoolchildren will get a kick out of the Hall of Sculpture, patterned after a real Greek temple. Family, youth, and children's programs are available. There's a **free** audio tour, including a kid-friendly version hosted by Art Cat, the museum's mascot for children's programs.

Since the museum of natural history and the museum of art are attached, one admission gets you into both, and there are often joint programs such as tours of both facilities. Also adjacent you'll find the Carnegie Music Hall and the Carnegie Library of Pittsburgh. There are two restaurants and a brown-bag lunchroom at the facility, as well as a six-level parking garage.

Nationality Rooms (ages 6 and up)
Fifth Avenue entrance, Cathedral of Learning; (412) 624-6000; www.pitt.edu/~natrooms. Reservations are recommended. Tour fees are $.

At the University of Pittsburgh's Cathedral of Learning you can compare New England Colonial architectural style with French Empire, Japanese, Indian, Austrian, Russian, Byzantine, Chinese Empire, first-century Israeli, or Irish Romanesque. Twenty-six different nations are represented in the Nationality Rooms Tours. Funded by gifts from Pittsburgh's ethnic communities, the Nationality Rooms are functioning classrooms in which your family can tour "around the world" with a university student guide who has been trained to adapt the tour to different ages and interests.

Younger children enjoy patting the laughing lion in the Chinese Room or identifying the fairy tales depicted in the German Room. The gift shop carries many unusual publications and an array of international gifts.

Heinz Memorial Chapel (ages 8 and up)
Cathedral of Learning; (412) 624-4157; www.pitt.edu. Open 8:30 a.m. to 5 p.m. on weekdays. The chapel is nondenominational. On Sun, the chapel is open 1:30 to 5:30 p.m.

Stained-glass windows set a tone of Gothic otherworldliness.

PNC Carousel at Schenley Plaza (all ages)
Forbes Avenue; (412) 682-7275; www.schenleyplaza.org. Carousel operates May through Oct, Mon through Fri 10 a.m. to 6 p.m., Sat 10 a.m. to 7 p.m., and Sun 11 a.m. to 5 p.m. Tokens for rides on the carousel can be purchased at the token machine located by the

Pittsburgh **on Ice**

Our kids loved the "mascot skates" at the Schenley Park ice rink, with its stunning view of downtown. They wobbled around the open-air rink with the Pirate Parrot and other huge plushy figures on ice. At downtown's PPG Place rink, they loved being surrounded by the tall glass skyscrapers, which sparkled like icicles.

Amazing
Pennsylvania Facts

Pittsburgh has more than 275 public parks and playgrounds.

carousel for $1.25. An operator is available for assistance. Riders must be taller than 4 feet or accompanied by an adult. The carousel is wheelchair accessible.

Schenley Plaza includes gardens and a broad lawn and hosts a number of **free** concerts. Alongside, a tented area offers shade. There's **free** entertainment, and kiosks offer light meals and drinks for nearby tables.

Phipps Conservatory (all ages)

Schenley Park; (412) 622-6914; www.phipps.conservatory.org. Open year-round Tues through Sun 9 a.m. to 5 p.m. Admission: $$ for adults, $ for students and children 2 to 12. Outdoor gardens are open dawn to dusk, **free.**

Inside the Victorian glass structure of the Phipps Conservatory, you can see hundreds of orchids, palms, ferns, and other plants. The conservatory also exhibits sculptures by famous artists like Dale Chihuly among the greenery. The Japanese Courtyard Garden has an excellent collection of bonsai. In winter the indoor gardens soothe your cabin fever, and in warm weather you can enjoy both indoor and outdoor gardens and fountains. Kids will especially enjoy the stegosaurus topiary in the Fern Room. During the winter holiday season, the conservatory hosts a Garden Railway and winter flower show.

A recent expansion includes a tropical-forest conservatory, greenhouses, and a spectacular below-ground welcome center with gift shop and cafe.

The Frick Art and Historical Center (ages 8 and up)

7227 Reynolds St.; (412) 371-0600; www.frickart.org. Open year-round Tues through Sun 10 a.m. to 5 p.m. Closed Mon. Admission to the museum is **free.** Admission to Clayton is $$. **Free,** secure parking at the Reynolds Street entrance.

Another one of Pittsburgh's leading citizens was Henry Clay Frick, who lived here at Clayton until 1905, when he moved to New York City (in a house that also became a museum). The Frick Art and Historical Center is a six-acre site that includes Clayton, the Frick Art Museum, historic Car and Carriage Museum, visitor center, and cafe. The Victorian home has been meticulously restored, and about 95 percent of the furnishings are original. The Car and Carriage Museum displays old-fashioned automobiles, sleighs, and carriages. Little ones will be interested in the visitor center, which was once the playhouse of Helen, the Fricks' daughter. (Please note that neither backpacks nor strollers are permitted in Clayton.) A cafe in the garden offers lunch and high tea.

Out of the **Mouths of Babes**

As we waved good-bye to his grandparents, who were boarding the magnificent *Delta Queen* stern-wheeler in downtown Pittsburgh for a weeklong cruise down the Ohio River, our preschool son, Bill, decided he'd go along. "We want tickets!" he told the nearest steward. It was a no-go; hardly any three-year-olds sail solo on these voyages.

Pittsburgh Zoo and PPG Aquarium (all ages)

One Hill Rd., in Highland Park (ten minutes from downtown Pittsburgh); (412) 665-3640; www.pittsburghzoo.com. Open daily except Dec 25. In winter the gates are open 9 a.m. to 4 p.m. If you're already inside the gate, you can stay until 5 p.m. In summer the gates open at 10 a.m. and close at 5 p.m., and you can stay inside until 6 p.m. Parking is $ per vehicle. Admission is $$.

The Pittsburgh Zoo and PPG Aquarium boasts the only public aquarium in Pennsylvania—a 45,000-square-foot, state-of-the-art facility featuring more than 4,000 aquatic animals: penguins, barracuda, piranhas, stingrays, jellyfish, sharks, a rare Amazon River dolphin, and much more. Innovative tank designs include a crawl-through stingray tunnel and a two-story shark tank. Another impressive water feature is the polar bear pool, which floats above visitors strolling through a tunnel.

Kids Kingdom, the Children's Zoo at the Pittsburgh Zoo, has been ranked one of the top three children's zoos in the country. Kids Kingdom includes exciting interactive exhibits. Parents enjoy the fact that they can sit on the patio in Kids Kingdom while the kids swing like spiders, slide like penguins, and enjoy the playground and live animals.

The zoo's animals have natural enclosures and plenty of space. Highlights include the Siberian tigers in the Asian Forest; lions, leopards, rhinos, and gazelles of the African Savannah; and family groups of lowland gorillas, plus monkeys, gibbons, and orangutans of the Tropical Forest. A number of baby elephants have been born here in the past several seasons.

Some of the zoo's pathways are hilly, but stroller-friendly.

ALSO IN THE AREA

Pittsburgh offers plenty of action for sports enthusiasts. The Pirates play in the **PNC Park** and the Steelers at **Heinz Field.** For information and tickets for the Pirates, call (800) BUY–BUCS or check the Web site at http://pittsburgh.pirates.mlb.com. For the Steelers call (412) 323-1200 or visit www.pittsburghsteelers.com. The Pittsburgh Penguins (NHL hockey) still play in the same arena, but it's now called the **Mellon Arena** (formerly the Civic Arena). Call (800) 642-PENS, or visit www.pittsburghpenguins.com.

For self-propelled fun, take a bike tour of Pittsburgh's riverfront on the **Three Rivers Heritage Trail.** Nearly 37 miles of paved or crushed-limestone trails run through downtown, South Side, and along the North Shore from Neville Island to Millvale, 5 miles up the Allegheny River. Need a bike? The city's Blue Bikes program offers **free** loaners. To get a swipe card to access bike lockers on the South Side and North Shore, visit Friends of the Riverfront, 33 Terminal Way (just off East Carson Street in the South Side), Mon to Fri from 9 a.m. to 5 p.m. Call (412) 488-0212 or visit www.friendsoftheriverfront.org.

Pittsburgh visitors may also wish to take in a performance at one of the many cultural venues: The world-famous **Pittsburgh Symphony** sponsors kid-friendly concerts hosted by mascot Fiddlesticks throughout the season at Heinz Hall (412-392-4900; www.pittsburgh symphony.org). Other downtown theaters include the Byham, the O'Reilly, the Benedum, and the CLO Cabaret. You can see everything from ballet to the Pittsburgh Opera, Broadway shows, concerts, dance, and comedy. Get a full calendar and buy tickets at www.pgharts.org. In Oakland, Point Park University's Playhouse at 222 Craft Ave. has offered theater for more than fifty years. Call (412) 621-4445 or visit www.pittsburghplayhouse.com.

Millvale

In Millvale, families enjoy biking on the level Three Rivers Heritage Trail to downtown Pittsburgh and relaxing at Riverfront Park. Teens love the hip music at Mr. Small's Theater.

Mr. Small's Skatepark (ages 5 and up)

Riverfront Drive, Millvale, 6 miles from downtown Pittsburgh off PA 28 North; (412) 821-8188; www.mrsmalls.com. Open daily noon to 8 p.m. Parents must come in person to sign waivers for those under age 18. Admission $$ for four hours, $$$ all day; helmet and pad rental $.

Located along the Allegheny River in Millvale (3 blocks from Mr. Small's Theatre, a converted church that often hosts all-ages rock music shows), this skate park has an in-depth street course with a great variety of ramps for skateboarding, in-line skating and freestyle biking, including a 40-foot-wide vert ramp. By bike reach the park on the Three Rivers Heritage Trail.

West Mifflin

Memories of a childhood in Pittsburgh usually include scrambling around a rocking Noah's Ark in Kennywood. Voted "Favorite Amusement Park" for eleven years in a row by the National Amusement Park Historical Association (NAPHA), Kennywood has also been called the "Roller Coaster Capital of the World."

Kennywood (all ages)

4800 Kennywood Blvd.; (412) 461-0500; www.kennywood.com. Open daily mid-May through Labor Day 10:30 a.m. to 10 p.m. Tickets are $$$$. Junior (under 46") admission is $$$$. Senior general admission is $.

Amazing
Pennsylvania Facts

Kennywood is one of only two amusement parks that are National Historic Landmarks. DAFE (Darkride and Funhouse Enthusiasts) voted Kennywood the "best darkride park" in the country.

Offering old-fashioned fun for every member of the family, Kennywood is only minutes away from downtown Pittsburgh, off the Swissvale exit (exit 9) of I-376 (Penn–Lincoln Parkway). Although some rides will get you wet, none require bathing suits.

A Pittsburgh landmark since 1898, Kennywood is now also a National Historic Landmark. The carousel pavilion and a restaurant are the original structures. Others were added over the years. One roller coaster, for example, the Jack Rabbit, with its "camel back" (double dip), looks just the way it did in 1921. The Thunderbolt, the classic wooden coaster dubbed "King of the Coasters" by the *New York Times,* starts off with a thrilling downhill plunge.

"Pittsburgh's Lost Kennywood" re-creates Luna parks of the past. But Kennywood has continued to evolve, with rides like Phantom's Revenge, and the Pitt Fall, the world's tallest and fastest free-fall ride. Kennywood's Exterminator combines a roller coaster with virtual reality to give you the ride of your life, in the dark, through underground tunnels and sewers where you'll encounter who knows what.

Phantom Fright Nights take place every Fri and Sat evening in Oct—but beware! It is not suggested for children under thirteen.

There are changing tables in all the restrooms. In Kiddieland there are kid-size restrooms and an area for nursing mothers. Parking is **free.**

West Homestead

Sandcastle Water Park (all ages)

1000 Sandcastle Dr., on PA 837 between the Homestead High Level Bridge and Glenwood Bridge; (412) 462-6666; www.sandcastlewaterpark.com. Open daily in season, usually June through Labor Day weekend, 11 a.m. to 6 p.m. The park stays open until 7 p.m. in July and Aug. Admission: Whitewater Pass (includes all water activities—hot tubs, pools, Lazy River, and fifteen waterslides) is $$$ for adults and children three and older.

Sandcastle Water Park, Kennywood's sister park in West Homestead, began life as an abandoned steel mill and was opened as a water park in July 1990. Sandcastle is a major riverside water park with a boardwalk, fifteen water slides, three pools, and a Lazy River. It also has two race-car tracks, video games, and miniature golf. Mon-Tsunami is a 20,000-square-foot wave pool with huge roller waves as well as diamond waves.

Only the bravest watersliders should attempt the Lightning Express twin body slides, 60 feet high and 250 feet long, each with a double dip, followed by a monster free fall. (AAAH!)

Another slide, Cliffhangers, uses a new concept in waterslide design: sky ponds. Each pond is at a different level above the ground. You and your inner tube can float in one pond before sliding down to the next.

If that doesn't sound like your speed, relax on the Lazy River, with its whirlpools, fountains, and gentle current. Wet Willie's Waterworks is recommended for younger children, and The World's Largest Hot Tub is perfect for stressed-out parents.

Parking and boat docking are **free.** Special events and picnics are held in Sandcastle's Riverplex entertainment complex. Parking is $.

Springdale

Rachel Carson said, "Those who contemplate the beauty of the earth find reserves of strength that will endure as long as life lasts." The famous author of *Silent Spring* was born in 1907 in the farmhouse now known as the Rachel Carson Homestead, in Springdale, within minutes of Pittsburgh. As your family travels this region that is so much a part of our industrial heritage, a visit to Carson's home is a healthy reminder of the downside of "progress."

Rachel Carson Homestead (ages 8 and up)
613 Marion Ave., approximately thirty minutes from downtown Pittsburgh; (724) 274-5459; www.rachelcarsonhomestead.org. Open Sat and Sun 10 a.m. to 4 p.m. At other times you may call (724) 274-5459 for an appointment. Admission is $.

Tour this nineteenth-century house and find out about one woman who made a difference. This is the birthplace and childhood home of Rachel Carson, author of *Silent Spring*, published in 1962. Carson's books pointed out for the first time the dangers of DDT and other pesticides. Her special interest in exposing children to nature was illustrated by her 1956 article "Help Your Child to Wonder." You'll also enjoy the nature trail that Rachel Carson walked and the gardens, especially the Butterfly Garden.

Special children's programs are offered. In May Rachel Carson's birthday is celebrated.

Tarentum

In Tarentum, only a few miles northeast of the Rachel Carson Homestead, you can find out what life was like for miners in this area.

Tour-Ed Mine and Museum (ages 8 and up)
748 Bull Creek Rd. at exit 14 of PA 28 North, located on the Allegheny Valley Expressway, opposite Woodlawn Golf Course; (724) 224-4720; www.tour-edmine.com. Open Memorial

Day to Labor Day, Wed to Mon 10 a.m. to 4 p.m. Admission is $$ for adults, $ for children 12 and under. Group rates available.

You'll have to wear a miner's hard hat and mind your head as you board a mining car, modernized for comfort and electrically powered, to travel a 0.5-mile underground at Tour-Ed Mine and Museum into a genuine coal mine. Your tour guide, a real miner, will help you learn about the history of coal mining. It's chilly down here, so bring your sweater. This is not for the claustrophobic.

Kids will enjoy a tour in a locomotive on the surface to see a demonstration strip mine and auger mine. You can also see the company store, 1785 log home, and sawmill. You can even see a bedroom set up like the ones where the miners slept. There are covered picnic areas and snacks available.

Butler

The Butler County Historical Society administers several historic sites in the county, which are open seasonally. For information on any of these sites or to arrange a group or off-season tour, call the historical society at (724) 283-8116, or visit www.butlerhistory.com.

Big Butler Fair (all ages)
Butler County Fairgrounds, 6.5 miles east of I-79 on US 422, Prospect; (724) 865-2400; www .bigbutlerfair.com. $, children age two and under **free.** Does not include ride tickets, all-day pass available.

Traveling north from Pittsburgh, you'll begin to see plenty of farm country on these rolling hills. That's why the annual Big Butler Fair has been a favorite around here for more than 150 years. Livestock exhibitions, rides, concerts, a demolition derby, and grandstand events are the big draws at the fair, always held the week of the Fourth of July. Admission charged. **Free** parking.

Butler County Heritage Center (ages 8 and up)
119 W. New Castle St.; (724) 283-8116; www.butlerhistory.com. Hours vary seasonally.

This center presents temporary exhibits on the history of this area. On permanent display are artifacts from Butler County's many industries, including a tin shop, a Bantam jeep, Spang oil tools, Franklin glasswork, and farm tools.

Cooper Cabin (ages 8 and up)
Off PA 356 on Cooper Road; (724) 283-8116; www.butlerhistory.com. Hours vary seasonally.

Built around 1810, Cooper Cabin was an original county homestead. On Halloween families gather around a bonfire at the cabin to hear ghost stories. On weekends from May to Sept, the cabin offers special events including horseshoeing, basket weaving, quilting, spinning, and weaving, as well as an herb garden and outbuildings such as a spinning house, springhouse, and toolshed.

How Do You Spell Pittsburgh?

In 1768 the descendants of William Penn purchased land from the Native American tribes known as the Six Nations, calling it the "Manor of Pittsburgh"—with an "h." Officially, Pittsburgh has always been spelled with an "h," except for the period from 1890 to 1911, when the U.S. Post Office Department dropped the "h" in accordance with the U.S. Board of Geographic Names.

And yet people all over the country persist in misspelling Pittsburgh.

In 1921 *Pittsburgh First,* "the official organ of the Chamber of Commerce of Pittsburgh," urged all Patriotic Pittsburghers to assist the general public in the spelling of the name of their city. The "h" was important, they maintained, because it distinguished Pittsburgh, Pennsylvania, from all the other cities of the same name across the country.

Little Red School House Museum (ages 6 and up)
200 E. Jefferson St.; (724) 283-8116; www.butlerhistory.com. Hours vary seasonally.

At the Little Red School House, built in 1838, you sit down in a real old-fashioned desk as your tour guide transforms into a teacher.

Maridon Museum (ages 10 and up)
322 N. McKean St.; (724) 282-0123; www.maridon.org. Open Tues to Sat 11 a.m. to 5 p.m., Sun noon to 5 p.m. $, children under 8 free.

Little ninjas and others who love a glimpse of other countries may like the Maridon Museum in downtown Butler. It houses 800 Chinese and Japanese art objects that date back to 3,000 B.C. Ivory, jade, paintings, and scrolls are on display.

Harmony

The village of Harmony was founded in 1804 by members of a religious communal group, the Harmony Society. This group eventually built about 130 buildings including two outlying villages.

The Harmony Museum (ages 8 and up)
218 Mercer St.; (724) 452-7341 or (888) 821-4822; www.harmonymuseum.org. Open year-round 1 to 4 p.m. daily except Mon. Appointments strongly recommended for weekends. Closed holidays. Admission is $; children under 6 enter free.

The Harmony Museum displays Native American artifacts, as well as artifacts of the Harmonists and Mennonites. The museum also offers walking tours of the historic district of Harmony, as well as the Ziegler Log House and the Wagner House. Limited wheelchair accessibility.

Amazing
Pennsylvania Facts

The Pittsburgh Crawfords are considered the greatest Negro League baseball team of all time.

Portersville

Moraine State Park (all ages)

225 Pleasant Valley Rd., off US 422; (724) 368-8811;www.dcnr.state.pa.us. Open year-round 8 a.m. to sundown. **Free** admission, but there are rental fees for boats, cabins, etc. The beach is **free.**

Moraine State Park offers 17,000 acres of family-oriented nature programs. There are nature walks and canoe trips. Having recently reintroduced ospreys to Lake Arthur, the park offers educational programs about these birds of prey and local waterfowl. You can rent motorboats, pontoons, or sailboats. A 0.7-mile paved bike trail winds around the north shore of the lake.

McConnell's Mill State Park (all ages)

Five miles west of Moraine State Park, off US 422; (724) 368-8091 or (724) 368-8811; www .dcnr.state.pa.us. The gristmill is open for **free** guided tours Memorial Day to Labor Day, 10 a.m. to 6 p.m. This scenic park features a covered bridge and a waterfall. For more information and park hours, call (724) 368-8091.

Also administered by Moraine State Park is McConnell's Mill State Park. It's definitely worth the walk to see the 400-foot Slippery Rock Creek Gorge, formed by the glaciers thousands of years ago. The huge boulders literally "slipped" down the walls of the gorge, creating a strange and wonderful landscape. You can also explore the 2,500 acres of parkland, have a picnic, hike one of the trails, or take a **free** guided tour. If you have your own boat, you can go kayaking or rafting.

Jennings Environmental Center (all ages)

2951 Prospect Rd.; (724) 794-6011; www.dcnr.state.pa.us. The education center is open Mon through Fri, 8 a.m. to 4 p.m. or whenever educational programs are offered. **Free** admission. Some programs have fees. Call for information.

Jennings Environmental Center is the only state park environmental education center in western Pennsylvania, and one of only four in the state. This site is a true relict prairie ecosystem.

A what? A relict prairie ecosystem is a prairie formed by prehistoric glacial activity. Here the glacier left only 4 to 6 inches of topsoil, with clay underneath. As a result, trees don't grow here, but grasses and wildflowers do. If you visit in late July or Aug, you can see spectacular wildflowers in bloom, such as the spiky purple blazing star. The prairie also supports unusual wildlife, such as the eastern massasauga rattlesnake, one of Pennsylvania's three species of poisonous snakes and an endangered species in the state.

You can hike or picnic here from dawn to dusk, seven days a week. Public interpretive programs are offered on weekends. Please call for program schedules. In spring and summer special programs highlight the wildflowers in bloom. In March you can learn about maple sugaring, and in April Earth Day programs teach about biodiversity and related topics. Many other programs are also available.

Volant

Main Street in the quaint rural town of Volant offers more than fifty shops and restaurants featuring Victorian collectibles, arts and crafts, Christmas specialties, housewares, pottery, and special events such as a Quilt Show and Sale in July, an Autumn Pumpkin Festival, Old Fashioned Christmas, and more. Volant is located north of New Castle, on PA 208, ten minutes from I-79 and I-80. It is just minutes away from McConnell's Mill State Park and Living Treasures Animal Park. There's also a thriving Amish community in this area.

The shops are open daily except for New Year's Day, Easter, Thanksgiving, and Christmas. Hours are 10 a.m. to 5 p.m. Mon through Sat and noon to 5 p.m. on Sun. For more information visit www.volantshops.com.

New Castle

Bet you didn't know that New Castle, Pennsylvania, is the "Fireworks Capital of America." Two of the largest fireworks manufacturers, Pyrotecnico and Zambelli Internationale, are based in this city northwest of Pittsburgh.

So, if you happen to be in the area around Independence Day, check out the **"Fireworks Capital of America Fireworks Festival"** here on the Saturday after July Fourth. Besides the fireworks festival, there's also "Back to the Fifties Weekend" at Cascade Park and the Ellwood City Arts, Crafts, and Food Festival at Ewing Park. All of these events feature fireworks, all are in June or July, and all are within a few miles of each other.

Riverplex, a dining and entertainment center, is helping revive New Castle's Main Street.

For details contact Lawrence County Tourism at (724) 654-8408 or (888) 284-7599. Or check the Web at www.visitlawrencecounty.com.

Harlansburg Station's Museum of Transportation (all ages)
US 19 and US 108; (724) 652-9002; www.harlansburgstation.com. Open seasonally, so call for current hours. Generally the museum is open weekends only in fall and winter, Sat 10 a.m. to 5 p.m. and Sun noon to 5 p.m. In summer and fall, it is open Tues through Sat 10

a.m. to 5 p.m. and Sun noon to 5 p.m. Closed Mon, and Jan through Feb. Admission is $. Group tours available by appointment.

Family-owned, family-operated, and family-friendly, Harlansburg Station's Museum of Transportation looks just like an old railroad station, with four Pennsylvania Railroad cars in front. Inside one of the cars, you can see displays of railroad memorabilia such as uniforms, silver, linens, and more. As you enter the museum, a model conductor greets you. Inside the museum you're surrounded by planes, trains, trolleys, cars, and trucks—all kinds of transportation.

Hoyt Institute of Fine Arts (ages 8 and up)

124 E. Leasure Ave.; (724) 652-2882. Open Tues and Thurs 11 a.m. to 8 p.m., Wed, Fri, and Sat 11 a.m. to 5 p.m. Closed Sun and Mon. General admission is **free.** Period House Tours $ by appointment only.

This regional arts center is housed in two neighboring 1917 mansions on five manicured acres of New Castle's historic North Hill. Collections include significant regional artwork, decorative arts, and Shenango china. Adult and youth art classes are offered year-round. Every year the Hoyt hosts a Summer Art Camp and a **free** Children's Summer Arts Festival.

Living Treasures Animal Park (all ages)

US 422, 4 miles west of I-79 in Moraine; (724) 924-9571; www.ltanimalpark.com. Open daily 10 a.m. to 6 p.m. in May, Sept, and Oct and 10 a.m. to 8 p.m. Memorial Day through Labor Day. Admission is $$ for adults, $ for children 2 to 12; children under 2 are **free.** Please note that there are two "Living Treasures Animal Park" locations: this one in Moraine and the other in Donegal on PA 711 south of PA 31. For the Donegal location, please call (724) 593-8300.

Get up close to more than one hundred species of friendly animals from all over the world at Living Treasures Animal Park.

New Brighton

Merrick Art Gallery (ages 8 and up)

Fifth Avenue at Eleventh Street; (724) 846-1130; www.merrick artgallery.org. Open Tues through Sat 10 a.m. to 4:30 p.m. and Sun 1 to 4 p.m. **Free** admission.

The Merrick Art Gallery houses the collection of French, German, English, and American paintings of the eighteenth and nineteenth centuries that belonged to Edward Dempster Merrick. It has a display of artifacts belonging to the New Brighton Historical Society as well. The gallery also mounts many special exhibits, such as its annual Victorian Christmas Toy Show.

Amazing
Pennsylvania Facts

Its three rivers give Pittsburgh another distinction: It has 446 bridges—
more than Venice, Italy!

Ambridge

Old Economy Village (ages 8 and up)

Fourteenth and Church Streets, 18 miles northwest of Pittsburgh on PA 65; (724) 266-4500; www.oldeconomyvillage.org. Open Tues through Sat 9 a.m. to 5 p.m., Sun noon to 5 p.m. Closed Mon and winter holidays and Jan through Feb. Admission: ages 6 to 12 and 60 and over $; ages 12 to 59 $$; family rate $$$; children ages 5 and under enter free.

Old Economy Village was built by the same Christian communal society that built Harmony (see previous entry in this section). Here you can visit seventeen restored buildings and gardens and learn about how this unusual community lived. Your whole visit takes about an hour and a half, including the orientation film *Economy: A Place of Promise* and a tour of the exhibits, gardens, and buildings. The society had its own textile mill, as well as a tailor, printer, shoemaker, cabinetmaker, locksmith, and more, and the village store still posts the 1827 price list. Kids will enjoy using the hand pump to pour themselves a drink.

Many special events and tours are available, including events such as the Family Festival in June, Erntefest (food festival) in Sept, and Candlelight Christmas at the village in Dec. Wheelchair-accessible restrooms, diaper-changing areas.

Raccoon Creek State Park and Wilderness
Reserve (all ages)

Located in southern Beaver County, 25 miles west of Pittsburgh (take US 22 or US 30; access to the park is via PA 18); (724) 899-2200; www.dcnr.state.pa.us. Trails are open year-round from 8 a.m. to sunset. Free admission.

One of the largest and most beautiful state parks in Pennsylvania, Raccoon Creek State Park has about 7,000 acres and Raccoon Creek Lake, which itself is more than one hundred acres.

Located within Raccoon Creek State Park, only steps east of the park entrance, is the 315-acre Wildflower Reserve, where you can choose between easy walking trails and trails with gentle grades. Your best bet to see the most blooms is Apr or May, but something is blooming from late Mar through summer. If you're lucky, you might see deer, raccoons, wild turkeys, mink, birds, and other wildlife. Comfortable shoes are a must. On Soldier Days you can view historic reenactments, military displays, and more.

Recreational facilities include boating, hiking, camping, swimming, and picnicking. Modern family cabins are available year-round, with electric heat, kitchens, and toilets.

While you're in Raccoon Creek State Park, you may wish to visit Frankfort Mineral Springs, about 0.5-mile south of the park entrance. From the 1790s to 1932, this was the site of a popular spa where many people were attracted to the purported medicinal properties of the spring water. Call (724) 899-2200.

Avella

Meadowcroft Museum of Rural Life (ages 6 and up)

401 Meadowcroft Rd.; (724) 587-3412; www.meadowcroftmuseum.org. Open weekends in June, July, and Aug; Sat noon to 5 p.m., Sun 1 to 5 p.m., otherwise open by appointment. Admission: $$ for adults, $ for children 6 to 16; children under 6 enter free. The last complete tour starts at 3 p.m. Call for information about group reservations and many special workshops and events.

Sixteen thousand years of history and prehistory in western Pennsylvania are brought to life at the Meadowcroft Museum of Rural Life, which is operated by the Senator John Heinz Pittsburgh Regional History Center, in association with the Smithsonian Institution. The grounds here include the archaeological site that contains the earliest evidence of human life in eastern North America. At the Rockshelter, visitors can see evidence of the tools and campfires made by the first Americans 16,000 years ago.

Meadowcroft Village recreates nineteenth-century rural life. Explore log houses, a covered bridge, a blacksmith's shop, and other exhibits.

Located off PA 50, less than an hour from Pittsburgh, the museum offers many hands-on educational programs for groups. Wear good walking shoes, because the paths between the buildings are natural. There is a snack bar and gift shop.

Washington

The Pennsylvania Trolley Museum (all ages)

One Museum Rd.; (724) 228-9256 or (877) PA–TROLLEY; www.pa-trolley.org. Open 11 a.m. to 5 p.m. daily from Memorial Day to Labor Day; weekends 11 a.m. to 5 p.m. Apr 1 through Dec 30. Admission is $$ for adults and $ for children 2 to 15.

Here in Washington, you'll find the only museum where you can see, learn about, and actually ride historic electric-rail vehicles from Pittsburgh, Philadelphia, Johnstown, and other cities. Take several generations along for an opportunity for reminiscing and intergenerational storytelling.

First go to the visitor education center to buy your tickets and view an exhibit. Stop and browse through the exhibits or take in a film. During the winter holidays you can even find yourself at the controls of a model-train layout.

Rides leave from the Richfol Shelter across the picnic area and next to the car barn. You just won't believe how beautifully these streetcars have been restored. Your motorman and most of the staff are volunteers. You'll clatter on a 3-mile journey past a scenic section that was once an old coal-mining railroad. After you climb off the trolley, you may view about twenty-five trolley cars from the museum's collection, including the real "Streetcar Named Desire" from New Orleans. You can even peek in on the car shop where volunteers restore the cars. Bring along a picnic lunch if you like.

Just 25 miles southwest of Pittsburgh, off I-79, exit 41 southbound or exit 40 northbound, the trolley museum is convenient to Meadowcroft Village in Avella. Special events include: the Anything on Wheels Fair in June, with a trolley parade, antique vehicle display, and motorcar and caboose rides; the Pumpkin Patch Trolley in Oct; and the Santa Trolley in Dec.

Washington County Historical Society's
Lemoyne House (ages 8 and up)

49 East Maiden St.; call (724) 225-6740 for admission prices; www.wchspa.org. Open Feb to mid-Dec, Tues to Fri 11 a.m. to 4 p.m. Sat group tours available by appointment. Admission is $.

Dr. Francis Julius LeMoyne, a successful nineteenth-century physician, took the courageous step of opening his home and properties as stops along the Underground Railroad. LeMoyne House is now the headquarters of the Washington County Historical Society, including its military museum, collection of Civil War weapons, and a time capsule prepared by President Ulysses S. Grant. The beautiful stone home, which also served as Dr. LeMoyne's medical office, still contains some of his old medical instruments and books. In Sept the Historical Society hosts its annual African-American Cultural Festival.

Where to Eat

IN PITTSBURGH

Buca di Beppo, 3 Station Sq., South Side; (412) 471-9463; www.bucadibeppo.com. Casual atmosphere and giant platters of Italian specialties, from pasta to pizza. Kid's menu for under-10s.

Dozen Bake Shop, 807 Liberty Ave. (downtown; four other locations throughout the city); (412) 621-4740; www.dozenbakeshop .com. Two words: fabulous cupcakes.

Klavon's Cream Parlor, 2801 Penn Ave.; (412) 434-0451; www.klavonsicecream.com. This 1920s-era drug store soda fountain is lovingly maintained in the Strip District. Try the pecan ball, a local favorite. Treats range from gigantic to "baby wee cones."

Lulu's Noodles, 400 S. Craig St.; (412) 687-7777. Casual Asian food, close to the universities and the Carnegie Museums in Oakland.

Riverview Cafe, Carnegie Science Center, One Allegheny Ave., North Side; (412) 237-3417. Casual atmosphere, city view on the Ohio River. Kid-friendly foods, booster seats.

Where to Stay

IN PITTSBURGH

Best Western University Center Hotel, 3401 Blvd. of the Allies; (412) 683-6100 or (800) 245-4444. Nearby: Oakland, downtown, museums, universities, Station Square, zoo, Kennywood.

Courtyard by Marriott Downtown, 945 Penn Ave.; (412) 434-5551.

Pittsburgh Hilton & Towers, 600 Commonwealth Place, Gateway Center; (412) 391-4600; www.pittsburgh.hilton.com. Overlooks Point State Park. Walking distance to Cultural District, sports stadiums, and History Center.

Springhill Suites, 223 Federal St., Pittsburgh; (412) 323-9005; www.marriott.com. On the North Shore. Walking distance to the Children's Museum, Carnegie Science Center, and pro sports stadiums.

For More Information

VisitPittsburgh; (800) 359-0758; www.visit pittsburgh.com.

Northeastern
Pennsylvania

With the Delaware and Susquehanna Rivers, the Pocono Mountains, wilderness areas, numerous lakes, and crystal-clear rivers, northeastern Pennsylvania has attracted vacationers since the 1800s. But northeastern Pennsylvania is more than just a resort area. The discovery of one of the world's largest deposits of anthracite coal made the region a center for industry. Entrepreneurs, immigrant workers, and others came to the area to make money or find work. The country's first railroads were built to transport the coal to the cities. Other industries moved their operations here to take advantage of the cheap fuel.

Thanks to its history—both natural and industrial—northeastern Pennsylvania offers a special mix to family vacationers today. Those looking for hiking, skiing, boating, and

TopPicks in Northeastern Pennsylvania

- **Float trip on the Delaware River**
- **Mountain biking in the Lehigh Gorge**
- **Skytop Lodge,** Skytop
- **World's End State Park,** Forksville
- **Pocono Environmental Education Center (PEEC),** Dingmans Ferry
- **Steamtown National Historic Site,** Scranton
- **Electric City Trolley Museum,** Scranton
- **Lackawanna Coal Mine tour,** Scranton
- **Woodloch Pines Resort,** Hawley
- **Inn at Starlight Lake,** Starlight

NORTHEASTERN PENNSYLVANIA

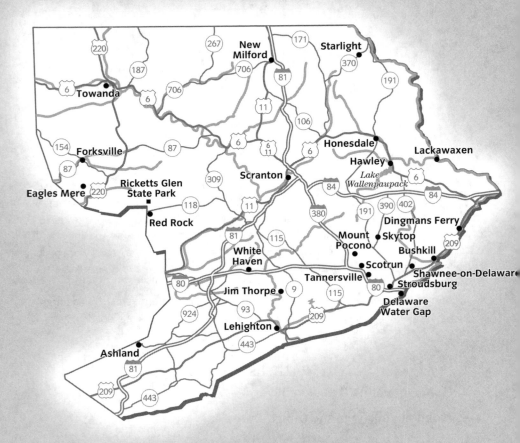

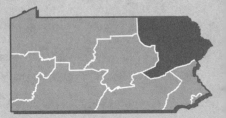

relaxing resorts will not be disappointed. But the region's industrial history adds some more unusual attractions, such as factories, railroad excursions, and coal-mine tours. The Poconos are the classic vacation destination—and there's good reason, especially where families are concerned. With so many resorts to choose from, every family can find one that fits its needs.

Despite overdevelopment in some areas, the unspoiled areas of the Poconos are absolutely beautiful—and very accessible. We're not talking huge snowcapped mountains; we're talking gentle hills, lovely trails, and babbling brooks that are easy for all members of the family to enjoy.

For example, the Poconos ski resorts are perfect for families. The vertical drops are steep enough to keep it interesting for Mom and Dad while gentle enough for kids to learn easily. Most of the resorts have great learn-to-ski programs for kids, starting as young as three years old.

One of the hottest things on the slopes in recent years is snow-tubing. This is also very good news for families. Though parents may worry a bit the first time the kids take to the slopes on skis or snowboards, snow-tubing—with its cushy, fit-the-whole-family inflatable rafts—is something everyone can do together.

TopEvents in Northeastern Pennsylvania

- **Elk Mountain Spring Carnival,** Union Dale, Mar; (570) 679-4400.

- **RiverFest,** Scranton, May; (570) 347-6311.

- **Delaware River Sojourn** at sites along the Delaware, mid-June.

- **Patch Town Day at Eckley Miner's Village** in Weatherly, mid-June; (570) 636-2070.

- **Northeastern Pennsylvania Bluegrass Festival,** Tunkhannock, June; (570) 721-2760.

- **Pittston Tomato Festival,** mid-Aug; (570) 655-1424.

- **Wildflower Music Festival** in Hawley, Lake Wallenpaupack, July and Aug; (570) 253-5500.

- **Moscow Country Fair,** mid-Aug; (570) 842-9804.

- **Rail Expo at Steamtown National Historic Site** in Scranton, early Sept; (570) 340-5200 or (888) 693-9391.

- **Shawnee Mountain Lumberjack Festival** in Shawnee-on-Delaware, early Oct; (570) 421-7231.

Delaware Water Gap and the Stroudsburg Area

For vacationers arriving in Pennsylvania from New Jersey, the Delaware Water Gap serves as a gateway to the Poconos. This natural land formation along the Kittatinny Ridge is a dramatic backdrop for a host of outdoor activities. The town of Delaware Water Gap is a good place to start exploring.

Stroudsburg and East Stroudsburg are the commerce centers of this part of the Poconos. You'll find restaurants and some lodgings in these towns, but most of the tourist attractions and resorts are located in the surrounding smaller towns. For information on this area, visit www.delawarewatergap.com.

The Delaware Water Gap National Recreation Area (all ages)

Bushkill; (570) 426-2435; www.nps.gov/dewa. Grounds are open year-round. Visitor centers, open seasonally, and hiking are free; day-use fee at beaches and some picnic areas.

The 37-mile portion of the Delaware River extending from the Delaware Water Gap north to Milford was designated a National Recreation Area in the 1960s. The river offers great family canoeing, fishing, and rafting opportunities, and the hills on either side offer some fun trails and historic sites to explore on foot, skis, or snowmobile. There's excellent hiking in the area—the Appalachian Trail cuts through at the Gap—with some shorter trails that even little legs can handle without problems.

Other attractions that kids enjoy are visiting Millbrook Village (actually, it's about 16 miles from the Gap on the New Jersey side), gazing at dramatic waterfalls located around the area, and swimming in the cool, clear river at Milford and Smithfield beaches. Best of all, the park is less than two hours from New York or Philadelphia.

The best places to view the Gap itself are three overlooks along PA 611 just south of I-80. US 209 going north offers a nice family drive along the river valley, with the Pocono Plateau rising to the west. (The Poconos are not a typical mountain range but rather a plateau.)

There's a visitor center at Kittatinny Point, just off I-80 on the New Jersey side of the river. It's open daily May through Oct and on weekends year-round. Another visitor center, located at Dingmans Falls, about 30 miles north of I-80 on US 209, is open during the summer. To find out what's happening in the park during your visit and to get a ranger's recommendation on what to do and see, stop by one of the visitor centers. While you're there, pick up a Junior Naturalist Discovery Pack, a self-guiding booklet that helps children six to twelve explore the park. Kids who complete the pack are eligible to become Junior Rangers.

Delaware River **Canoe and Rafting Trips**

The Delaware is a wonderful, calm river for family rafting and canoeing. Although children eight to twelve get the most out of this kind of trip, most liveries will accommodate younger children—even toddlers. Rafting is recommended over canoeing for children under twelve, says David Jacobi of Adventure Sports in Marshalls Creek. His organization is one of several that offer Delaware River rafting and canoe trips. Typical excursions range from a couple of hours to all day. Be sure to specify your family members' ages and abilities when talking with the liveries; they'll help you decide which excursion is best for you.

- **Adventure Sports in Marshalls Creek,** US 209, Marshalls Creek; (570) 223-0505 or (800) 487-2628; www.adventuresport.com. Trips run seven days a week in summer. Fees: $$$$ for adults, $$$ for children ages 13 through 17, and $$ for children ages 2 to 12.

- **Chamberlain's Canoes, Inc.,** River Road, Minisink Hills; (570) 421-0180 or (800) 422-6631; www.chamberlaincanoes.com.

- **Shawnee River Adventures** (offered by Shawnee Inn and Golf Resort), River Road, Shawnee-on-Delaware 18356; (570) 424-4000, ext. 1120 or (800) SHAWNEE; www.shawneeinn.com. Midweek specials. Open daily Apr through Oct.

Water Gap Trolley (ages 2 and up)

Main Street, Delaware Water Gap; (570) 476-9766. Open Apr through Oct (weather permitting) 10 a.m. to 4 p.m. Admission: $$ for adults, $ for children ages 2 to 12, children under 2 **free.**

The Water Gap Trolley takes vacationers from the depot on PA 611 near the town's center (actually, it's right across from the town's only stoplight) into the National Recreation Area. The one-hour narrated tour covers the geological and cultural history of the region.

Shawnee Place Play and Water Park (ages 2 and up)

Hollow Road, Shawnee-on-Delaware; (570) 421-7231; www.shawneemt.com. Open weekends from Memorial Day to June 15 and daily from June 16 to Labor Day, 10 a.m. to 5 p.m. Admission is $$$ for adults and children, $$ for spectators; children under 40 inches **free.**

Kids will enjoy swimming and sliding at Shawnee Place Play and Water Park, located just north of I-80 (take exit 52 to US 209 and follow signs). Especially geared for children under age twelve, the park has two slides and two pools, both about 3 feet deep. There are three magic shows daily, as well as fifteen unique play elements.

Shawnee Mountain (ages 4 and up)

Hollow Road, Shawnee-on-Delaware; (570) 421-7231; www.shawneemt.com. Open mid-Dec to mid-Mar, 9 a.m. to 10 p.m. weekdays, 8 a.m. to 10 p.m. weekends. Varying prices for lift tickets, rentals, and learn-to-ski programs.

Shawnee Mountain has twenty-three trails, a snowboarding area, snow-tubing, and a vertical drop of 700 feet. It also has an extensive ski program for kids. There's a Ski Wee program for six- to twelve-year-olds. Little ones (four to five years) can join the Pre-Ski Wee group. More adventurous kids ages ten to fifteen will want to hook up with the Mountain Cruisers. Beginning to early-intermediate snowboarders can join the Young Riders for eight- to fifteen-year-olds. Programs are $$$$. Three- and five-day packages are available (reservations required). For non-skiing children eighteen months and up, the Little Wigwam Children's Center is open daily for babysitting 9 a.m. to 5 p.m. on weekdays and 8 a.m. to 5 p.m. on weekends.

Shannon Inn and Pub (all ages)

Exit 52 off I-80, East Stroudsburg; (570) 424-1951 or (800) 424-8052. A wide variety of ski and golf packages are available, custom-tailored to your needs, at reasonable prices.

Several of the attractions nearby recommend the Shannon Inn for families. With an indoor pool, on-site casual restaurant, and a kids-stay-**free** policy, this 120-room hotel has everything a family needs for a quality, budget-priced vacation. Through cooperative agreements with Shawnee and Camelback ski areas and other nearby sites, the Shannon Inn offers two-day ski and golf packages.

Quiet Valley Living Historical Farm (ages 3 and up)

US 209, 3.5 miles south of Stroudsburg; (570) 992-6161; www.quietvalley.org. Open June 20 through Labor Day, Tues through Sat 10 a.m. to 5:00 p.m.; and Sun noon to 5:30 p.m. Admission: $$ for adults, $ for children ages 3 to 12.

Take a trip back in time at the Quiet Valley Living Historical Farm. Here your family will spend time with the Zeppers, a German immigrant family that settled this land back in 1765.

After a brief welcoming presentation, leave the present day and step back into the 1800s. The farmhand will introduce you to the animals, demonstrate the farm equipment, and let your kids jump in the hayloft. In addition to regular tours during the summer months, the museum also has a summer program for children, and special presentations, such as a Farm Animal Frolic in May, a Harvest Festival in Oct, and an Old Time Christmas celebration in Dec. Call for more information and specific dates. The Farm Animal Frolic is especially recommended for small children, with baby bunnies, hatching chicks, piglets, lambs, and more for children to touch and learn about.

Mount Pocono and Eastern Poconos
(Tannersville, Scotrun, Skytop)

Mount Pocono is in the heart of Pocono resort country. There are lots of resorts and attractions—everything from petting zoos to cheesecake factories—to choose from within a few miles of Mount Pocono, but here are some of our top picks.

Great Wolf Lodge (all ages)
Scotrun; www.greatwolflodge.com.

There are 300 suites available for overnight stays, with a variety of themed bedrooms for children. Chief among activities to keep families busy is the massive indoor water park, kept at 84 degrees year-round, with ten waterslides for all different ages and speeds. Climb the 12-level tree house, with sixty geysers and water effects, and the 1,000-gallon tipping bucket that will douse you every fifteen minutes.

Camelback Ski Area and Camelbeach Waterpark
(ages 4 and up)

Camelback Road, off I-80 (exit 45), Tannersville; (570) 629-1661; www.skicamelback.com (winter) or www.camelbeach.com (summer). Open for skiing late Nov through late Mar, weather permitting. Water park open late May through Labor Day. Call for specific dates. Lift tickets: $$$$. Children's ski instruction: $$$$ per lesson (includes lift ticket, lesson, and rental). Check the Web site for "Value Days." $$$$ for adults (12 to 64), $$$ for children (3 to 11) and seniors. Children 2 and under enter free.

The Camelback Ski Area is worth a stop in any season. In winter Camelback is one of the Pocono's largest ski resorts, with thirty-three trails, thirteen lifts, and a vertical drop of 800 feet. One of the newer additions is snow-tubing, a great family activity. There's a full-scale ski program where children ages four to twelve can spend the day learning to ski or snowboard.

From May until the end of fall, Camelback transforms from a ski resort to Camelbeach Waterpark, with eight waterslides, an action river, swimming pool, kids' play area, minia-ture golf, an alpine slide, and more. Ride the chairlift to the top of the mountain, enjoy the view of the Pocono Mountains, and take the alpine slide down. Buy a full ticket and enjoy the waterpark attractions all day. There's also a summer day-camp program at the facility; kids ages five to twelve can sign up for a day, a week, or the whole summer.

Caesar's Brookdale-on-the-Lake Resort (all ages)
PA 611, Scotrun; (800) 233-4141; www.caesarspoconoresorts.com. Open year-round. Call for package rates.

Okay, I have to admit it: There's something a little comical about visiting a renowned couples resort with your toddler, but Caesar's really has something here. Though families don't have full use of all the couples-oriented facilities here (we were disappointed to know we weren't eligible for breakfast in bed), it is a great way to combine some time for yourselves and still have a family vacation. (After the kids are asleep, you can sneak into the bath and enjoy the Jacuzzi for two.) Kids five and older can join the Brookdale Kids Kamp and participate in a wide range of special activities just for kids, from face painting to special meals and magic shows.

We visited with our two youngest children, two and one-half and one and one-half at the time. The staff couldn't have been more accommodating, spreading out a tablecloth under the high chair at each meal, filling our sippy cups and bottles each day, and making us bagels for the road. At each meal we sat with a different family, which was fun for adults and children alike. While we ate, a clown, magician, or other entertainer made the rounds of the tables, creating animals from balloons or cracking jokes with the kids.

Many rooms sleep up to eight people, and some have 36-inch TVs or Bose Wave radios.

During the summer and winter seasons, there are lots of activities at the nearby ski resorts, National Recreation Area, petting zoos, and other Poconos attractions.

Skytop Lodge (all ages)

PA 390, Skytop; (800) 345-7759; www.skytop.com. Open year-round.

Classic resorts have a few great elements in common: a stately lodge, a rocking-chair porch, great trails for hiking and walking, and a casual but classy approach to everything.

Skytop Lodge is one of those places—and it has only been improved with the addition of a spa and renovated guest rooms.

Rather than a resort that caters to kids, Skytop accommodates families the same way it accommodates all of its guests: with individual attention and concern for detail. Families can check into Skytop for a weekend or a week and find plenty to do for everyone: There are hiking and cross-country ski trails from 1 mile to 10; guided nature walks and self-guided fitness trails; downhill skiing, mountain bikes, rowboats, canoes, and sporting clays available on site; a swimming lake and indoor and outdoor pools; a game room; and a gorgeous golf course.

Skytop offers Camp in the Clouds for children ages four to ten every day in summer and weekends year-round. The program, which runs from 9 a.m. to 4:30 p.m., includes arts and crafts, nature walks, swimming, and other supervised activities. The cost is $$$ per full or half day.

Winter Camp in the Clouds is offered every Sat, Jan through Mar, 6 to 9 p.m. **free** of charge. Parents can dine alone while kids ice skate, watch movies, and more after a kid's dinner.

Skytop is a splurge; however, if you can swing it, it's an excellent family vacation. Accommodations are on the American plan, which means all meals are included. The menu includes some excellent entrees for adults and some favorites for kids. There is a per-day charge ($$$$) for children under sixteen who stay in their parents' room.

ALSO IN THE AREA

Pocono Cheesecake Factory, PA 611, Swiftwater; (570) 839-6844. Open daily 10 a.m. to 6 p.m. See cheesecakes made fresh daily.

Callie's Candy Kitchen and Pretzel Factory, PA 390, Mountainhome; (570) 595-2280 or (800) 252-7750; www.calliescandy.com. The Pretzel Factory is open daily Apr through Dec, weekends only Jan, Feb, and Mar. The candy factory is open year-round except Jan.

Located about 5 miles apart on PA 390, Callie's factories let you watch while candy and pretzels are made. Of course then you'll want to buy some in the gift shop.

Bushkill

US 209 from I-80 up to Milford is a lovely drive along the Pennsylvania side of the Delaware River. Here are some suggested stops on the way.

Mary Stolz Doll Museum (ages 3 and up)

US 209 North and McCole Road; (717) 588-7566. Open daily 11 a.m. to 5 p.m. Admission is $.

The Mary Stolz Doll Museum is definitely a don't-touch place, but if you have a doll lover in the family, the collection of more than 125 dolls from around the world makes it well worth resisting the temptation. Kids especially like the impressive array of Barbie and Jem dolls. There's also a fine display of miniature rooms, bears, and old toys.

Pocono Indian Museum (ages 6 and up)

US 209 North; (570) 588-9338; www.poconoindianmuseumonline.com. Open daily (call ahead for hours and admission prices).

The Pocono Indian Museum says it's the only museum in Pennsylvania dedicated to portraying the life and times of the Delaware Indian. Its six rooms display artifacts unearthed within a 20-mile radius of the museum. The museum also has a large gift shop. Your admission includes a thirty-minute taped, self-guided tour.

Bushkill Falls (all ages)

US 209; (570) 588-6682; www.visitbushkillfalls.com. Open Apr through Oct, 9 a.m. to dusk. Admission: $$ adults, $ for children ages 4 through 10; under 4 enter free. Free parking.

The Peters family started charging admission to see these eight magnificent falls, sometimes called the "Niagara of Pennsylvania," on their 300 acres one hundred years ago. The tourists haven't stopped coming since. Take a short nature walk back to the falls. Small children can usually manage the easy forty-five-minute to one-hour stroll. For the more energetic, there's a 2-mile hike that affords an even better view. A gift shop, food facilities, picnic area, and restroom facilities are available to visitors. There are also paddleboat rides, fishing, miniature golf, an ice-cream parlor, a Pennsylvania wildlife exhibit, and a Native American exhibit.

Fernwood Hotel and Resort (all ages)

US 209, Box 447, Bushkill 18324; (570) 588-9500 or (888) FERNWOOD; www.fernwoodhotel .com.

Fernwood Hotel and Resort offers year-round vacation possibilities, including an eighteen-hole golf course, snow-tubing, ice skating, two lakes, themed restaurants, live entertainment, indoor and outdoor pools, and a planned schedule of daily activities for children and adults. There's also "The Zone," a 10,000-square-foot game center. Fernwood is convenient to many popular ski resorts.

Dingman's Ferry

Can you picture one of Dingmans Ferry's most famous natives, Chief Thundercloud? If you've got an old nickel, it's easy. He's thought to be the model for the famous beaked profile on the heads side of the coin (and for the last five-dollar gold piece minted in the United States). Though he was a Boy Scout in his youth, Thundercloud went on to quite a show-biz career, traveling with Buffalo Bill's Wild West show and P. T. Barnum. He also served as a model for sculptor Frederick Remington and artist John Singer. He's buried back in his hometown cemetery on US 6/PA 309 in Delaware Township.

You can learn more about Thundercloud at The Columns, the home of the Pike County Historical Society in Milford. That's where you'll find a treasured piece of Americana reverently displayed. The Lincoln Flag is so called because it's the one that adorned the balustrade at Ford's Theater on April 14, 1865. When the president was shot by John Wilkes Booth, the stage manager placed it under Lincoln's head. Its bloodstains, still clearly visible, have been confirmed as Lincoln's.

Located at 608 Broad St., the society welcomes visitors 1 to 4 p.m. Wed through Sun. Admission is $; children **free.** For information call (570) 296-8126 or visit www.pike countyhistoricalsociety.org.

Pocono Environmental Education Center (PEEC)
(ages 3 and up)

RR2 Box 1010, Dingmans Ferry 18328; (570) 828-2319; www.peec.org.

For families interested in learning about the environment in a national park, there's no better deal than a weekend at the Pocono Environmental Education Center (PEEC). PEEC offers Family, Nature Study, and Recreational Weekends that help children and adults learn about the natural world around them. Enjoy activities such as hiking, canoeing, cross-country skiing, nature study, orienteering, natural history investigation, crafts, and field trips such as the Waterfall Hunt. PEEC's thirty-eight-acre campus is located within the borders of the Delaware Water Gap National Recreation Area and includes classrooms, an indoor pool, craft center, darkroom, library, bookstore, and overnight cabins.

Accommodations are in one-room cabins with private bathrooms that sleep between two and fourteen people. Group tenting is also available in the tent platform area. Meals are served at the dining hall. Weekends include lodging in a PEEC cabin, all meals, and programmed activities (everything from square dancing to live-animal presentations). Children under two are **free,** four and under are half price, and ages five to eight are 25 percent off. PEEC provides linens and towels for an additional cost.

ALSO IN THE AREA

Grey Towers, Milford; (570) 296-9630; www.fs.fed.us/na/gt. Grey Towers, a National Historic Landmark, was once the home of Gifford Pinchot, the first chief of the USDA Forest Service and twice governor of Pennsylvania. It is managed and maintained by the USDA Forest Service in cooperation with the Pinchot Institute for Conservation. Public tours of the house are conducted daily, on the hour, 10 a.m. to 4 p.m. weekdays and 10 a.m. to 4 p.m. on weekends. Many conservation programs are also offered.

Promised Land State Park, PA 390, 5 miles south of I-84; (570) 676-3428; www.dcnr .state.pa.us. Promised Land State Park is a 3,000-acre park surrounded by state forestland—creating a total of 11,000 acres of preserved wilderness. The area is home to a wide variety of wildlife, including one of eastern Pennsylvania's bigger populations of black bear. There are numerous housekeeping cabin resorts along PA 390, and camping is available in the park. There are environmental programs for children during summer. One primitive campground stays open year-round for cross-country skiers who can't bear to go home at the end of the day.

Hawley–Lake Wallenpaupack

Lake Wallenpaupack, the state's third largest man-made lake, is 15 miles long with 52 miles of shoreline. It was created in the 1920s by Pennsylvania Power & Light (PPL) as part of a major hydroelectric project. The PPL Wallenpaupack Environmental Learning Center offers exhibits exploring the environment as well as cultural and historical resources of the lake region. Open weekdays only, 8 a.m. to noon and 12:30 to 4:30 p.m. For information call (800) 510-0130 or go to www.pplprojectearth.com. PPL also maintains Shuman Point, Ledgedale natural area, and Beech House Creek Wildlife Refuge for public use. They are great places for short nature hikes and spotting wildlife such as beavers, herons, hawks, and more.

Just north of the lake is the town of Hawley, a great town for antiquing. Kids will be more interested in the following area attractions.

Tanglwood Ski Area & Winter Park (ages 3 and up)
PA 507, Lake Wallenpaupack; (570) 226-SNOW; www.tanglwood.com. Open daily Dec through Mar.

If you're in the area during winter, check out nearby Tanglwood Ski Resort, which offers nine trails of downhill skiing, a snowboarding area, a snow-tubing park, and several cross-country ski trails. There's also a Ski Wee children's program and a nursery available for small children. The ski shop is one of the only ones in the area to rent cross-country as well as downhill equipment.

Lake **Cruises**

Along the lake in Greentown there are resorts and marinas geared to vacationers who want to spend time on the water. Your family might try:

- **Pine Crest Yacht Club, Inc.,** PA 507; (570) 857-1136. Open May through Oct. Boat rentals available.

- **Pocono Action Sports,** PA 507; (570) 857-1976. Sailboats, rowboats, fishing, and waterskiing boats available.

Claws 'N' Paws Wild Animal Park (ages 2 and up)

Off PA 590, near Hamlin; (570) 698-6154; www.clawsnpaws.com. Open daily May 1 through late Oct, 10 a.m. to 6 p.m. Admission: $$$ adults, $$ ages 2 through 11 and seniors; children under 2 are **free.**

Claws 'n' Paws Wild Animal Park is a unique private zoo with 120 species of animals. Kids may feed the giraffes and lory parrots at scheduled feeding times. There are two different live animal shows through Labor Day. During the reptile show kids can pet an alligator and a python. Other exhibits include bears, otters, primates of several types, many species of birds, and rare white tigers. The new Dinosaur Outpost area lets kids dig for buried dinos, discover fossils at three dig sites, sit on a triceratops, and mine for gemstones. The easy-to-follow trails through the woods and the size of the facility help keep younger children from getting overwhelmed and overtired by the experience.

Triple "W" Riding Stables (ages 6 and up)

Follow blue-and-white state signs. Beechnut Drive, off Owego Turnpike near Lake Wallenpaupack; (570) 226-2620; www.triplewstable.com or www.doublewranchbnb.com. Stable: (800) 450-2620. Open year-round (except hunting season).

Take a step beyond "follow-the-leader" riding at this 200-acre horse ranch in a secluded area on the top of the mountain, featuring western riding experiences tailored to the individual. The staff at Triple "W" ensure a fun and rewarding ride for all members of the family by taking into consideration level of expertise and ambition. Overnight camping on horseback, hayrides, and pony rides for children under seven are also available.

Triple "W" offers Wild West shows, complete with a beautiful stagecoach, at many local events, fairs, and rodeos. There are also Murder Mystery weekends, day trips, school trips, reunions, weddings, and company outings.

In winter there's enough snow at the top of the mountain to get a lot of use out of the horse-drawn sleigh with jingle bells.

If you're looking for overnight accommodations, stay at the Double "W" Ranch Bed and Breakfast, located on the same property. The B&B boasts a large dining room, ski lounge with fireplace, a game room, and a three-level outdoor deck with a hot tub and a great view. The grounds include flower gardens, gazebos, and hiking paths. For the bed-and-breakfast call (877) 540-RANCH.

Woodloch Pines Resort (all ages)

PA 590, Hawley; (800) 572-6658 or (800) 272-9428; www.woodloch.com. Open year-round.

If you follow PA 590 east from Hawley, you'll arrive at an excellent family resort, Woodloch Pines Resort, named "one of the most exceptionally family-friendly resorts we've seen in many years" by Family Travel Network. Woodloch Pines was established as a small inn back in 1958. Since then it has grown into a complex with 160 hotel rooms, a nightclub, several restaurants, game rooms, recreation complex, and more family activities and children's programs than you can cram into a seven-day stay.

The resort is located right on Lake Teedyuskung, sixty-five acres of crystal-clear waters with a sandy swimming beach and rowboats, paddleboats, canoes, kayaks, and sailboats for exploring on your own. Woodloch Pines has the space and the layout that allow some families to be quiet and relax with one another while other groups applaud and cheer one another in games and contests. Other seasonal activities include hiking, biking, golf, snow-tubing, snowmobiling, ice-skating, bumper cars, go-karts, rifle range, batting cages, and more.

Woodloch Pines rates include three meals a day, activities, and entertainment. For families who prefer a more independent vacation, homes are available for rent at Woodloch Springs, a planned village centered around an award-winning golf course. Rates vary according to package length and accommodation type. Please call for current rates and availability.

ALSO IN THE AREA

Lacawac Wildlife Sanctuary (ages 6 and up), Lacawax Road, Ledgedale; (570) 689-9494; www.lacawac.org. Open year-round. One-mile self-guided nature trail overlooking Lake Wallenpaupack (pick up a trail guide at the parking lot), plus a host of special programs May through Oct.

Dorflinger–Suvdam Wildlife Preserve, White Mills; (570) 253-1185. Located off US 6 between Hawley and Honesdale, this private preserve features hiking and cross-country ski trails and a great series of outdoor concerts in the summer months. The glass museum on the same property is interesting to adults and older children but not a great choice for toddlers and active kids.

Fly **Fishing**

Both the Delaware and Lackawaxen Rivers are known by anglers as prime fly-fishing areas. Licensed guides will take you and your older kids out on the river for lessons. Check the list published by the Park Service.

Lackawaxen

PA 590 continues east from Woodloch Pines to the state line at Lackawaxen and the Delaware River. This tiny Pennsylvania town was the home of Zane Grey, author of such famous Western novels as The Riders of the Purple Sage and more than fifty others. Today the property is owned by the National Park Service as part of the Upper Delaware Scenic and Recreational River, which encompasses a 74-mile stretch of river from Sparrowbush, New York, to Hancock. Rafting is a popular activity in this area.

Upper Delaware **River Trips**

The Upper Delaware River is one of the last and longest free-flowing rivers in the northeastern United States. There are some rapids here, but most of the river is Class I, which means it is safe for beginning boaters and children over five. (Always wear life jackets and exercise caution when on or near the water.)

There are several river accesses along the Upper Delaware, including one in Lackawaxen. If you don't have your own boat to launch here, contact one of the liveries that rent canoes, rafts, and tubes and conduct guided trips down the Delaware. The Park Service publishes a list of liveries and licensed guides. Most outfitters provide boats, life jackets, and drop-off and pickup service at various river access points. They also have campsites available, although most are located on the New York side of the river. Remember, although the river is open to the public, the land on either side is privately owned. Please respect the rights and privacy of landowners.

Some of the bigger operations on the northern portion of the river include the following:

- **Lander's River Trips & Campgrounds,** 5666 NY 97, P.O. Box 500, Narrowsburg, NY 12764; (800) 252-3925; www.landersrivertrips.com. Children must weigh at least fifty pounds. With landings in Hancock, Hankins, Callicoon, Skinners Falls, Narrowsburg, Ten Mile River, Minisink, Pond Eddy, Knights Eddy, and Matamoras, Lander's has the Upper Delaware covered. In addition to conducting rafting and canoe trips, the company rents equipment for self-guided expeditions. Facilities include campgrounds, a motel (Ten Mile River Lodge in Ten Mile River, New York), and large grassy areas for playing near the river.

- **Wild and Scenic River Tours,** 166 NY 97, Barryville, New York; (800) 836-0366.

Zane Grey Museum (ages 8 and up)

River Road; (570) 685-4871; www.nps.gov/upde/historyculture/zanegrey.htm. Open season-ally. No park entrance fee. A program fee is charged for the museum. Admission is $; chil-dren under 10 are free. Call ahead for museum hours.

This museum, operated by the National Park Service as part of the Upper Delaware Scenic and Recreational River, houses an impressive collection of memorabilia of Grey's life and his passion for the West.

Little ones will be frustrated by the "don't touch" policy of the museum, but school-age and older kids interested in stories of the Wild West will enjoy the twenty-minute guided tour. The paintings on the walls of Grey's study depict scenes from the Southwest.

Also at the museum is a gift shop (many of Grey's novels are on sale for some light vacation reading). The ranger on duty will be able to point out some of the highlights of the park, including Roebling's Delaware Aqueduct and the locks of the D&H Canal. Be sure to ask for the Junior Ranger Program Activity Book. Children who successfully complete six of the twelve activities in the pamphlet are awarded a certificate of achievement and a Junior Ranger patch.

Roebling's Delaware Aqueduct (ages 6 and up)

PA 590; (570) 685-4871; www.nps.gov/upde. Information center open seasonally. The bridge operates year-round.

Down the road about 0.5 mile from the Zane Grey Museum is the Delaware Aqueduct, also known as the Roebling Bridge. Believed to be the oldest existing wire suspension bridge in the Western Hemisphere, it was designed and built in 1848 by John Augustus Roebling, the man who later designed the famous Brooklyn Bridge in New York City. The Tollhouse, on the New York Side, contains historic photos from the canal era (1825 to 1898). It is open seasonally.

Honesdale

Honesdale, located at the intersection of US 6 and PA 191, is in many ways the quintes-sential American small town. Its Main Street is lined with shops and stores that have been operated by the same families for years. Through a special Main Street program, many of the stores have been renovated to reflect the town's historic architecture. The Victorian homes and big porches of north Main Street are classic examples of American design.

Wayne County Historic Society Museum (ages 2 and up)

810 Main St.; (570) 253-3240; www.waynehistorypa.org. Open year-round; call for current hours. Admission is $; children under 12 are free.

Here you can see a replica of the original Stourbridge Lion, the first commercial steam locomotive to run on an American rail in 1829. (The original is in the Smithsonian Insti-tution in Washington, D.C.) Another exhibit traces the history of the D&H Canal, which connected Honesdale to the Hudson River, 108 miles away. There's also an impressive collection of Native American artifacts found in the Upper Delaware River Valley by a local archaeologist.

Stourbridge Line Rail Excursions (all ages)

303 Commercial St.; (570) 253-1960; www.waynecountycc.com. Call or check the Web site for current schedule. Rates vary according to season and itinerary.

The Stourbridge Line Rail Excursions run on weekends in summer and for special occasions at other times. The excursions follow the Lackawaxen River to Hawley and Lackawaxen. Different themes include fall foliage tours, dinner-theater tours, the Great Train Robbery Run, the Halloween Fun Run, the Easter Bunny Run, and the Santa Express.

The Wayne County Visitor Center, at the same address, houses a number of railroad exhibits and there's a gift shop featuring railroad souvenirs.

ALSO IN THE AREA

Carousel Water and Fun Park, PA 652, Beach Lake; (570) 729-7532; www.carousel-park .com. Open May through Oct. Go-karts, waterslides, bumper boats, minigolf, and batting cages are among the attractions here. Pay one price or pay by the ride.

Fun and Games, Route 6 Plaza, US 6; (570) 253-9111. A pay-and-play center with indoor minigolf that can be just the ticket on rainy days.

Wayne County Fair, PA 191; www.waynecountyfair.com. The first week in Aug, the Wayne County Fairgrounds hosts a fairly traditional county fair. There are rides and food, but the best part is watching local 4-H kids with the animals they've raised and trained themselves.

Starlight and New Milford

Head north from Honesdale on PA 191 and you'll find yourself in northern Wayne County. The thick forests of this corner of the state add to the feeling of an escape from civilization.

Inn at Starlight Lake (all ages)

Lake Road, Starlight; (800) 248-2519; www.innatstarlightlake.com. Open year-round.

One of the best places to enjoy northern Wayne County is the Inn at Starlight Lake, which has been attracting vacationers since 1909. Guests can stay in the inn itself, but families will generally prefer the cottages. Each cottage is a little different: Some have fireplaces, others have sleeping lofts for kids. All have private bathrooms.

As the name suggests, the inn is located right on Starlight Lake, a pretty little body of water that's great for swimming and exploring by rowboat or small sailboat (no powerboats allowed). There is a tennis court, shuffleboard, and a library and game room for evenings and rainy days. In winter visit nearby Mount Tone and Elk Mountain for downhill and cross-country skiing.

The inn is also the first stop on the four-day self-guided Inn-to-Inn bike tour of Wayne and Susquehanna Counties. For families with older children, this is a great combination of an active vacation and lovely accommodations.

Old Mill Village Museum (ages 5 and up)

Located 1 mile south of New Milford on PA 848 (exit 223 of I-81) and accessible from US 11; (570) 465-3448; www.oldmillvillage.com. Hours vary seasonally. Admission is $ for adults, free for children under 2 with an adult.

Follow the signs from the interstate to this group of historic buildings and artifacts depicting life in the area in the 1800s. During summer artisans demonstrate different crafts, from blacksmithing to quilting. There are also special events and festivals throughout the season, including an Annual Arts and Crafts Day, an antique doll show, Old Time Country Music Contest, and more.

Scranton

Tricks, trains, and really fast automobiles: Scranton has a lot to offer family travelers.

Pocono Raceway (all ages)

Long Pond; (800) 722-3929; www.poconoraceway.com. Open seasonally. Admission: $$$ per vehicle for grandstand.

Do your kids love NASCAR? Then you already know about Pocono Raceway, home to two of the biggest races on the NASCAR circuit. The Pocono 500 in June and the Pennsylvania 500 in Aug draw thousands of fans to this famous 2.5-mile track, just south of Scranton. Local resorts offer packages that include tickets and lodging.

Steamtown National Historic Site (all ages)

Entrance off Lackawanna Avenue, just west of Steamtown Mall; (570) 340-5200 or (888) 693-9391; www.nps.gov/stea. Open daily 9 a.m. to 5 p.m. (closed major holidays). Museum entrance fee: $$ adults; children free.

Railroad buffs of all ages won't want to miss Steamtown. Occupying fifty-two acres of a working railroad yard in downtown Scranton, Steamtown traces the history of railroading in the region and throughout the country. The structure includes a visitor center, a theater, an operating turntable, technology and history museums, a renovated roundhouse, and a museum store.

Watch the eighteen-minute film *Steel and Steam* to learn about the history of American steam railroading. At the history museum meet the people (actually lifelike statues) who worked, used, and depended on the railroad. Visit the roundhouse to see several examples from the Steamtown collection of locomotives and railroad cars. Learn about locomotive design and railroad communications at the technology museum.

From Steamtown you can board a rail excursion along the Pocono Mainline or ride the Heritage Valley Station Stops on the former D&H Mainline ($$$ for adults, $$ for seniors and children) or to the historic Radisson Lackawanna Hotel (included in general admission). According to one park ranger, children are "glued to the window or fast asleep during these trips. Either way, it's great for parents!" Call the park for current information and train schedules.

The Steamtown site is wheelchair accessible, and there are restrooms with changing tables. The excursion is accessible, but prior reservations are required. There are chemical toilets on the train, and snacks are available during a brief stop at Moscow.

After touring Steamtown, walk up the long ramp to the mall at Steamtown. (On rainy days, or when little ones are tired, it may be better to drive to the mall and park in the lot there.) There's a food court with fast food for every taste. If you prefer a more leisurely dining experience, head downstairs, or into town where there are many restaurants to choose.

Electric City Trolley Museum (all ages)
300 Cliff St. on property of Steamtown; (570) 963-6590; www.ectma.org. Open daily 9 a.m. to 5 p.m. Ride and museum combo tickets are $$; children under 3 are free.

The Electric City Trolley Museum shares a parking lot with Steamtown, making one-stop shopping for kids who love the rails. This museum tells the story of electric traction and trolley systems in northeastern Pennsylvania. Trolley excursions depart regularly from the same platform as the Steamtown trains and go through the Crown Avenue tunnel. The Children's Gallery teaches "painless geography" through models set on maps of the area. Kids can generate their own electricity, run a trolley system, and build their own model anthracite communities.

Radisson Lackawanna Station Hotel (all ages)
700 Lackawanna Ave.; (570) 342-8300; www.radisson.com/scranton.pa.

Sticking with the railroad motif, why not stay in a glorious old railway station? The Lackawanna Station Hotel, a building on the National Register of Historic Places now operated by the Radisson chain of hotels, is just a few blocks from Steamtown. You can actually take the Steamtown Excursion train to Steamtown. The station's waiting area has been transformed into a palatial lobby with two restaurants and complete hotel facilities—including a game room that's a hit with kids.

Houdini Museum (ages 3 and up)
1433 N. Main Ave.; (570) 342-5555; www.houdini.org. Open daily Memorial Day through Sept 15; other times by appointment. Admission is $$.

Featured on the Travel Channel's Magic Road Trip, the Houdini Museum is a must-see for budding magicians. The museum takes visitors back to the days of vaudeville, when traveling performers like Houdini frequently visited the Scranton area. There are continuous guided tours, a film, and nonstop magic shows, along with Houdini memorabilia and exhibits about Scranton's vaudeville past. A wonderful magic show is performed by nationally known magicians such as Dorothy Dietrich and Bravo the Great. Lots of laughs, live animals, and audience participation.

The Halloween "Spook-tacular" Theater of Illusion takes place from Columbus Day through Halloween. Appropriate for all ages, this magic show features classic illusions with nothing too scary for little ones.

Lackawanna Coal Mine (ages 3 and up)

McDade Park; (570) 963-MINE or (800) 238-7245; www.lackawannacounty.org. Open daily Apr through Nov. Admission: $$ adults, $ children ages 3 to 12; children under 3 are **free.**

Coal is a major part of this region's history. One of the best places to gain an understanding of the life of a coal miner is on the Lackawanna Coal Mine Tour at McDade Park in Scranton. Here visitors ride 250 feet down into a real underground coal mine. Former miners and sons of miners tell the story of what a typical workday was like for the men and boys (as young as seven years old!) of the mines. Children who are afraid of the dark should be forewarned, but most children's favorite part of the tour is when the guide turns out the lights and the group stands in total darkness for a long couple of seconds.

The tour is partially wheelchair accessible, as long as the person can move from a wheelchair to the car. It's chilly and damp down below (55 degrees year-round), so be sure to bring along a sweatshirt.

Montage Mountain (ages 2 and up)

1000 Montage Mountain Rd.; (570) 969-7669 or (800) GOT–SNOW; www.skimontage.com. The summer park is open from mid-June to Labor Day, weekdays noon to 5 p.m. and weekends 10 a.m. to 7 p.m.

Another center of family-oriented activity is Montage Mountain, located right off exit 182 of I-81. Summer activities include waterslides, batting cages, chairlift rides, children's activity park, playground, and more. During the colder months, Montage is home to a top ski resort offering skiing, snowboarding, and snow-tubing. Sat night is Family Night. A new Northeastern Pennsylvania visitor center is located here.

ALSO IN THE AREA

Lackawanna County Stadium (ages 5 and up), Montage Mountain Road; (570) 969-BALL; www.redbarons.com. Home to the Red Barons, an AAA farm club for the Philadelphia Phillies. Call for game information and schedules for the upcoming season.

Everhart Museum (all ages), Nay Aug Park, 1901 Mulberry St., Scranton; (570) 346-7186; www.everhart-museum.org. Open year-round. Admission is $$ for adults, $ for seniors and children; children under 5 are **free.** Permanent exhibits include a dinosaur hall, rock and mineral display, a bird gallery, and children's gallery, as well as examples of American and European painting, prints, and more. The Everhart often attracts high-quality traveling exhibits, so be sure to call ahead and see what will be there during your stay.

Eckley Miners' Village (all ages), RR 2, Box 236, Weatherly 18255; (570) 636-2070; www.eckleyminers.org. Open daily year-round. Admission: $ per person, $$ for families. Just 9 miles east of I-81, Eckley Miners' Village offers the chance to visit an authentic

McDade **Park**

The Lackawanna Coal Mine may be the main attraction, but there's lots more to do in McDade Park. Next door to the mine is the Anthracite Heritage Museum, which traces the history of coal and its influence on the people of this area, including immigrant workers in the coal mines. Call (570) 963-4804 for more information.

McDade Park is also home to a summer theater festival, a fall balloon festival, and other special events. In addition, it's a great place for a family picnic and outdoor play. For more information and a schedule of upcoming events, call (570) 963-6764.

nineteenth-century "patch" town. The town was originally built in 1854 by the mining firm of Sharpe, Leisenring and Co. for its workers, mostly new immigrants to the United States. The town, which was restored in the late 1960s for the filming of the movie The Molly Maguires, is now a historic site, administered by the Pennsylvania Historical and Museum Commission. Throughout the summer season the village holds various special events, including Patch Town Days, a Living History Weekend, and Family Sunday, which features a community picnic typical of the 1800s.

The Lehigh Gorge and Surrounding Area
(White Haven, Jim Thorpe, Lehighton)

The Lehigh River cuts through the section of the Pocono Plateau south of Wilkes-Barre and creates a gorge that has become a mecca for recreation enthusiasts. A bike path along the river is a dramatic but easy ride (especially going north to south), and the river itself offers challenging white water for boating. There's also great skiing in the area, as well as some terrific resorts for families.

For a family that wants to combine outdoor activities like biking, hiking, and swimming with more urbane pursuits such as museums, shops, and restaurants, the town of Jim Thorpe has a winning combination.

Mauch Chunk Lake Park (all ages)　

625 Lentz Trail, Jim Thorpe; (570) 325-3669; www.carboncounty.com/park. Open year-round.

In the late 1800s and early 1900s, tourists flocked to Mauch Chunk (now Jim Thorpe) to ride the famous Switchback Railroad. This 18-mile figure- eight of track was more like a roller coaster than a train ride—at some points on the trip, cars reached speeds of 60 miles per hour. Now, a century later, the Switchback is again attracting tourists. Although the railroad has not operated in many years, its railbed has been transformed into one of the best-known mountain-bike trails on the East Coast.

Much of the Switchback trail is located within or near Mauch Chunk Lake Park, a county park that offers more than a vacation's worth of activities. The park features nice campsites, a sandy beach on a beautiful lake, excellent programs at the environmental center, picnic pavilions, a food and refreshment stand, and 18 miles of biking, hiking, or cross-country skiing trails. Trails include scenic overlooks, one of which offers a spectacular view of the Lehigh Gorge and Glenonoko Falls. On weekends during the month of Oct—peak foliage time—the park offers hayrides along the Switchback Trail.

Other special attractions of the park include wheelchair access to the lake, a wheelchair-accessible fishing pier, restrooms with changing tables, and a nice playground for kids. Fees are charged for many of the park's activities, including swimming, hayrides, equipment rentals, and camping. Eight camping cottages are available for rent.

Mauch Chunk Museum and Cultural Center (ages 4 and up)
41 W. Broadway, Jim Thorpe; (570) 325-9190; www.mauchchunkmuseum.com. Open Tues through Sun year-round. Call ahead for current hours. Admission is $.

Stop here to learn about the history of the Switchback Railroad and the town that grew up around it. An exhibit called "The Story of Mauch Chunk" (the town that changed its name to Jim Thorpe) portrays the history of the coal mining industry in Mauch Chunk; the Lenni Lenape Indians; and the life of Jim Thorpe, the Native American Olympic athlete for whom the town was renamed in the 1950s. Although Thorpe was never a resident of the town, his widow heard of the area's efforts to revitalize its economy and offered her husband's memorabilia in exchange for naming the town in his honor.

The museum is housed in a beautiful redbrick Victorian church built in 1843.

The Old Jail Museum (ages 6 and up)
128 W. Broadway, Jim Thorpe; (570) 325-5259. Open daily except Wed, Memorial Day through Labor Day. Open weekends only in Sept and Oct. Admission is $.

Asked what kids like best about his museum, Thomas McBride answers, "It's a real jail and it's spooky. Real 'bad guys' were here!" Indeed, this building served as the Carbon County jail from 1871 to Jan 1995. It was also the site of the hanging of the Molly Maguires. It has now been preserved as a museum. Tour guides take visitors through the kitchen, cell blocks, and even down to the dungeon, where prisoners were kept in solitary confinement. Yes, it's a bit spooky, but there are lessons to be learned here. Older kids especially seem fascinated. Look for the "mysterious handprint" left by a prisoner in 1871. No matter how many times the room is repainted, the ghostly handprint always bleeds through!

Blue Mountain Sports and Wear (ages 8 and up)
US 209, Jim Thorpe; (800) 599-4421; www.bikejimthorpe.com. Open daily.

According to *Outside* magazine, Jim Thorpe offers the "best biking in Pennsylvania." If mountain biking or other outdoor sports are your pleasure, stop in at the Blue Mountain Sports and Wear shop for information about the excellent trails in the area. The store offers top-quality bike rentals and shuttle service to various trailheads. Tell the experienced staff your skill level and how much time you want to spend, and they'll guide you to the right trail. In addition to bike rentals, the store has camping equipment, kayaks, rowboats, canoes, cross-country skis, and snowshoes for rent.

Pocono Whitewater Rafting (ages 5 and up)

PA 903, Jim Thorpe; (570) 325-8430 or (800) WHITEWATER; www.whitewaterrafting.com.

Another option for outdoor enthusiasts is a rafting trip down the Lehigh River. Pocono Whitewater Adventures offers "Family-Style Floatrips" for kids from "five to eighty-five," including riverside barbecue. One child per two paying adults rides **free.**

Asa Packer Mansion (ages 8 and up)

Packer Hill, Jim Thorpe; (570) 325-3229; http://asapackermansionmuseum.homestead.com. Open daily Memorial Day through Oct 31. Call ahead for hours. Admission is $$ for adults and $ for children under 12.

Although not a place to take your wound-up preschooler, older kids will enjoy ogling the opulent furnishings in this Victorian mansion.

Old Mauch Chunk H.O. Scale Model Train Display (all ages)

41 Susquehanna St., Jim Thorpe; (570) 386-2297 or (570) 325-4371. Open year-round. Hours vary. Admission is $; children under 4 enter free.

Across the street from the visitor center, in the Hooven Mercantile Co. building, head up to the second floor to see the Scale Model Railroad Display. With 1,000 feet of track, 60 cars, 200 miniature buildings, and 100 bridges, it sure is an impressive display.

The Inn at Jim Thorpe (all ages)

24 Broadway, Jim Thorpe; (570) 325-2599; www.innjt.com.

With a restaurant on-site and kid-friendly policies, this is a great place to stay right in Jim Thorpe. You can walk to all the sights. Suites have dining areas, whirlpools, VCRs, refrigerators, microwaves, and coffeemakers—things that make a family vacation much easier.

ALSO IN THE AREA

Big Boulder and Jack Frost Ski Resorts, Lake Harmony; (570) 722-0100 or (800) 468-2442; www.big2resorts.com. Big Boulder and its neighbor, Jack Frost, offer a great vacation deal for families. Families can try skiing (downhill and cross-country), snow-tubing, snowboarding, motorsports, and paintball and stay in a vacation home on the property. Even better, kids under five stay **free.** Both resorts also offer babysitting, ski lessons in winter, music festivals in summer, and nightlife all year long. Jack Frost has TRAXX, a 15-mile course through the woods with divisions for motocross, ATV, and BMX bikes. This

Pennsylvania **State Parks**

With 116 parks adding up to more than 300,000 acres, Pennsylvania has the largest state park system east of the Mississippi—and one of the best travel bargains anywhere. From the majesty of old-growth forests to the drama of waterfalls, from the solitude of fishing to the camaraderie of a multigenerational family vacation, these parks offer something for just about everyone. And admission is free.

But while many families are aware of the recreational offerings of the state parks, many don't know about the cozy cabins and excellent campgrounds that offer an escape from ordinary life. Fifty-five of Pennsylvania's state parks offer camping. Located in the woods, on the edge of a lake, by a babbling brook, or at the edge of an inspiring vista, these accommodations are the stuff vacation dreams are made on—at prices that make wishes come true.

Cabin rentals include tiny rustic cabins for two and modern cabins with living room, bathroom, kitchen, and bunk beds for six. You'll have to reserve a weekday for the best rates, but even on weekends, the cabins are still a bargain. In summer the cabins are available by the week. Bring your own food, linens, and cooking utensils, and you've got a terrific vacation.

Leave your tent behind and try two new overnight choices in the state park system: yurts and camping cottages. A yurt is a round tent on a wooden deck, equipped with a cooking stove, refrigerator, table, chairs, electric heat and outlets, fire ring, water pump, two bunk beds, and other simple amenities. The camping cottages are rustic wooden structures with electric lights and outlets, windows, screened porches, heaters, and minifridges. Each cottage sleeps five.

Modern campsites rent for as low as $$$ per night—rustic for even less.

By calling (888) PA–PARKS, you'll be able to make reservations up to eleven months in advance at any of the state parks in Pennsylvania. If one park has no available cabins for the dates you select, the operator will locate another that does. You can also check the Web site at www.dcnr.state.pa.us.

Your best bet is to call the individual parks if you have specific questions.

course is available for people ten and up. Bring your own equipment, but you can rent bicycles only. Also at Jack Frost is nighttime snow-tubing on Sat nights.

Ashland

Pioneer Tunnel Coal Mine & Steam Train (all ages)
Nineteenth and Oak Streets; (570) 875-3850; www.pioneertunnel.com. Open Apr through Nov. Call ahead for specific times. Mine tour: $$ for adults, $ for children under 12. Steam train: $$ for adults, $ for children under 12.

If you didn't visit the Lackawanna Coal Mine in Scranton—or if you and your kids enjoyed it so much you're ready for another mine tour—then head to Ashland and the Pioneer Tunnel Coal Mine. Like the Scranton mine, this is an actual coal mine. When the coal company shut it down, some local volunteers and former miners transformed it into a fascinating study of a coal miner's life. Visitors enter the mine in open mine cars, just as the miners did when they started their workdays.

After the thirty-five-minute mine tour, take a ride on a narrow-gauge steam locomotive, the Henry Clay. Along the 1.5-mile round-trip, you'll see two other examples of coal mining: a strip mine and a bootleg coal mine, where men snuck past guards to get coal to sell or to heat their own homes. You can see the smoke rising from the ground as a result of the famous Centalia mine fire.

Red Rock

Ricketts Glen State Park (ages 2 and up)
PA 487; (570) 477-5675 or (888) PA–PARKS (camping reservations only); www.dcnr.state.pa.us. Open year-round. Free.

Ricketts Glen State Park may well be the most beautiful and least well known of Pennsylvania's many state parks. The park, which spills into Luzerne, Sullivan, and Columbia Counties, covers 13,050 acres with lakes, waterfalls (twenty-two in all!), hiking and cross-country skiing trails, and many opportunities for fishing, boating, camping, horseback riding, and more.

The Glens Natural Area, a registered National Natural Landmark, is the centerpiece of the park. Here, where two branches of Kitchen Creek create deep gorges, there are rare stands of virgin hemlock and other trees, some more than 500 years old. Much of the hiking in the park covers pretty steep territory, but with the help of a park ranger, you can choose trails that may be easier for children. For example, the Evergreen Trail, just 0.5-mile long, takes hikers through giant hemlocks and pine trees and to a view of several waterfalls. There are 120 tent and trailer campsites available year-round at the park. In summer there are flush toilets and hot showers. In winter only pit toilets are available.

If camping sounds a bit too rustic, consider staying at one of the ten comfortable family cabins in the park. Each has a living area, kitchen, bath, and two or three bedrooms. Advance reservations are required for the cabins.

Hunting is permitted in parts of the park. If you visit during the hunting season (primarily in late fall), check in with park rangers to find out what safety precautions are appropriate.

Eagles Mere

This little town is a Victorian charmer. Parents and grandparents will love the Newport-style "cottages" built for wealthy Philadelphia vacationers more than a century ago; the Eagles Mere Inn is a still a chic choice. Kids will find seat-of-the-pants fun.

Eagles Mere Ice Toboggan Slide (all ages)
PA 43, Eagles Mere; recorded message (570) 525-3244; www.eaglesmere.org. Open Fri 6:30 to 9:30 p.m., Sat 10 a.m. to 8 p.m., and Sun 10 a.m. to 6 p.m. Admission $$ per hour.

Local lore says that back in 1909, the first user of this 1,200-foot-long toboggan run hopped aboard a shovel to ride down the ice. As he gathered speed, smoke trailed behind: He actually burned off the seat of his pants! Nowadays riders use the small or large toboggans provided to zip down the 120-ton ice chute (no children may ride alone—parental supervision is required). The slide is open winter weekends, and food and beverages are sold.

Forksville

World's End State Park (ages 6 and up)
PA 154; (570) 924-3287 or (888) PA–PARKS; www.dcnr.state.pa.us. Open year-round. Free.

Despite its small size (less than 1,000 acres), it's easy to feel as if you're at the edge of the world in this remote valley. If you're looking for a good place to introduce your children to wilderness camping, this is the spot. There are seventy tent and trailer sites and nineteen cabins, equipped with refrigerator, range, fireplace, table, chairs, and beds. (There's a central shower facility.)

The park includes numerous hiking trails, including the 59³/₁₀-mile-Loyalsock Trail, part of which runs through the park. Most of the trails are pretty steep, so this park is a better choice for older kids and more-experienced hikers.

Festivals of Forksville

Forksville might as well be called Festiville, with all the annual events planned for the fairgrounds and other locations around town. The fun starts in winter with the annual Endless Mountains 50 Sled Dog Race. The 50-mile race, which is run in the state game lands near Forksville, attracts six-dog racing teams from as far away as Canada. When and if the weather gets cold enough, folks in the area start calling (570) 525-3255 to find out if the Ice Toboggan Slide has been set up in Eagles Mere.

In February the Forksville fairgrounds is the site of the Sullivan County Sleigh Ride and Rally. Here, horses pull the sleighs. In addition to divisions for men, women, and children, there's a timed obstacle-course race and a "Currier & Ives" class, where contestants are judged on the "postcard" quality of their sleighs. Visitors can get a ride in a bobsled. Labor Day weekend brings the Sullivan County Fair, held at the Forksville Fairgrounds. In October it's time for the Fall Festival, with demonstrations by quilters, woodcarvers, and apple-butter and apple-cider makers. There are wagon rides, draft horses, and lots of activities for children.

For more information: Sullivan County Chamber of Commerce (570-482-4088) or Endless Mountains Visitors Bureau (570-836-5431). Web site: www.endlessmountains.org. The calendar portion of this Web site can be searched like a database for events of special interest.

Towanda

Not to be confused with the Bradford County Heritage Farm Museum, the Bradford County Historical Society and Museum recently opened in the newly renovated jail building in Towanda.

Bradford County Historical Society and Museum
109 Pine St.; (570) 265-2240. Open Thurs through Sat.

The new Bradford County Historical Society and Museum houses many interesting exhibits that preserve the history of Bradford County and the building's role as the local jail. Portions of the jail were left in their natural state to preserve a sense of the building's past. You can peek at the jail cells through a peephole actually used by the guards.

Where to Eat

IN THE DELAWARE WATER GAP AND STROUDSBURG AREA

Brownie's in the Burg, 700 Main St., Stroudsburg; (570) 421-2200.

The Sarah Street Grill, 550 Quaker Alley, Stroudsburg; (570) 424-9120. Casual dining including steaks, seafo0od, and pasta. Children's menu offers chicken fingers, grilled-cheese sandwiches, and pizza.

IN THE MOUNT POCONO AND EASTERN POCONOS AREA

Memorytown, Grange Road, Mount Pocono; (570) 839-1680. Shops, snack bar, restaurant, and amusement area all in one.

Smuggler's Cove, PA 611, Tannersville; (570) 629-2277.

IN THE HAWLEY–LAKE WALLENPAUPACK AREA

Ehrhardt's Lakeside Restaurant, PA 507, 1 mile south of US 6, Hawley; (570) 226-2124. Dining with a view of Lake Wallenpaupack.

Falls Port Inn & Restaurant, Main Street, Hawley; (570) 226-2600. Children's menu, Sunday brunch, historic building.

IN THE HONESDALE AREA

Beach Lake Cafe, PA 652, Beach Lake. Open year-round. The most popular place around for weekend breakfasts, this little coffee shop serves up omelets and pancakes. Get there early on Sat to avoid a wait.

IN SCRANTON

Coney Island Lunch, 515 Lackawanna Ave.; (570) 961-9004. Downtown Scranton's oldest restaurant has served baseball, hot dogs, and apple pie since 1923.

Cooper's Seafood House, 701 N. Washington Ave.; (570) 346-6883. Kids' menu.

The Mall at Steamtown, Lackawanna Avenue; (570) 343-3400. Food court upstairs and a sit-down restaurant downstairs.

Pat McMullen's Restaurant, 217 E. Market St.; (570) 342-3486.

Where to Stay

IN THE DELAWARE WATER GAP AND STROUDSBURG AREA

Quality Inn, 1220 W. Main St., Stroudsburg; (570) 424-1930 or (800) 777-5453; www.choicehotels.com.

Pocono Inn, Delaware Water Gap; (570) 476-0000.

Shawnee Inn & Golf Resort, River Road, Shawnee-on-Delaware; (570) 424-4000 or (800) SHAWNEE; www.shawneeinn.com.

Timothy Lake, RD 6, Box 6627, East Stroudsburg 18301; (570) 588-6631 or for reservations (800) 588-2221. Part of the "Outdoor World" group of camping resorts.

IN MOUNT POCONO AND EASTERN POCONOS

Hampton Court Inn, PA 611, Mount Pocono; (570) 839-2119.

Pocono Super 8 Motel, PA 611, Mount Pocono; (570) 839-7728.

IN THE SCRANTON AREA

Holiday Inn Scranton–East, 200 Tigue St., Dunmore; (570) 343-4771. Indoor pool, renovated rooms.

Howard Johnson Inn Scranton, 320 Franklin Avenue, Scranton; (570) 346-7061. Near Steamtown National Historic Site.

Outdoor World Scotrun Resort, PA 611, Scotrun; (570) 629-0620 or for reservations (800) 588-2221; www.rvthereyet.cc. Part of the national chain of camping resorts.

IN THE HONESDALE AREA

Beach Lake is on PA 652, a great home base for exploring the Upper Delaware Valley and Honesdale.

Central House. Off PA 652; (570) 729-7411 or (570) 729-8341; www.centralhouseresort .com. Open year-round. An on-the-lake location, family-style meals, and on-site swimming pool and volleyball court—a nice spot for a value-priced vacation.

Pine Grove Cabins. Off PA 652; (570) 729-8522. Open May through Oct. For families who prefer to cook their own meals, these cabins can't be beat. Owners Jerry and Barbara Zimmerman keep this bungalow colony immaculate. Kitchens, small living rooms, bathroom with showers, and two bedrooms are crammed into each cabin. There's a beach for swimming and boats for guest use. Weeklong packages are available.

For More Information

Endless Mountains Visitors Bureau; (570) 836-5431 or (800) 769-8999; www.endless mountains.org.

Jim Thorpe Tourist Agency; (570) 325-3673; www.jimthorpe.org

Luzerne County Tourist Promotion Agency; (888) 905-2872; www.tournepa .com.

Pennsylvania's Northeast Territory Visitors Bureau; (570) 457-1320 or (800) 22WELCOME; www.visitnepa.org.

Pocono Mountains Convention and Visitors Bureau, 1004 Main St., Stroudsburg 18360; (800) 762-6667; www.800poconos .com.

Schuylkill County Visitors' Bureau; (570) 622-7700 or (800) 765-7282; www.schuylkill .org.

Central
Pennsylvania

The center of Pennsylvania holds a wonderful array of cultural, historical, and recreational opportunities for families. Two cities, Williamsport and State College, have great museums, cultural events, and a wide variety of amenities, such as accommodations, shopping, and restaurants. Either one makes a good base for exploring the surrounding areas.

Dotted around the region are charming small towns, wonderful state parks, farms, and other rural attractions. Campgrounds are plentiful, and little bed-and-breakfasts often welcome families. The local county tourism organizations and chambers of commerce are great resources for planning your trip. Here are our recommendations.

TopPicks in Central Pennsylvania

- **Knoebels Amusement Park and Campground,** Elysburg
- **Peter J. McGovern Little League Baseball Museum,** Williamsport
- **Mountain Dale Farm,** McClure
- **Shaver's Creek Environmental Center,** State College
- **Penn State University Creamery,** State College
- **Children's Discovery Workshop,** Williamsport
- **Clyde Peeling's Reptiland,** Williamsport
- **T&D's Cats of the World,** Mifflinburg
- **Camp Woodward,** Woodward
- **Walking tour of the Victorian downtown in Lewisburg**

CENTRAL PENNSYLVANIA

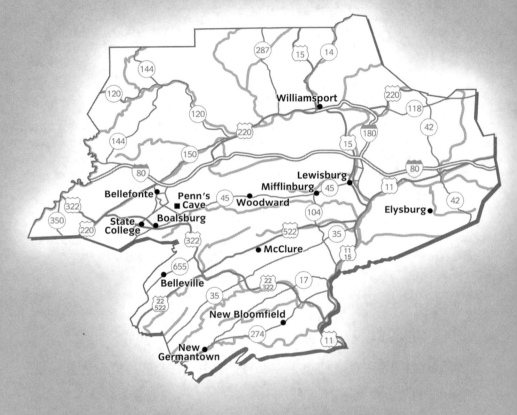

Williamsport

If you have a child in Little League, then Williamsport—the home of the Peter J. McGovern Little League Baseball Museum—is a required stop on your vacation in central Pennsylvania. Once you get to the city, you'll find that the museum is a great destination. So is a Crosscutters game. To find out more about Williamsport's own minor league baseball team, including schedules and ticket information, visit www.crosscutters.com.

In Williamsport you can also access the Pine Creek Rail Trail, which stretches for 64 miles from Ansonia in Tioga County to Jersey Shore in Lycoming County.

Peter J. McGovern Little League Baseball Museum
(ages 5 and up)

US 15 South; (570) 326-3607; www.littleleague.org. Memorial Day through Labor Day: Open Mon through Sat 10 a.m. to 7 p.m., Sun noon to 7 p.m. Labor Day through Memorial Day: Open Mon, Thur, and Fri 10 a.m. to 5 p.m., Sat noon to 5 p.m., and Sun noon to 4 p.m. Closed Tues and Wed and major holidays. Adults $$; children 5 to 13 $.

The Peter J. McGovern Little League Baseball Museum traces the history of Little League from its founding in 1939 to the present, when millions of children in scores of countries participate in the program. There are interactive displays and batting and pitching cages with instant replay monitors so that kids can see themselves on "instant replay." You can watch highlights of the Little League World Series—a truly international sporting event that takes place here each Aug. The Hall of Excellence includes tributes to such famous

TopEvents in Central Pennsylvania

- **Belleville Farmers Market** in Belleville, Wednesdays; (717) 935-2146.
- **Big Spring Film Festival in Bellefonte**, mid-May; (814) 355-2917.
- **Mifflinburg Buggy Days in Mifflinburg**, end of May; (570) 966-1355.
- **Memorial Day,** Boalsburg, May; (814) 466-9266.
- **Historic Car Cruise,** Bellefonte, June; (814) 355-2917.
- **Central Pennsylvania Festival of the Arts in State College,** July; (814) 237-3682.
- **Ag Progress Days in State College,** mid-Aug; (814) 865-2081.
- **Arts and Crafts Fair,** Bellefonte, Aug; (814) 355-2917.
- **Little League World Series,** Williamsport, Aug; (570) 326-1921.
- **Victorian Christmas,** Dec, Bellefonte; (814) 355-2917.

former Little Leaguers as Tom Seaver, Kareem Abdul-Jabbar, columnist George Will, and former New Jersey Senator Bill Bradley.

Children's Discovery Workshop (ages 3 to 11)

343 W. Fourth St. at Elmira Street; (570) 323-7134; http://williamsportymca.org. Open Sept through May, Tues through Fri 10 a.m. to 5 p.m., Sat 11 a.m. to 5 p.m. and Sun 1 to 5 p.m.; June through Aug, Tues through Sat 10 a.m. to 4 p.m. Admission: $ per person; children under 2 are **free.**

Located inside the Williamsport YMCA, the Children's Discovery Workshop is a hands-on museum for children ages three to eleven. The interactive exhibits are designed to inspire children's imaginations, explorations, and discoveries. Features include a toddler area, bricks to build a castle, a pretend ice-cream parlor, and changing exhibits. One of the most popular features is the 129-foot-long "FUNnel," which children can crawl through.

Thomas T. Taber Museum of Lycoming County (ages 5 and up)

858 W. Fourth St.; (570) 326-3326; www.lycoming.org/lchsmuseum. Open year-round Tues through Fri 9:30 a.m. to 4 p.m. and Sat 11 a.m. to 4 p.m. Open Sun from May to Oct 31, 1 to 4 p.m. Adults $$, children 12 and under $.

Model-train enthusiasts will want to stop here to see the Larue Shempp Model Train exhibition, with more than 300 toy trains and two working layouts—reputed to be one of the finest displays of its kind in the country. There's a frontier room, which re-creates the furnishings from the county's first European settlement in 1769; a general store from the turn of the twentieth century; a one-room schoolhouse; a working gristmill; and a collection of farming, blacksmithing, and milling tools from the 1700s to 1900s. You can board the Historic Williamsport Trolley here, too.

Historic Williamsport Trolleys (all ages)

Downtown; (800) CITYBUS or (570) 326-2500; www.citybus.org. Open Tues, Thurs, and Sat during June, July, and Aug. Tours are $ per person.

The Historic Williamsport Trolleys are run by the City Bus company of the Williamsport Bureau of Transportation. The three trolleys, the Herdic, the Weightman, and the Stotz, are actually replicas of historic streetcars. Each makes a ninety-minute narrated trip around the historic areas of Williamsport. The route takes you past Millionaire's Row (6 blocks of magnificent mansions), the field where the first Little League game was played, and other sights of the city. Riders can get on and off at one of the downtown stops and each of the two outlying stops. On Tues and Thurs you can get off the trolley and onto the Hiawatha for a cruise—another great way to tour the sights of this city.

Hiawatha Riverboat (all ages)

Susquehanna State Park; (570) 326-2500 or (800) 248-9287. In season only (570) 326-1221; www.ridehiawatha.com. Cruises operate Tues through Sun, May through mid-Oct. Public cruises: Adults $$, children 3 to 12 $. Family Night cruises: Adults $$, children 3 to 12 $. First come, first served after tickets go on sale at 10:30 a.m.

The other way to tour the town is aboard the *Hiawatha*, a paddle wheeler that plies the Susquehanna River. The hour-long public cruise includes a narration that relates the history of the area, from the time when the Susquehannock Indians lived along these shores through the European settlements and boom years of the lumber industry. On Tues nights in June, July, and Aug, come aboard for a special cruise just for families, ninety minutes long, with a different featured activity every night. Sunday brunch cruises, for $$$ per person, will sail you to the Antlers Country Club for brunch, then take you back by Historic Williamsport Trolley.

Clyde Peeling's Reptiland (ages 4 and up)

US 15, south of Williamsport; (570) 538-1869 or (800) REPTILAND; www.reptiland.com. Open year-round daily 10 a.m. to 5 p.m. on weekdays, until 6 p.m. on weekends. Closed major holidays. Admission is $$; children under 4 are free.

Don't miss Clyde Peeling's Reptiland, an accredited zoo with a collection of sixty different species of reptiles and amphibians. Poison dart frogs, a giant toad, a gaboon viper, a green tree python, a king cobra, alligators, giant tortoises, turtles, iguanas—they're all here. There are educational programs five times during the day that give visitors a chance to see and touch the animals up close.

The newly renovated indoor exhibit complex allows comfortable viewing of animals year-round. You may dine at a Subway restaurant in the entrance building. And on the third weekend of Oct, come learn about nocturnal animals at Reptiland's Flashlight Safari.

Although it doesn't offer wheelchair rentals, Reptiland is wheelchair accessible.

Elysburg

Knoebels Amusement Park and Campground
(ages 2 and up)

PA 487, about 12 miles south of Bloomsburg; (570) 672-2572 or (800) ITS–4FUN; www .knoebels.com. Open weekends in Apr, May, and Sept; daily in June, July, and Aug. Admission free to park; camping and cabins are $$$$. Individual ride prices are $. Pay-One-Price plans available Mon through Fri during the in-season.

If you've ever wondered what happened to the traditional amusement parks you remember from your own childhood, head to Knoebels (pronounced with a hard "k"). This park got its start at the turn of the twentieth century, when Henry Hartman Knoebel charged 25 cents to water, feed, and brush the horses that brought groups to swim on his property. After a few years he added picnic tables and sold ice cream and other snacks to the visitors. A pool, overnight cottages, and a carousel were added in 1926. By the 1940s Knoebels had graduated to an amusement resort.

Today Knoebels offers fifty rides (including two world-class roller coasters, the Phoenix and the Twister), a huge swimming pool, and a good selection of kiddie rides. There are several restaurants, snack bars, and picnic areas as well as a collection of shops and regularly scheduled entertainment. All of this is nestled among natural streams and shady hemlock trees that keep the temperatures here a good 10 degrees lower than elsewhere in the area.

If this sounds like too much for a day trip, stay the night—or longer—at one of 500 campsites and log cabins. Cabins sleep six and have electricity. Call (570) 672-9555 for campground information.

Lewisburg

A pretty Victorian town that is home to Bucknell University, Lewisburg is a good place to stop and stretch your legs or grab some lunch. There are some great historic homes in town that are open for tours. Although not geared for small children, older ones enjoy the tours.

Slifer House Museum (ages 6 and up)

80 Magnolia Dr.; (570) 524-2245; www.albrightcare.org/slifer-house. Open Apr 15 through Dec 31, Tues through Sun 1 to 4 p.m.; Jan 1 through Apr 14, Tues through Fri 1 to 4 p.m. or by appointment. Admission is $; children under 10 are free.

House tours aren't on most kids' Top 10 list, but the Slifer House has several exhibits that children six and older enjoy. An artifact quiz is designed to stimulate minds, both young and old. Among the favorites are the children's bedroom and old toys, a Regina music box, and the doctor's office, with antique medical tools. A sure hit with kids. Slifer House also hosts family activities such as Civil War encampments, storytelling, and workshops. The house is wrapped in Victorian excess for the Christmas holidays, including a floor-to-ceiling tree with nineteenth-century ornaments and garlands of roses over the dining-room table.

Packwood House Museum (ages 6 and up)

15 N. Water St.; (570) 524-0323; www.packwoodhousemuseum.com. Open Tues through Sat 10 a.m. to 5 p.m. Admission is $; children under 6 are free.

One of the oldest log-built structures in Pennsylvania, the Packwood House was originally constructed between 1796 and 1799. Christmas is a special time for children at the Packwood. Even younger children love seeing the decorations and lights. The rest of the year, the museum is more geared for school-age children. There is an impressive collection of antique furniture, glass, ceramics, textiles, and more at the Packwood.

Mifflinburg

In addition to the following sights, Mifflinburg serves as the headquarters for no fewer than four Pennsylvania state parks: McCalls Dam State Park (known for its fishing); R. B. Winter State Park (with lake swimming, environmental education, and camping); Ravensburg State Park (fishing, hiking, and camping); and Sand Bridge State Park (known for snowmobiling trails). For information on any one of these parks, call (570) 966-1455 or (888) PA–PARKS.

Mifflinburg Buggy Museum (ages 3 and up)

598 Green St.; (570) 966-1355; www.lycoming.org/buggy. Open May through Oct, Thurs through Sat 10 a.m. to 5 p.m., Sun 1 to 5 p.m. From Nov through Mar, closed Sun. Admission is $$ for adults and $ for children 6 to 17. Children under 6 enter free. Free parking.

The Mifflinburg Buggy Museum gives you a chance to see horse-drawn buggies up close. Through the late nineteenth century, Mifflinburg earned the nickname "Buggy Town" by producing roughly 5,000 horse-drawn vehicles a year, more per capita than any other town in Pennsylvania. Over an eighty-year period, the town was home to seventy-five separate buggy makers. Only one of these factories remains, the W. A. Heiss Coachworks, now part of the museum. The Mifflinburg Buggy Museum is the only known preserved nineteenth-century carriage shop, and it has all its original contents.

First stop at the visitor center to view the seven-minute introductory video and self-guided exhibit. The hands-on workbench includes a wheel that can be disassembled, tools to handle, a buggy engraving, coloring and word-find sheets kids can complete at the museum or take home, and more.

Then take a guided tour of the original factory, complete with tools and supplies; the Repository (showroom) with vehicles on display; and the family home. Recently reopened after restoration, the museum has also upgraded accessibility for wheelchair users and for the visually and hearing impaired. Each May the museum hosts the annual Mifflinburg Buggy Day Festival, featuring craft vendors, antiques dealers, live entertainment, food, activities for children, demonstrations, and buggy rides.

Christkindl Market (ages 2 and up)

Downtown Mifflinburg; (570) 966-1666; www.mifflinburgchristkindlmarket.com.

Another Mifflinburg traditional celebration is Christkindl Market, held Thurs through Sat, the second week of Dec. The festival re-creates a traditional German Christmas Market, with authentic food, seasonal music, and handmade gifts for sale. At 6 p.m. on Fri night, children participate in a beautiful Children's Lantern Parade. There's also a Santa's Workshop with crafts and games.

T&D's Cats of the World (all ages)

Penn's Creek; (570) 837-3377; www.tdscats.com. Open weekends May through Sept noon to 6 p.m. Admission is $$; children under 2 enter free. Group tours can be arranged throughout the year.

According to the Web site, the purpose of T&D's Cats of the World is "to rescue wildlife, especially exotic felines, from situations of abuse, mistreatment, and abandonment, when they are no longer wanted as pets." This effort began as a labor of love when the Mattive family (Terry, Donna, Jennifer, and T. J.) discovered how many exotic animals are abandoned when they outgrow the baby stage. Today, the entire Mattive family is involved in the care of eleven Bengal tigers, one Siberian tiger, eight African lions, nineteen cougars, five bobcats, three leopards, and twelve servals, plus smaller mammals such as skunks, coyotes, raccoons, river otters, and more.

McClure

Mountain Dale Farm (all ages)
Rural Route 2, Box 985, McClure 17841; (570) 658-3536; www.mountaindale.net. Open year-round.

If your family wants to experience farm life firsthand, then a vacation at Ken and Sally Hassinger's Mountain Dale Farm is just the ticket. This 175-acre farm is surrounded by state forest and game land, making it a complete getaway from civilization. But you don't have to rough it completely. The farm offers accommodations in a variety of cabins and efficiencies. Children under twelve are half price, and those under two years old stay **free.** Meals are provided at an extra cost upon request, but most visitors enjoy cooking in their own kitchens or in the common kitchen.

Kids love helping out with the barn chores and getting to know the sheep, goats, cattle, horses, geese, ducks, chickens, and dogs. Other activities include boating, fishing, swimming, or ice-skating on three ponds; cross-country skiing or hiking in the woods; or just relaxing on the front porch of your cabin. Come before Christmas and choose your own tree from the Christmas tree farm.

New Bloomfield

Little Buffalo State Park (all ages)
PA 34; (717) 567-9255; www.dcnr.state.pa.us/stateparks/parks/littlebuffalo.aspx. Open year-round. Free for most activities.

In Perry County, 830-acre Little Buffalo State Park has both historic and natural attractions. There's an eighty-eight-acre lake, a swimming pool (fee charged), hiking trails, fishing, and picnic areas. But there are also a covered bridge, a working gristmill from the 1800s, an old farmhouse, and a narrow-gauge railroad trace with an original railroad car. In winter there are 7 miles of cross-country trails, a sledding and tobogganing area, and a skating area on the lake (the rest of the lake is open for ice fishing in winter). There is no camping in the park, but the park ranger can furnish names of other campgrounds in the area.

Box Huckleberry Natural Area (all ages)
PA 34; (717) 536-3191; www.dcnr.state.pa.us. Open year-round. Free.

Just a few miles south of Little Buffalo State Park and technically part of Tuscarora State Forest, on PA 34 is the Box Huckleberry Natural Area, a special reserve for a box huckleberry plant estimated to be 1,300 years old. A short interpretive nature trail around the area is a favorite of small children. This is a good place to teach your kids about the importance of preserving our natural resources. Trail maps and a written history of the plant are available on-site.

New Germantown

Tuscarora State Forest (all ages)
PA 274, southwest of New Germantown; (717) 536-3191; www.dcnr.state.pa.us/forestry/
stateforests/tuscwild.aspx. Open year-round. Free.

Traveling southwest on PA 274 from New Germantown, you'll come upon the entrance to the Tuscarora State Forest—90,512 acres of amazing vistas, undisturbed areas, trout streams, state parks, hiking, snowmobiling, and more. The forest roads are well maintained, making a great route for a mild "off-road" driving experience. The Bureau of Forestry has developed a brochure that will guide you on a 26-mile auto tour of the forest. The dirt roads are in good shape, so you shouldn't need four-wheel drive to navigate the route in good weather.

Highlights in and around the state forest include: Hemlocks Natural Area, a 120-acre area of virgin hemlock forest with 3 miles of hiking trails; the Iron Horse Trail, a rails-to-trails project that provides 10 miles of hiking with only moderate climbing necessary; the Tuscarora Trail, a 22-mile side trail of the Appalachian Trail; Fowler Hollow State Park, with eighteen campsites and fishing in the creek; and Colonel Denning State Park, with fifty-two trailer and tent sites, excellent hiking, and an extensive environmental education program during summer months. For more information about the state forest and natural areas, contact the Bureau of Forestry, RD 1, Box 42-A, Blain 17006. For more information about the state parks within the forest, call (888) PA–PARKS.

Belleville

Everyone loves a farmers' market: rows of fresh vegetables, home-baked goods, handmade crafts, and the chance to meet the people who produce them. The town of Belleville may have the ultimate farmers' market.

Belleville Farmers Market (all ages)
South Penn Street, PA 655; (717) 935-2146. Open Mar through Dec, Wed during daylight hours. Free admission.

The Belleville Farmers Market takes place every Wed from six in the morning to six at night. The ten-acre Amish market has livestock yards, auction barns, and 400 flea-market stalls. It's a popular event, so be prepared to walk a ways from your car to the auction areas. For more information about the area, call the Juniata Valley Area Chamber of Commerce at (570) 248-6713. For information on this and other farmers' markets, check www.ams.usda.gov and select "Farmers Markets."

ALSO IN THE AREA

Mifflin County Trout Hatchery (ages 4 and up), PA 655, between Belleville and Reedsville; open Wed and Sat. While you're in the area, check out the hatchery, where children can fish for trout and pay only for what they catch. Fishing poles and bait are provided.

State College

A visit to a college campus is a great way to inspire a child's educational dreams. The home of Penn State University, one of the country's best public universities, State College has much to offer families.

Bolstered by the university population, State College is a thriving town with many hotels, shops, and restaurants. Many of the area's attractions are within an easy drive, making the town an ideal base for your explorations.

Penn State Creamery (all ages)

119 Food Science Building; (814) 865-7535; www.psu.edu. Open daily.

Kids of all ages scream for ice cream, and a trip to this ice-cream parlor is a tradition for Penn State alumni and their families. It's the largest university creamery in the nation. Each year approximately 3.5 million pounds of milk pass are processed into more than one hundred fabulous fresh flavors. Many are named for famous Penn Staters (try the Peachy Paterno). About half the milk comes from the university's own cows, the other half from an independent producer. The creamery's new location features a casual outdoor cafe with umbrella tables as well as indoor seating for eighty.

Central Pennsylvania Festival of the Arts (all ages)

Downtown State College; (814) 237-3682; www.arts-festival.com. Five days in July. Free admission.

State College is the site of the Central Pennsylvania Festival of the Arts, a five-day celebration that takes place in July each year. The first day of the festival is traditionally Children and Youth Day, featuring the creations of local children ages eight through eighteen and a wonderful procession through town in which children wear masks and carry their works of art. Life-size puppets also take part in the procession. Storytelling, marionette performances, concerts, and more round out this not-to-be-missed event. Organizers have made special attempts to include people with special needs, including those with visual impairments.

An O'Toole **Family Adventure**

After a summer week at sports camp on Penn State's beautiful campus, we scooped up our son James and headed for home. But first we stopped for another kind of scoop. The university's Creamery, with more than one hundred delicious ice cream and sherbet flavors, is a sweet end to any campus visit.

Frost Entomological Museum (ages 5 and up)

Headhouse 3, halfway between Shortlidge and Bigler Roads; (814) 863-2865; http://ento .psu.edu/facilities/frost. Open Mon through Fri 9:30 a.m. to 4:00 p.m. Free.

The Insect Zoo features a functional beehive plus a variety of insects and other arthopods such as scorpions, tarantulas, and cockroaches. Kids will get a kick out of it; parents may or may not.

Earth and Mineral Sciences Museum (ages 5 and up)

16 Deike Building, Pollock Road; (814) 865-6336; www.ems.psu.edu/museum. Open year-round Mon through Fri 9:30 a.m. to 5 p.m. Closed holidays. Free.

The halls of the Deike Building are lined with crystals, gems, carvings, and fossils. Kids especially like the ultraviolet light room that highlights minerals invisible under normal incandescent lights. The shrunken heads also get an enthusiastic reception from most kids.

Penn State Ice Pavilion (ages 2 and up)

Pollock and McKean Streets; (814) 865-4102.; www.pennstateicerink.psu.edu. Open to the public for part of most days. Call ahead for current hours. Admission is $. Skate rental is $.

After checking out the museums, you might want to take a spin around the indoor ice-skating rinks at the Ice Pavilion, in the Greenberg Indoor Sports Complex. The complex offers two rinks with superior surfaces.

Beaver Stadium (ages 5 and up)

University Drive and Curtin Road; (814) 863-1000 or (800) 833-5533. Various prices.

For many people the most famous aspect of Penn State is its football team. The Nittany Lions play in the Big Ten College Football League, and sports fans come from around the country to see a game at Beaver Stadium. For current schedules and tickets, call the aforementioned phone numbers or log onto www.psu.edu.

Bryce Jordan Center (ages 5 and up)

University Drive and Curtin Road; (814) 863-5500; www.psu.edu/sports/tickets.

Men's and women's basketball as well as a variety of special events take place across the street from Beaver Stadium at the Bryce Jordan Center. Call for schedules and tickets.

College of Agricultural Sciences (all ages)

Agriculture Administration Building, University Park; (814) 865-4433. Open 9 a.m. to 4 p.m. Free.

Check out the animals at the agricultural facilities of the College of Agricultural Sciences, near Beaver Stadium. See white-tailed deer, sheep, cattle, horses, and pigs. There's also an exhibit of flowering plants and vegetables.

Throughout the year special events are scheduled for the nearby Ag Arena. Check the marquee outside to see what's scheduled, or call ahead. Children especially enjoy the shows of horses or dairy cattle. Around Christmas, the Festival of Trees features more than one hundred different trees, decorated by area businesses and organizations.

Ag Progress Days and Jerome K. Pasto Agricultural Museum (all ages)

Russell E. Larson Agricultural Research Center, PA 45; (814) 863-1383; http://apd.psu.edu (for information on Ag Progress Days) or http://pasto.cas.psu.edu (museum information). Free.

Penn State's Ag Progress Days is one of the largest agricultural shows in the country. It takes place in mid-Aug each year and features live animal exhibitions, a petting zoo, computer-based games, demonstrations of the latest farming technologies, and displays of antique farm equipment. The Family and Youth Building has special programs just for kids.

On the same site as the Larson Agricultural Research Center, the Jerome K. Pasto Agricultural Museum traces the history of farming in America with displays of old tools and appliances from the days before electricity. It's open Apr 15 to Oct 15. Call ahead for scheduling information (814-865-8301). Admission is **free,** but donations are encouraged.

Millbrook Marsh Nature Center (all ages)

614 Puddintown Rd., State College; (814) 231-3071. Open year-round. Call ahead for current hours. Free admission.

A cooperative venture of many local educational organizations, this is the site for several nature programs conducted by the Shaver's Creek Environmental Center. The mission of the center is to educate and inspire people about the natural world and to instill a passion for the environment through science, history, culture, and art. Call for updated information and a schedule of events.

Stone Valley Recreation Area (all ages)

PA 1029, off PA 26 South; (814) 863-1164; www.psu.edu/stone_valley. Open year-round sunrise to sunset. Free.

After the hubbub of the active campus, this is a great place to come and wind down. Administered by Penn State, the Stone Valley Recreation Area has a wide variety of activities for all ages. Depending on the season you can enjoy boating (canoes, rowboats, or sailboats—all of which are available for rent), fishing (trout and bass), hayrides, hiking, ice-skating (rentals available), sledding, ice fishing, or cross-country skiing (lessons available). There are eleven wheelchair-accessible cabins for overnight accommodations. The one-room cabins are equipped with bunk beds, refrigerator, electric range top, electricity, and gas heat. There are central bathroom and shower facilities nearby. Bring your own linens and cooking and eating utensils. Call for rates and reservations.

Shaver's Creek Environmental Center (all ages)
PA 1029 (Charter Oak Road) off PA 26 South; (814) 863-2000; www.shaverscreek.org. Open mid-Jan to mid-Dec, 11 a.m. to 5 p.m. daily. Visitor and Raptor Center admission is $ per person; children under 3 are free.

Learn about the local wildlife and how injured eagles, hawks, owls, reptiles, and amphibians are cared for at this lovely environmental center. There's a bookstore with a good selection of books for children; you'll also find other wildlife accessories there. Special gardens attract butterflies, bees, and hummingbirds.

Shaver's Creek is the site of a wonderful day-camp program for children six and up. For children six to eleven, the Discovery and Explorer Camps run from Tues through Fri and end up with a family overnight at the camp.

Children twelve and up can choose from several different camp experiences. Raptor and More Camp (in which campers work with rehabilitated birds of prey), is for campers ages fourteen to seventeen.

Boalsburg

Looking for a special way to spend an upcoming three-day weekend? The town of Boalsburg has several claims to fame that make it a good destination any time of year. For Memorial Day weekend, how about visiting the place where the holiday got its start? Boalsburg has been commemorating this day since 1864, and today there are community picnics and parades to enjoy.

In July Boalsburg is the site of the Peoples' Choice Festival of Pennsylvania Arts and Crafts. The weekend of activities includes free museum tours for children, a petting zoo, and a stuffed-animal vet.

Columbus Day weekend coming up? What better place to get in touch with the explorer than at the Christopher Columbus Family Chapel, part of the Boal Mansion and Museum. And for Veterans Day, learn the history of our nation's veterans at the Pennsylvania Military Museum across US 322.

Boal Mansion and Museum (ages 6 and up)
300 Old Boalsburg Rd.; (814) 466-6210; www.boalmuseum.com. Open Tues through Sat 10 a.m. to 5 p.m., Sun noon to 5 p.m. summer to Labor Day; 1:30 to 5 p.m. in spring and fall; closed Mon. Admission is $$$ for adults and $$ for children 7 to 11; children under 7 enter free.

This historic house has an added attraction: original objects belonging to Christopher Columbus. Originally part of the Columbus family castle in Spain, the chapel contains heirlooms that date back to the 1400s. The *Wall Street Journal* called the collection "a strong tangible link to Columbus in the New World." Kids especially enjoy looking at the antique weapons and dresses and hearing stories about nine generations of the Boal family, across more than 210 years in the same house, continuing today.

Pennsylvania Military Museum and
Twenty-eighth Infantry Division Shrine (ages 7 and up)

PA 45 and Business US 322; (814) 466-6263; www.pamilmuseum.org. From Apr through Oct, open Tues through Sat 9 a.m. to 5 p.m. Nov through Mar, open Thurs through Sat 10 a.m. to 4 p.m., Sun noon to 4 p.m. Closed Mon except for Memorial Day, July Fourth and Labor Day. Call ahead for hours Nov through Mar. Admission fee charged. Senior citizen, youth, and group discounts available.

Built on the site of the Pennsylvania National Guard's shrine for service in the two World Wars of the twentieth century, the Pennsylvania Military Museum commemorates the service and sacrifice of Commonwealth veterans from the Spanish American War through Desert Storm. Pennsylvania citizen soldiers, sailors, airmen, marines, and industry are honored with exhibits on technology, tactics, and service. The shrine and museum are situated within a sixty-seven-acre parklike setting that includes walking/bike paths and a covered picnic pavilion, only a short walk away from historic Boalsburg. On-site public programming includes "Celebration of Service: Honoring Pennsylvania Veterans" on the third Sunday in May; "World War Two Revisited" with reenactors bivouacking on the ground on Memorial Day Weekend; and the People's Choice Arts Festival in July. For more information on these and other events, go to www.boalsburgcentral.com/specialevents.html. This museum is one of twenty-six sites administered by the Pennsylvania Historical and Museum Commission (www.phmc .state.pa.us).

Cave Exploration

Woodward Cave and Penn's Cave may get most of the attention, but central Pennsylvania actually has hundreds of fascinating caves and caverns. If you're interested in doing some cave exploring that's a bit off the beaten path, contact the Nittany Grotto, headquartered in State College. This group of enthusiastic cave explorers encourages safe and responsible cave exploring. Its members are pleased to arrange Beginner Trips. In order to take advantage of this service, families may be asked to join the group at a cost of $10 a year. For more information contact the group's Web site at www.clubs.psu .edu/nittanygrotto.

Tussey Mountain Ski Resort (ages 3 and up)

301 Bear Meadows Rd.; (814) 466-6266 or (800) 733-2754; www.tusseymountain.com. Open year-round.

Heading east from State College on US 322 is Tussey Mountain Ski Resort, a great place for family skiing and snowboarding. At the Kid's Mountain Learning Center, children ages three to six can ski in a specially designed learning area. They can even join a Paw Prints group and enjoy instructed play and an introduction to skiing. The Mountain Lion group, for children six to ten years old, is aimed at building children's skiing skills. Both classes run two hours and are scheduled twice a day on weekdays and three times a day on weekends. Tussey Mountain also offers Avalanche Canyon, a snow-tubing area. There's a Winter-Break Camp for kids six and up when they're off from school for the holidays.

Summer activities include concerts, batting cages, go-karts, fishing, and more.

Eastern Centre County

Just east of State College are several small towns with worthwhile attractions for families. Here are a few of the best.

Penn's Cave (ages 4 and up)

PA 192, 5 miles east of Centre Hall; (814) 364-1664; www.pennscave.com. Open 9 a.m. to 5 p.m. Mar 1 to Dec 31 (weekends only in Dec and Feb). Admission is $$$ for adults and $ for children 2 to 12.

Penn's Cave has been attracting visitors for centuries, since the Seneca Indians discovered it. It has been a tourist attraction since the late 1800s, when a hotel was built on the site.

Penn's Cave is the country's only water-filled cave, and tours are given by motorboat. Along the hour-long ride you'll see amazing stalactites and stalagmites in a series of "rooms." Colored lights illuminate formations with names like the Statue of Liberty, Chinese Dragon, and Niagara Falls. If you're lucky, you'll spot some of the bats that live in the cave.

No matter what the temperature outside, it's always 52 degrees inside the cave, so bring a jacket in summertime. Some children are initially scared by the dark and the idea of being underground; however, most become more comfortable as they get involved in spotting the formations and enjoying the colored lights. According to tour guides, the temperament of the child is more of a factor than age.

But there's more to Penn's Cave than the cave. There's also 1,000 acres with an operating farm and a wildlife sanctuary with elk, mountain lions, deer, wolves, and mustangs. Professional guides take you through the park in four-wheel-drive vehicles, pointing out animals and telling about their habits. Tours last about one and a half hours. The sanctuary is open daily Mar through Nov. Call ahead for rates and reservations.

In Sept Penn's Cave is also the site of the Nittany Antique Machinery annual show. Model trains, tractor parades, demonstrations of antique machinery, toy tractors, and a children's pedal pull are among the attractions.

Woodward Cave and Campground (ages 4 and up)

PA 45, Woodward; (814) 349-9800; www.woodwardcave.com. Open daily 9 a.m. to 5 p.m. in summer, 10 a.m. to 4 p.m. in spring and fall. Closed Nov through Mar. Admission is $$ for adults, $ for children 3 to 12, and **free** for children 2 and under.

If Penn's Cave has whet your appetite for spelunking, head back to PA 45 and continue east to Woodward Cave and Campground, one of the largest caverns in Pennsylvania. A sixty-minute tour takes you through the five rooms of the cavern, each filled with rock formations. The Hanging Forest features a large collection of stalactites. In the Hall of Statues, see one of the largest stalagmites in the United States: the Tower of Babel. If you're planning to camp in the area, inquire about the nineteen-acre campground with sites for tents as well as RVs. Cabin rentals are also available.

Camp Woodward (ages 7 to 18)

134 Sports Camp Dr., Woodward; (814) 349-5520; www.woodwardcamp.com.

"A school for how to have fun" is how Camp Woodward describes itself. It's an extreme sports paradise, with runs, ramps, tramps, and rails for skateboarders, BMXers, cheerleaders, gymnasts, and snowboarders, who attend one-week training sessions. There's also the Woodward Getaway, which invites families to visit for weekends. Stay in the lodge and try out all the coolest offerings, including exclusive use of the Lot-8 and Cloud Nine indoor training facilities (the camp requires that parents stay to watch kids' every death-defying move). The package is offered weekends from mid-Sept to May.

Bellefonte

About 12 miles north of State College on PA 26, you'll find Bellefonte, the county seat for Centre County. This lovely Victorian town celebrated its bicentennial in 1996, and things are hopping still.

With a historic district of more than 300 buildings, taking a walking tour through this town is like taking a walk back in time. The town is especially beautiful when decked out for a Victorian Christmas each December (call 814-355-2917 or check www.bellefonte .com for more information).

Bellefonte Museum for Centre County (ages 5 and up)

133 Allegheny St.; (814) 355-4280; www.bellefontemuseum.org. Open year-round. Admission charged. Call for schedule and rates.

The goal of the Bellefonte Museum is to promote appreciation of the area's heritage, especially among children. The hard-working volunteer staff visits schools and has set up exhibits around town. The museum is now housed in the historic Benner–Linn House, donated to the town by the Omega Bank next door. The exhibits change at least three times per year and are designed for both children and adults.

Bellefonte Festivals

The Victorian Christmas is the biggest festival in Bellefonte's schedule, but there are several more that are worth checking out. In mid-May come for the Big Spring Festival, which celebrates the spring that supplies the town with water. For more information and this year's schedule, call (814) 355-1458.

In June the streets of Bellefonte fill with antique and vintage automobiles as the town re-creates a Historic Cruise, that lapping-the-block ritual favored by teens in the 1950s. August brings the annual Bellefonte Arts and Crafts fair, with area craftspeople exhibiting and selling their creations and with special events for children.

Bellefonte Historical Railroad (all ages)

Train Station, High Street; (814) 355-1053; www.bellefontetrain.org. Various excursions throughout the year, mostly on weekends. Call (814) 355-2917 for schedules and prices,

On weekends from Memorial Day to Labor Day, the railroad offers trips to Curtin Village (described below), Sayers Dam (a nice place for a picnic), the town of Lemont, or the gliderport at Julian. In fall the route takes you to Bald Eagle Ridge, aflame with autumn leaves. The Santa Claus Express in Dec features a visit from you-know-who. Other excursions are offered throughout the year.

Eagle Iron Works and Curtin Village (ages 4 and up)

PA150, 2 miles north of I-80; (814) 355-1982; www.boggstownship.org. Open weekends in May, Sept, and Oct; Wed through Sun during summer. It is also open in mid-Dec for Christmas at Curtin. Call for current hours and rates.

Heading north on PA 150 from Bellefonte, stop off at Eagle Iron Works and Curtin Village, a historic site that gives a glimpse of life in the 1800s. Or take an excursion on the Bellefonte Historic Railroad to Curtin. There's a restored iron furnace, the iron master's mansion, and a worker's log cabin. Throughout the year the museum holds special events, including craft shows, Civil War encampments, and antique tool demonstrations.

Where to Eat

IN WILLIAMSPORT

Bonanza Steak House, 1503 E. Third St.; (570) 326-7114.

Hoss's Steak and Sea House, 1954 E. Third St.; (570) 326-0838.

Manhattan Bagel, 1790 E. Third St.; (570) 322-4500.

Olive Garden, 1825 E. Third St.; (570) 321-9250.

Peter Herdic House, 407 W. Fourth St.; (570) 322-0165. A little more formal but family oriented, offering a variety of traditional meats, seafood, pasta, and salad. Open Tues through Sat.

Red Lobster, 1951 E. Third St.; (570) 323-0423.

Vinnie's Italian Eatery, 44 W. Fourth St.; (570) 326-1998.

IN STATE COLLEGE
Original Waffle Shop, 1610 W. College Ave.; (814) 235-1816. Open daily. A campus tradition, with fast service and massive breakfasts.

The Tavern Restaurant, 220 E. College St.; (814) 238-6116. Offers a variety of steaks, seafood, chicken, and salads. Children's menu has chicken nuggets, burgers, etc., and side dishes. Relaxed atmosphere.

Where to Stay
IN WILLIAMSPORT
Best Western Williamsport, 1840 E. Third St.; (570) 326-1981 or (800) 780-7234; www .bestwesternpa.com. This hotel complex offers some great features for families—an outdoor pool, free Disney channel, on-site restaurants—plus kids stay and eat free. In summer a "Pool-side King Room" may be the best choice for families. Features include a king-size bed plus pull-out sofa just steps from the pool.

Genetti Hotel, 200 W. Fourth St.; (800) 321-1388. Located in downtown Williamsport, this full-service historic hotel offers suites as well as standard guest rooms. An on-site pool and restaurant make it a good choice for families.

Holiday Inn, 100 Pine St.; (800) 325-3535. The Holiday Inn has two clinchers that make this hotel a hit with kids: an indoor pool and Nintendo-equipped televisions. And the hotel's kids-eat-free policy at the on-site restaurant makes it a hit with parents, too.

IN LEWISBURG
Best Western Country Cupboard Inn, US 15 North; (570) 524-5500. Hotel, restaurant, and gift shop all in one complex.

Days Inn Lewisburg, US 15; (570) 523-1171. Perkins Family Restaurant on premises.

IN THE STATE COLLEGE AREA
Many of the major hotel/motel and restaurant chains have facilities in and near State College. Here are a few to check out:

Bellefonte/State College KOA Campground, 2481 Jacksonville Rd., Bellefonte; (814) 355-7912 or (800) KOA–8127. Full-service campground with cabin rentals available. Heated outdoor pool.

Courtyard by Marriott, 1730 University Dr., State College; (814) 238-1881. An indoor pool, suites, and an on-site restaurant make this a good choice for families.

Days Inn Penn State, 240 South Pugh St., State College; (814) 238-8454 or (800) 258-DAYS. Just blocks from campus, the Days Inn has on-site parking, a restaurant/sports bar, and an indoor pool. Mad Mex restaurant on-site.

The Nittany Lion Inn, 200 W. Park Ave., State College; (814) 231-7500 or (800) 233-7505. Colonial-style inn on the Penn State campus.

Ramada Inn State College, 1450 S. Atherton St., State College; (814) 238-3001 or (800) HOLIDAY. Two outdoor swimming pools make this an especially good choice in the summer.

State College Super 8 Motel, 1663 South Atherton St., Business US 322, State College; (814) 237-8005 or (800) 635-1177. Continental breakfast on-site included; restaurant across parking lot.

For More Information

Bellefonte Tourism Commission; (814) 355-2917; www.bellefonte.com.

Central Pennsylvania Convention and Visitors Bureau, 800 E. Park Ave., State College 16803; (814) 231-1400 or (800) 358-5466; www.visitpennstate.org or www.central pacvb.org.

Columbia–Montour Visitors Bureau; (570) 784-8279 or (800) 847-4810; www.itour columbiamontour.com.

Lycoming County Tourist Promotion Agency; (570) 377-7700 or (800) 358-9900; www.williamsport.org.

Susquehanna Valley Visitors Bureau; (570) 524-7234 or (800) 525-7320; www.visit centralpa.org.

Pennsylvania's
Northern
Tier

Pennsylvania has the largest rural population in the country. That means there are more people living in towns of fewer than 2,500 people here than in any other state. Although all of the regions covered in this book have many towns that meet that description, along Pennsylvania's Northern Tier it's hard to find towns that don't. There are large stretches of this region that remain wilderness—and provide wonderful opportunities for camping, boating, hiking, skiing, and more.

Scenic US 6 traverses the northern tier of Pennsylvania, passing some of the region's best-loved sights and towns. For information about scenic US 6, call 1-87-PAROUTE6 or

TopPicks in Pennsylvania's Northern Tier

- **Splash Lagoon Indoor Waterpark,** Erie

- **Pine Creek Gorge,** Ansonia

- **Ole Bull State Park,** Cross Fork

- **Crook Farm and Country Fair,** Bradford

- **expERIEnce Children's Museum,** Erie

- **Heart's Content National Natural Landmark,** Allegheny National Forest, Warren

- **Cook Forest Sawmill Center for the Arts,** Cooksburg

- **Presque Isle State Park,** Erie

- **Erie Maritime Museum and the U.S. Brig *Niagara***

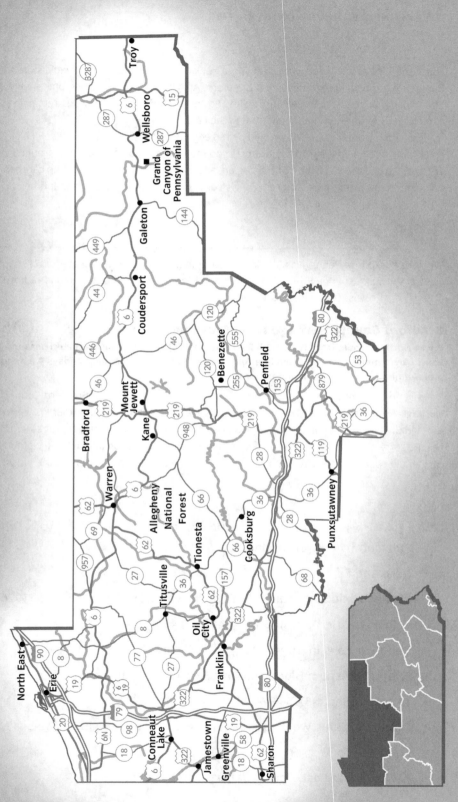

PENNSYLVANIA'S NORTHERN TIER

check the Web at www.paroute6.com. Pine Creek Gorge, billed as Pennsylvania's Grand Canyon, is a spectacular achievement of nature. Allegheny National Forest, one of only fifteen national forests in the eastern United States, harbors some of the last remaining virgin stands of northern hardwoods left in the East.

This is a big area. Our advice would be to keep your ambitions within limits. Pick a state park, a town, or a sight that interests you most, and build your vacation around it. Try to see more than a portion of this region, and you'll spend more time in the car than enjoying its many offerings. You can always come back to see more at another time.

Troy

We start our tour of Pennsylvania's Northern Tier in the town of Troy, located on US 6 just west of the Susquehanna River. Please note that the town of Bradford is not in Bradford County, but Troy is. This leads to some confusion.

Bradford County Heritage Farm Museum (all ages)
PA 14 North, 0.5 mile from Troy; (570) 297-3410 or (570) 297-3405 during the off-season; www.troyfarmmuseum.org. Open late Apr through Oct, Fri to Mon and holidays 9 a.m. to 4 p.m. Admission is $; children under 6 are free.

Young and old alike will enjoy "The Farm Museum," established by the Bradford County Heritage Association on the Troy Fairgrounds. Local resident and dairy farmer Wilmer Wilcox's impressive collection of farm antiques is on display. The displays work together to tell the story of rural farm life in Bradford County. There's a kitchen and antique clothing and an old country store. The association has recently begun work to restore the oldest

TopEvents in Pennsylvania's Northern Tier

- **Punxsutawney's Groundhog Day**, Feb; (800) 752-PHIL.
- **Herb and Fiber Festival in Cooksburg**, June; (814) 927-6655.
- **Pennsylvania State Laurel Festival in Wellsboro**, June; (570) 724-1926.
- **Celebrate Erie Days in Erie**, Aug; (570) 454-7191.
- **Dan Rice Days in Girard**, Aug; (814) 774-3535.
- **Erie Art Museum Blues and Jazz Festival**, Aug; (814) 459-5477.
- **Troy Fair**, Sept; (570) 297-3648.
- **Fabulous 1890s weekend in Mansfield**, end of Sept; (570) 662-3442.
- **Erie ZooBoo**, Oct; (814) 864-4091.
- **Fall Pumpkin Fest**, Conneaut Lake; (814) 213-0022.

house in Troy Township, built in 1822, adjacent to the current museum. Formerly an inn on the stagecoach route, it houses period furniture, glassware, and antique toys and clothing. Portions of this house are open for tours.

During the Fall Carriage, Wagon, and Sleigh Festival in mid-Sept, children six and older enjoy the flax demonstration, blacksmithing, carpentry, tinsmithing, and stories of how chores were done in the past—from butter making with a dog-treadle butter churn to laundry with washboards and wringers. Throughout the season the heritage gardens display heirloom varieties of vegetables, plants used to make dyes, herbs, and perennials.

The museum is open daily during the Troy Fair, a typical country fair with farm animals, agricultural displays, and amusements. The fair has usually been held each year, for more than one hundred years, toward the end of July. For more information about the Troy Fair, call (570) 297-3648.

Wellsboro Area

Located on scenic US 6 in Tioga County, Wellsboro is an ideal base for adventures in Pine Creek Gorge, Pennsylvania's Grand Canyon. Forty-seven miles long with a maximum cliff height of 1,450 feet, this majestic canyon is surrounded by four state parks and hundreds of thousands of wilderness acres to explore by boat, foot, horseback, snowmobile, cross-country skis, mountain bike, and more. For information check www.visittiogapa.com.

Colton Point State Park (ages 8 and up)

Five miles south of US 6 at Ansonia; (570) 724-3061; www.dcnr.state.pa.us/stateparks/ parks/coltonpoint.aspx. Open year-round.

Perhaps the easiest way to get a glimpse of the Pine Creek Gorge is to head south from US 6 at Ansonia. There's a sign there that directs you to the park. The drive follows the rim, with short trails that lead to views over the canyon. Although there are guardrails at official overlooks, make sure children don't run ahead or roughhouse near the edge.

In addition to great views, Colton Point offers family camping, hiking trails, snowmobiling, and picnic areas. Most of the trails involve steep terrain and are recommended for experienced hikers aged eight and up.

Leonard Harrison State Park (ages 8 and up)

PA 660, 10 miles west of Wellsboro; (570) 724-3061; www.dcnr.state.pa.us/stateparks/ parks/leonardharrison.aspx. Open year-round.

Leonard Harrison State Park is on the east rim of the canyon. It offers one of the best views of the canyon anywhere. Stop at the visitor center to learn about the history of the canyon. Camping is available, and there are hiking trails of varying length and difficulty. Experienced family hikers (ages eight and up) won't want to miss the Turkey Path, a steep, 1-mile journey that takes you from the rim of the canyon down to Pine Creek.

Greater Mansfield Chamber of Commerce Celebrates the **Fabulous 1890s**

Every September, the town and university team up to host the Fabulous 1890s weekend. The event commemorates the first night football game, in which Mansfield University played Wyoming Seminary on September 28, 1892. The entire Mansfield community comes out to celebrate with a motorless parade, a balloon rally, a football reenactment, and fireworks. For more information on other events and festivals in Mansfield, call (570) 662-3442 or check www .mansfieldorg.com.

Pine Creek Trail (all ages)

Trailheads at US 6 in Ansonia and at PA 414 in Blackwell. Open year-round. Restrooms at trailheads. Call (570) 724-3061.

In an ongoing rails-to-trails project, 60.5 miles of the abandoned Conrail Railway along Pine Creek have been converted into a trail for hiking, biking, horseback riding, and other nonmotorized transportation. The relatively flat, groomed trail is wonderful for family hiking. The trail is wheelchair accessible and perfect for all-terrain strollers. The less strenuous Ansonia access is recommended for families.

If you'd like to tour Pine Creek Trail on a covered wagon, call Mountain Trail Canyon Wagon Rides at (877) 376-5561, or go to www.mountaintrailhorse.com.

Pine Creek Outfitters (ages 6 and up)

5142 US 6, Wellsboro; (570) 724-3003; www.pinecrk.com.

Whether you're looking for trail maps, equipment rentals, shuttles to trailheads, camping permits, guide service, or you-name-it, the folks at Pine Creek Outfitters are the ones to talk to. From kayaking to canoeing, biking to hiking, if they can't provide it themselves, they'll point you in the right direction. For families with young children, they particularly recommend their Upper Pine half-day trip, which navigates a calm section of the creek. There is no minimum age on this trip; others have a minimum age of seven. Pine Creek Outfitters also rents bikes and offers several useful guidebooks to the canyon.

Tioga Trail Rides (ages 8 and up)

PA 105, 536 Broughton Hollow Rd.; (570) 724-6592.

Tioga Trail Rides offers western riding on day rides or overnight trips. Children without experience must be at least twelve years old; younger children are allowed on shorter rides if they can control their horses and have an inseam of at least 21 inches (gotta be able to reach the stirrups!). Sunset and supper rides are also available. During winter Tioga Trail Rides offers bobsled rides.

Mountain Trail Horse Center (ages 8 and up)

Wellsboro; (877) 376-5561; www.mountaintrailhorse.com. Open spring through fall.

Mountain Trail Horse Center offers a wide variety of horseback rides designed as wilderness adventure. Covered-wagon rides are good for families of varying ages and abilities. There's no age minimum on the rides through the gorge. During the twice-yearly Family Vacation Horseback Adventures, the minimum age for overnight trips is dropped to eight (from the usual twelve). Longer trips are available. Rates go down per person with groups of more than four people.

Tioga Central Railroad (all ages)

P.O. Box 269, Wellsboro 16901; (570) 724-0990; www.tiogacentral.com. Various rates.

Take the 24-mile round-trip excursion from the station near Wellsboro to the north end of Hammond Lake, near the New York State border. The trip takes about an hour and twenty minutes and runs three times a day on weekends.

ALSO IN THE AREA

Hills Creek State Park, East of Wellsboro; (570) 724-4246; www.dcnr.state.pa.us/state parks/parks/hillscreek.aspx. One hundred ten campsites, cabins available; 137-acre lake.

Geocaching in Pennsylvania

It's the latest thing! Geocaching is a new kind of outdoor adventure for the twenty-first century. All you need is a GPS receiver, a set of coordinates, and some friends. GPS refers to Global Positioning System, a handheld electronic device that monitors your approximate position by satellite. The satellite determines your coordinates in latitude and longitude. In Pennsylvania, towns such as Allentown, Bethlehem, Easton, Harrisburg, Lancaster, Philadelphia, Pittsburgh, Punxsutawney, Scranton, St. Marys, Williamsport, and York all have caches hidden.

The goal of the game is to use your GPS to locate a "cache"—a "treasure"—hidden somewhere, using your GPS unit to navigate from your original position to the cache. Usually the cache turns out to be a strongbox containing surprises like small toys, CDs, or objects hidden by other geocachers. Some contain a disposable camera, but that isn't one of the prizes; it's so that the finder can take a picture of him or herself and leave it behind for the owner of the cache. After opening the cache, leave something behind for the next geocacher to find.

If you'd like to see what all the fun is about, go to www.geocaching.com and type the name of the area you want to visit.

Little Pine State Park, Waterville; (570) 753-6000; www.dcnr.state.pa.us/stateparks/parks/littlepine.aspx. One hundred four campsites; ninety-four-acre lake; hiking, biking, and cross-country ski trails; nature programs and swimming in summer.

Galeton Area

Home of the Pennsylvania Lumber Museum and headquarters for four state parks, Galeton has a full roster of events and activities for families.

Pennsylvania Lumber Museum (ages 6 and up)

5660 US 6 West, P.O. Box 239, Galeton 16922; 12 miles west of Galeton; (814) 435-2652; www.lumbermuseum.org. Open daily Apr through Nov 9 a.m. to 5 p.m. Closed major holidays. Admission is $; children under 6 are free.

From Wellsboro head west on US 6 to the Galeton area to enjoy a visit to the Pennsylvania Lumber Museum. Antique tools and other logging artifacts tell the story of this area's logging history. Tour a real logging camp and sawmill. A restored Barnhart Log Loader also included in the display. The museum is the site for several unusual special events throughout the year, including the Bark Peeler's Convention the weekend closest to July Fourth.

Lyman Run State Park (all ages)

454 Lyman Run Rd., Galeton; (814) 435-5010; www.dcnr.state.pa.us/stateparks/parks/lymanrun.aspx. Open year-round.

Lyman Run acts as the headquarters for three other state parks in the area: Cherry Springs, Patterson, and Prouty Place. Lyman Run offers trout fishing, ice fishing, swimming, and camping. Cherry Springs has picnic areas, hiking trails, hunting, snowmobile trails, and a campground. It's also the site of the Woodsmen's Carnival in early Aug. Patterson State Park offers picnicking, hiking, and camping. Prouty Place State Park is known for its picnic areas, cold-water fishing, hiking, and camping.

Ole Bull State Park (all ages)

Off PA 144, Cross Fork; (814) 435-5000 or (888) PA–PARKS for reservations; www.dcnr.state.pa.us/stateparks/parks/olebull.aspx. Open year-round.

About 20 miles south of Galeton is the Lodge at Ole Bull State Park, voted by *Condé Nast Traveler* magazine as Pennsylvania's top getaway. The lodge is actually a three-bedroom log cabin built by the Civilian Conservation Corps in the 1930s. It sleeps ten comfortably and is well equipped with everything you need for a woodsy adventure. It even has a playground out back for the kids. The first floor is wheelchair accessible. Book your reservations early (up to eleven months in advance). This is the kind of place where people come back each year.

Even if you're not lucky enough to book a week at the lodge, Ole Bull is still a great place for a family adventure. There are 81 tent and trailer sites along Kettle Creek, some with electrical hookups. Swimming, hiking, fishing, and biking also are all available in the secluded 125-acre park. During summer weekends there's a full schedule of environmental education programs.

Coudersport

Coudersport (pronounced *COW-dersport*) has the brightest lights in Potter County, which calls itself "God's Country." But folks here are actually proud of their dark nighttime skies—the better to see the stars.

Cherry Springs State Park (all ages)
4639 Cherry Springs Rd.; (814) 435-5010; www.dcnr.state.pa.us/stateparks/parks/cherry springs.aspx. Admission: **free.**

Located atop a 2,300-foot mountain, Cherry Springs has the darkest nighttime skies in the eastern United States. The 360-degree views from its Astronomy Field are favorites of professional stargazers. Once a month during warm weather, during the dark of the moon, Cherry Springs also offers public stargazing events. The evenings begin with a slide show that explains the basics of stargazing and the objects on view. As the sky gets darker, leaders use a special high-power green laser beam to point out the prominent constellations and other interesting sky sights. Then it's on to the binoculars to explore the skies. Children are welcome, but organizers ask parents to make sure they are quiet and well behaved.

Penfield

Parker Dam State Park and S. B. Elliot State Park (all ages)
Off PA 153; (814) 765-0630 or (888) PA–PARKS for reservations; www.dcnr.state.pa.us/stateparks/parks/parkerdam.aspx. Open year-round.

There are some great family programs available at Parker Dam State Park and S. B. Elliot State Park. Parker Dam offers a variety of naturalist programs for families, starting with Maple Sugar Weekends in March all the way through Apple Cider Sundays in the fall. During summer there are bat programs, evening campfire talks on the weekends, and even a guided trip to see the elk herd. In summer you can swim in the twenty-acre lake.

The camping here is class A, which means hot showers are available. There are also rustic log-frame and stone cabins available for rent year-round. There's no running water in the cabins, but there's a separate building with showers. A big fireplace supplies the heat, a refrigerator stores your perishables, and you can cook with an electric stove.

S. B. Elliot State Park offers a quieter setting on top of a hill. There are six cabins here and some class B campsites, but no flush toilets or showers.

Bradford

In Bradford your kids can get french fries with a side of crude oil. They'll get a giggle in the parking lot of the McDonald's restaurant on Main Street, where they'll see Cline Oil Well #1 pumping out dozens of gallons each day, just as it has since the 1870s. You'll see other private wells dotting front yards throughout the region—this is the heart of oil country, one of Pennsylvania's earliest industries. Please note that the town of Bradford is not in Bradford County. It's in McKean County.

Penn–Brad Oil Museum (ages 6 and up)

US 219; (814) 362-1955; www.pennbradoilmuseum.com. Open daily Memorial Day through Labor Day, Tues through Sat 10 a.m. to 4 p.m. and Sun noon to 5 p.m. Admission is $$ for adults and $ for seniors; children under 12 are free.

This museum traces the state's involvement in oil drilling and includes a working example of the 1890s-style wooden oil rig that once dotted the countryside.

Crook Farm and Country Fair (all ages)

US 219, third exit north of Bradford; (814) 362-6730 in spring through fall or (814) 362-3906 in the off-season. Open Tues through Fri afternoons during May through Sept and various times throughout the year. Call ahead for hours and admission prices. $

The Crook Farm is a collection of restored buildings from the 1800s, including a farmhouse, a one-room schoolhouse, barn, herb garden, tool house, train depot, and outbuildings. At the end of August, join the celebration at the Crook Farm Country Fair with crafts, food, entertainment, and special events for children. For information contact the Bradford Chamber of Commerce at www.bradfordchamber.com.

Zippo/Case Visitors Center (ages 6 and up)

1932 Zippo Dr., off US 219; (888) 442-1932; www.zippo.com and www.wrcase.com. Open Mon through Sat 9 a.m. to 5 p.m. and Sun 11 a.m. to 4 p.m. On Thurs open until 7 p.m. Admission is free.

Here's something you don't see every day: a collection of antique and rare Zippo lighters and cases. For the uninitiated, Zippo Manufacturing has been making "windproof" lighters with a lifetime guarantee since 1932. The company also makes steel tape measures, knives, money clips, pens, and key holders. Zippo products are popular among collectors, with swap meets and collector's clubs around the world. The Zippo/Case Visitors Center is the most-visited museum in Pennsylvania's Northern Tier.

Sights of **St. Mary's**

From Bradford head south on US 219 into Elk County, home of one of the two free-roaming elk herds east of the Mississippi—and the only one in Pennsylvania, now numbering more than 800. One of the best places to spot the herd is near the airport in St. Marys. The Winslow Hill viewing area is located near the town of Benezette, near Elk State Forest on PA 555.

Here's where you'll find an interpretive display about the herd, overlooking a beautiful valley where they are often found. Elk experts frequently make presentations at the nearby amphitheater.

Early morning and late afternoon are the best times to see elk. And once you hear them, you'll never forget the sound. A male elk's "bugle," or mating call, is one of the strangest songs you've ever heard. Or herd.

For information check the Web site www.pagreatoutdoors.com and click on "Elk Herd." You can download an Elk Scenic Drive map. You can even view the elk live via Web cam. For a free elk viewing guidebook, call Northwest Pennsylvania's Great Outdoors at (800) 348-9393. Remember, feeding the elk is against the law.

Zippo/Case Visitors Center attracts thousands of visitors from all over the world. More than 2,000 Zippo products are on display. New exhibits include "ZAC" (the Zippo/Case audio kinetic sculpture) and a 14-foot flag made entirely of Zippo lighters. Definitely not just another roadside attraction.

ALSO IN THE AREA

Holgate Toy Store and Museum (all ages), 200 Biddle St., Kane; (800) 343-8114; www.holgatetoy.com. Open daily year-round. Windows and a video allow you to see these charming toys being made at the toy factory. Kids love the trolley cars based on Mr. Rogers' Village of Make-Believe.

Allegheny Arms and Armor Museum (ages 5 and up), PA 46, Smethport; (814) 558-6112; www.armormuseum.com. Open daily 365 days a year, 10 a.m. to 6 p.m. Wheelchair accessible. Kids love this military museum with its changing displays of helicopters, tanks, vehicles, armor, and more. Living History Days, during the third week in June, offers the chance to see actual encampments and reenacted battles. Admission is free.

Warren

Allegheny National Forest　(all ages)　⊗◉Ⓐ

222 Liberty St., P.O. Box 847, Warren 16365; (814) 723-5150; www.fs.fed.us/r9/forests/
allegheny. Open year-round.

With more than a half million acres, there's room for many a family adventure within the
boundaries of Allegheny National Forest, the only national forest in Pennsylvania.

You will find a working forest when you visit the Allegheny. Congress mandates that
national forests be managed for a variety of uses, using techniques that ensure future
generations will be able to enjoy the benefits of these lands. Recreation, logging, and
wildlife habitat improvements are just some of the many activities going on in Allegheny
National Forest.

Several towns act as good bases for explorations of the forest, including Warren,
Marienville, Bradford, Ridgway, Tionesta, and Kane. Warren serves as the headquarters
for the forest, but there are information centers in Marienville and Marshburg. Before
planning your trip, be sure to get a copy of the **free** outdoor recreation map of the
Allegheny National Forest Region, available at tourist information centers or by calling
ahead. It displays the small roads of the forest much more clearly than most road maps.

The forest has just about everything a family adventurer looks for: camping (developed and backwoods), fishing, hiking, ATV trails, horseback riding, snowmobiling,
cross-country skiing, and hunting. There are nearly 200 miles of hiking trails, 700 miles of
streams, two Wild and Scenic Rivers, and several lakes and reservoirs within the forest.

But if you only have a few hours to explore the forest, head to Heart's Content, a
National Natural Landmark that harbors one of the last stands of old-growth forest in the
eastern United States. The turnoff from US 62 is easy to miss (it's just before the bridge to
Tidioute). Stop at the Tidioute Overlook, where an easy path leads to two vistas over the
river gorge. Look carefully; it's not unusual to see a bald eagle circling over the river. At
Heart's Content, there's a 1-mile interpretive trail. White pines and hemlocks that are hundreds of years old reach high into the sky.

Although no motorized vehicles are allowed in the old-growth forest, there are several excellent scenic drives through other parts of
the forest. US 62 follows the Allegheny
River from Tionesta to Warren; the
Allegheny Reservoir Scenic Drive
circles the large lake formed by
the Kinzua Dam; and the Long-
house Scenic Drive starts at the
Kinzua Dam and includes other area
highlights.

Mount Jewett

Kinzua Bridge State Park (all ages)

Off US 6, Ormsby Road; (814) 965-2646; www.dcnr.state.pa.us/stateparks/parks/
kinzuabridge.aspx. Open year-round.

Stop at the state park and take a look at the bridge and have a picnic. When it was built in
1882, it was the world's highest railroad bridge—called "the eighth wonder of the world."

Tionesta

Flying W Ranch (all ages)

PA 666; (814) 463-7663; www.theflyingwranch.com. Children must be 4 feet, 6 inches tall.

Another highlight of the Allegheny National Forest is the Flying W Ranch, on PA 666, 12
miles west of Tionesta. This 500-acre working ranch sits within the boundaries of the
national forest and offers countless opportunities for adventure. Spend an hour or a week
here taking western riding lessons, canoeing on the Allegheny River, hiking, fishing, and
more. In July come for the professional Allegheny Mountain Championship Rodeo. For a
real adventure, go on one of the overnight horseback trips into the national forest.

Accommodations range from bunkhouses to cabins, or you can bring your RV and
hook up at the campground. In summer the ranch offers a western riding camp for children ages six to fourteen.

Cooksburg

Not only does this area harbor one of the largest stands of virgin hemlock and pine forests in the East, it is also home to a thriving arts center. The combination is unbeatable for
a family vacation.

Cook Forest Sawmill Center for the Arts (ages 6 and up)

Off PA 666 in Volwinkel; (814) 927-6655; www.sawmill.org. Open summer and fall. Admission **free.** Ticket prices for live theater and special events and fees for classes vary. For
information on classes or festivals, call (814) 927-6655.

Cook Forest Sawmill Center for the Arts has two buildings full of crafts, art and craft
classes, various special events, and more. (Site I, which offers crafts, is open only in the
summer.) Festivals include a Herb Festival in June, Wood Competition and Show in July,
a Pyrography Festival (woodburning) in Aug, and Dulcimer and Folk Gathering in Sept.
There's also Creative HeARTS, for the mentally and physically challenged, and a young
people's drama workshop and dance camp.

Cook Forest State Park (all ages)

Exit 8, 9, or 13 off I-80 (P.O. Box 120, Cooksburg 16217); (814) 744-8407; www.dcnr.state. pa.us/stateparks/parks/cookforest.aspx.

Named one of the nation's top fifty parks, Cook Forest contains one of the last remaining old-growth forests of 200- to 350-year-old white pine and hemlock that reach 200 feet into the sky. At the Log Cabin Inn Visitor Center, check out the Historical Room, which displays logging and rafting tools as well as models and other artifacts of the logging industry.

There are 29 miles of trails that are wonderful for hiking, cross-country skiing, and more. Many of the trails are less than a mile in length—a distance that's just right for little hikers. Nature programs are offered on Fri and Sat nights, and guided walks are conducted year-round. The easy-flowing Clarion River is a great way to introduce yourself and your family to tubing or canoeing.

The twenty-three rustic cabins in the forest are a popular vacation option. The cabins are grouped in two areas. There are ten small, one-room cabins in the Indian area, located by the park office and near the accessible fishing pier. Flush toilet and shower facilities are nearby. The twelve River cabins are located on a hillside overlooking the Clarion River. These are some of the largest models built by the Civilian Conservation Corps (CCC), with a living room, kitchen, and two bedrooms. The park has completed work on two cabins to make the doors and kitchen appliances accessible to people in wheelchairs. Another bonus of these larger cabins: cold running water. Modern restrooms and showers are a five-minute walk.

Pine Crest Cabins (all ages)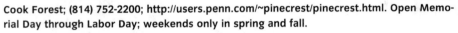

Cook Forest; (814) 752-2200; http://users.penn.com/~pinecrest/pinecrest.html. **Open Memorial Day through Labor Day; weekends only in spring and fall.**

For families who want to combine horseback riding with their vacation, one of the best choices is Pine Crest Cabins. Don't let the name fool you: There is a campground on the property as well as stables. There are also canoes, go-karts, bumper boats, and long-putt golf—all on a seventy-five-acre family-oriented resort. More than half of the land has been preserved in its natural state and provides great hiking territory for families. Log cabins sleep eight to ten people and have indoor and outdoor fireplaces and two or three bedrooms.

Double Diamond Deer Ranch (all ages)

PA 36, south of Cook Forest; (814) 752-6334; www.doublediamonddeerranch.com. **Open year-round. Call for current hours and admission prices.**

If you want to see your wildlife up a little closer, check out the Double Diamond Deer Ranch, near the entrance to the state park on PA 36 South. Here a herd of twenty-five deer have been raised since birth. The deer are tame, so they'll come right up and greet you, eat from your hand, and enjoy a good scratch behind the ears. Fawns are born each spring, and during June through August they are bottle-fed. Children are welcome to hold the bottles. The "Buck Barn" offers a chance to learn about the animals you've seen in the woods.

An O'Toole **Family Aventure**

James and Bill will never forget Groundhog Day in Punxsutawney. Unprepared for the crowds, we didn't reach Gobbler's Knob in time for Phil's official pronouncement. But when we finally arrived, the mob had thinned out to reveal Phil himself—fat, sleek, and toothy. His top-hatted handler kindly let my sons pet the fifteen-pound prognosticator—a thrill they remember fondly each February 2. Bill also remembers that we found a five-dollar bill in the snow.

Punxsutawney

On Groundhog Day each year, the world focuses its attention on the little town of Punxsutawney and on a groundhog named Phil. If he climbs out of his burrow on Gobbler's Knob and sees his shadow, the story goes, winter will be sticking around for a while longer. Phil's an old hand at this prediction stuff: He (or his ancestors) has been doing it every year since February 2, 1887.

Punxsutawney Groundhog Zoo (all ages)
124 W. Mahoning St.; (800) 752-PHIL; www.groundhog.org or www.punxsutawneyphil.com. Open year-round. Admission free.

You don't have to wait until February to get a glimpse of Phil. He can be found living with his family at the Punxsutawney Groundhog Zoo at the Civic Complex in town. Each summer the town celebrates its favorite son with a weeklong Groundhog Festival in July. Parades, dances, contests, flea markets, and lots of food are all part of the festivities.

This is also the site of the Punxsutawney Chamber of Commerce (124 W. Mahoning St.; 800-752-PHIL; www.punxsutawney.com), your source of information on accommodations, restaurants, attractions, and, of course, all things groundhog.

Franklin

Franklin is a great area for biking, hiking, and camping. Here are a couple of outfitters to help you plan your trip:

- **Outer Limits** (ages 8 and up), 2664 Bredinsburg Rd., Franklin; (814) 432-8432. Outer Limits offers customized outdoor adventures for families and other groups. From hiking, biking, and backpacking to canoeing and fishing, the guides provide everything you need, including equipment, meals, and transportation. All tour guides are certified in first aid and CPR.

- **Country Peddlers Recreational Rentals and Sales** (ages 8 and up), 2664 Bredinsburg Rd., Franklin; (814) 432-8055. Located near the Allegheny River and trailheads for two excellent family adventure trails: the Samuel Justus Recreational Trail (5.8 miles) and the Allegheny River Trail (14 miles). Country Peddlers rents the bikes, skates, or canoes you need to enjoy this beautiful area.

Oil City and Titusville

To get a better picture of the history of oil in this area, head to Oil City and Titusville.

Oil Creek & Titusville Railroad (all ages)

7 Elm St., Oil City; (814) 676-1733; http://octrr.clarion.edu. Open mid-June through Oct. Call for current fares.

You can board the Oil Creek & Titusville Railroad through "the valley that changed the world." The two-and-a-half-hour narrated trip describes the world's first oil boom. Ride in the open-air car for a perfect view of the beautiful northwestern Pennsylvania landscape. Or bring your canoe: The OCTRR will haul you upstream and leave you at Perry Street Station. Bicyclists can ride the 10-mile-long bike path through Oil Creek State Park. Riders and their bikes can board at Petroleum Centre, Rynd Farm Station, or Drake Well Station. Bikes can be rented Mon through Fri at Petroleum Centre by calling Oil Creek State Park at (814) 676-5915. See a variety of wildlife from groundhogs to bald eagles, with ducks, deer, and blue heron present nearly every trip, as well as the occasional black bear. Wheelchair accessible.

Oil Creek State Park (all ages)

Off PA 8, between Oil City and Titusville; (814) 676-5915; www.dcnr.state.pa.us/stateparks/parks/oilcreek.aspx. Open year-round.

The 9.5-mile paved bicycle trail through Oil Creek Gorge is the main attraction here. Bike rentals are available from the concession at the Old Egbert Oil Office. Hikers and, in winter, cross-country skiers are also welcome to use the trail.

Drake Well Museum (ages 6 and up)

Off PA 8, south of Titusville; (814) 827-2797; www.drakewell.org. Open year-round. Adults $$, children 6 to 12 $.

Heading up PA 8 toward Titusville, stop at the Drake Well Museum, where Edwin Drake drilled the first oil well and launched the petroleum industry in 1859. Here you'll find exhibits, videos, historic buildings, and operating oil machinery. Kids can make plastic, enjoy the fire-engine display, and blow the steam whistle in the full-size replica of Drake's engine house. Have fun "feeding" the horses in the oil transportation exhibit, but watch out for the nitro explosion! Trails in adjacent Oil Creek State Park provide great hiking, and there's a picnic pavilion.

Caboose Motel (all ages)
407 S. Perry St., Titusville; (814) 827-5730 or (800) 827-0690.

Got a train lover in your family? Stay at this twenty-one-caboose motel, where cabooses have been converted into accommodations complete with cable TV, air-conditioning, heat, telephones, and computer dataports. Pretty cool. It is adjacent to the Mill Restaurant, a renovated mill that has family dining.

Greenville

There are a couple of museums worth a look-see in Greenville. For information try Mercer County Tourism at www.mercercountypa.org.

Greenville Canal Museum (ages 6 and up)
60 Alan Avenue; (724) 588-7540; www.greenvillecanalmuseum.org. Open June through Aug, Sat and Sun only, 1 to 5 p.m.

This museum traces the history of the Erie Extension Canal, which was the major means of moving people and iron here from 1840 to 1871. You can see a full-size replica of a packet boat and a working model of a canal lock.

Greenville Railroad Park and Museum (all ages)
314 Main St.; (724) 588-4009; http://members.tripod.com/~greenville/rrpark.html. Open weekends only in May, Sept, and Oct 1 to 5 p.m. Open Tues through Sun during summer months, 1 to 5 p.m. Admission is free, but donations are gladly accepted.

Here your kids can climb aboard the largest steam switch engine ever built in the United States. There are also railroad cars, a 1914 Empire automobile, and the world's first parachute on display.

Greenville Farmers' Curb Market (all ages) 🔒
Corner of Penn Avenue and Main Street. Open Wed and Sat 7 a.m. to 2 p.m.

If you're in town on a Wed or Sat, check out this outdoor market that features the produce of farmers within a 20-mile radius of town.

Brucker Great Blue Heron Sanctuary (all ages) 🐘
PA 18, south of Greenville; (724) 589-2117. Open year-round. Admission is free.

More than 400 of these majestic birds nest at this wildlife reserve—the largest colony of herons in the state.

Conneaut Lake

You'll find lots of family fun around Pennsylvania's largest lake.

Conneaut Lake Area (all ages)

12382 Center St., Conneaut Lake; (814) 382-5115; www.conneautlakepark.com. Open daily early summer to late fall. Admission is free—you pay only for the rides you want.

For more than one hundred years, families have come to Conneaut Lake Park to enjoy the lake, ride the rides, and just plain have fun. There is a 167-room historic hotel, a 105-site modern campground with camping cabins, and a full range of rides and amusements. The classic Blue Streak wooden roller coaster is sure to thrill, and the Waterpark is a hit with most kids. When you've had enough of the rides, relax on the lake beach or take a ride on the stern-wheeler *Barbara J.* The park's operating status in the future is unclear, so call ahead.

Pymatuning State Park (ages 5 and up)

PA 58, Jamestown; (724) 932-3141; www.dcnr.state.pa.us/stateparks/parks/pymatuning .aspx. Open year-round. Generally open weekends mid-Apr to Memorial Day; daily through Labor Day; weekends again in Sept.

Almost everything about Pymatuning State Park is huge. At 21,122 acres, it is the largest state park in Pennsylvania. The 17,088-acre Pymatuning Reservoir is the largest lake in the state. And more people visit Pymatuning than almost any other Pennsylvania state park.

In addition to lots of fishing, boating, and other recreational opportunities, the park is noted for the Lineville Spillway Concession, where "the ducks walk on the fishes' backs." Hundreds of thousands of visitors come each year to feed the fish and view the wildlife in this area. Located 2 miles south of Lineville on Hartstown Road, the concession has refreshments, souvenirs, and fish food for sale. Although fish feeding and wildlife viewing are the main attractions, the scenery and sunsets are gorgeous on this causeway between the lakes. For more information contact the park office at (724) 932-3142.

Pymatuning Deer Park (all ages)

PA 58, Jamestown; (724) 932-3200; www.pymatuning.com/deerpark.htm. Open weekends in May and daily Memorial Day through Labor Day. Call for current admission prices.

This small zoo offers train and pony rides as well as an opportunity to pet and feed the animals. Small children especially seem to enjoy this stop. The park has over 200 animals, including lions, tigers, bears (oh my!), wallabies, kangaroos, and camels in addition to the favorite farm animals.

Sharon

Sharon is a very small town with some giant-size attractions. In Reyer's, it has the world's largest shoe store; in Daffin's Chocolate Kingdom, the world's largest candy store and in Quaker Steak and Lube, the best hot wings in the United States. (Your kids will agree.)

Daffin's Candies (all ages)

496 E. State St.; (724) 342-2892; www.daffins.com. Open Mon through Fri 9 a.m. to 9 p.m., Sun 11 a.m. to 5 p.m. **Free.**

This retail landmark boasts a chocolate menagerie that includes a 400-pound turtle, a 125-pound reindeer, and 75-pound frogs, plus rabbits, a train, a village, a Ferris wheel, and the castle of the Chocolate Kingdom. Kids remember the **free** samples.

Girard

The tiny town of Girard is close to the Ohio border and close to the hearts of Americans. It's the birthplace of Dan Rice, the circus master who created the character of Uncle Sam, the top-hatted embodiment of our country. The town celebrates in all-American fashion with Dan Rice Days each August.

Erie

Erie is the area's largest population center and the state's only Great Lake port. With Splash Lagoon Indoor Waterpark, Erie Otters hockey, Erie SeaWolves baseball, and so much more, Erie has never been better. For information on the Otters, go to www.ottershockey.com; for the SeaWolves, www.seawolves.com.

Presque Isle State Park (all ages)

Peninsula Drive (P.O. Box 8510, Erie 16505); (814) 833-7424; www.dcnr.state.pa.us/stateparks/parks/presqueisle.aspx. Open year-round. **Free** admission.

Presque Isle State Park is one of the most remarkable aspects of Erie. This narrow spit of sand (presque isle literally means "almost an island") juts out into Lake Erie, providing an unusual environment for wildlife and a beautiful retreat for humans. To plan your day at the park, stop at the interpretive center, where there is a wonderful nature gift shop and bookstore as well as exhibits about local wildlife.

An O'Toole **Family Adventure**

When a work assignment took me to Erie one spring day, I packed lightly: two pairs of Rollerblades and one happy, hooky-playing son. At Presque Isle Park, we parked, strapped on our skates, and zoomed along the paved lakefront path. Ten-year-old Bill had no trouble keeping up on the thirteen-and-a-half-mile loop. As we turned away from the lake, the wind at our backs pushed us along at top speed. It was a great way to welcome spring.

Choose the calm waters of Presque Isle Bay for boating or the almost oceanlike waves of Lake Erie for swimming. Water enthusiasts can rent canoes, rowboats, or motorboats to explore the waters on their own. Landlubbers can enjoy 13 miles of hiking trails. Some of the beaches at Presque Isle have occasionally been closed for a few days at a time due to unsafe water quality. It's carefully monitored, but call ahead to check the status of the area you plan to visit. Bring your binoculars; Presque Isle is touted as one of the best bird-watching sites in the country. More than 300 species live in or pass by the park.

B.O.A.T. (Best of All Tours, Inc.) runs the forty-nine-passenger Lady Kate from the Perry Monuments at Presque Isle. There's also a thirty-six-passenger water taxi, Presque Isle Express, that runs between Presque Isle and Dobbins Landing in downtown Erie. It's a great way to pack in a full day of Erie sights and fun.

Although busiest in summer, there's something to do year-round at the park. In winter hiking trails turn to cross-country ski trails, and Presque Isle Bay provides great ice fishing.

Tom Ridge Environmental Center (ages 3 and up)

301 Peninsula Dr., (814) 833-7424; www.trecpi.org. Open daily from 10 a.m. except Thanksgiving, Christmas, and New Year's Day. Admission to exhibits is free; tickets to the Big Green Screen, a large-format movie theater, is $ for adults and $ for children. After 3 p.m., movie tickets are discounted.

The Big Green Screen at the Ridge Environmental Center is four stories high and 45 feet wide—perfect for exciting, colorful films about the natural world, from hurricanes to humongous gorillas. Its free exhibits highlight the unique plants and animals of Presque Isle, which is a famous flyway for many migratory species.

Waldameer Park and Water World (ages 3 and up)

220 Peninsula Dr.; (814) 838-3591; www.waldameer.com. Open Tues through Sun, mid-May through Labor Day. Individual-ride and combo tickets available. Free parking and admission.

Right outside the entrance of Presque Isle State Park is Waldameer Park and Water World. If you don't spot it, your kids definitely will. There are five body slides, three double-tube slides, the Wild River tube slide, free-fall slide, speed slide, Endless River ride, three "tad pool" areas, and a heated pool. The amusement park has sixteen major rides and ten rides for children, including the fantastic log flume ride, Thunder River. The XScream is a 140-foot drop tower. Use of tubes and life jackets is free, and there is a variety of gift shops, snack bars, and midway games at the park. Or you can bring your own picnic. Puppet shows and musical shows are offered throughout the day.

Erie Maritime Museum (ages 6 and up)

150 E. Front St.; (814) 871-4596 or (814) 452-BRIG; www.eriemaritimemuseum.org. Open seven days a week year-round. Open Mon through Sat 9 a.m. to 5 p.m., Sun noon to 5 p.m. Last tickets sold at 4 p.m. Call for winter hours Jan 1 through Mar 31. Admission: adults $$, family ticket $$$, youth 6 to 12 $; children under 6 are free. Reduced rates when the Niagara is not in port.

The maritime attractions of downtown Erie have been united in the Erie Maritime Museum. This state-of-the-art facility is one of the few in the country that can teach children about the War of 1812. Exhibits explain North Coast maritime history, the reconstruction of the U.S. Brig *Niagara* and its role in the Battle of Lake Erie, and the soldiers and shipbuilders who lived here. You can take a look at how the *Lawrence* looked before and after cannon fire. Through the big windows that overlook the lake, you'll see the museum's flagship exhibit, one of the country's classic "tall ships." When it's in port, you can tour O. H. Perry's flagship, the *Niagara,* built to fight the naval battles of the War of 1812. The *Niagara* also offers day sails in the summer; these are restricted to children over 14.To avoid disappointing children with their hearts set on seeing this boat, call ahead.

Bicentennial Observation Tower (ages 3 and up)

Dobbins Landing; (814) 455-6055 or (814) 455-7557; www.visiteriepa.com/bicentennial_ tower.shtml. Open May to Sept. Call for current hours and days. Admission is $; children under 6 are free. Admission is free for all ages on Tues.

This 187-foot-tall tower gives an amazing view over Presque Isle, downtown Erie, and Lake Erie. Take the 210 stairs to the top observation deck or take the elevator. If you take the stairs, follow the sixteen stations that point out historic, geographic, and other landmarks.

Splash Lagoon Indoor Waterpark Resort (ages 2 and up)

I-90, exit 24; (866) 3-SPLASH; www.splashlagoon.com. Splash Lagoon opens every day at 10 a.m. Closing hours vary seasonally. Day passes are sometimes available on a first-come, first-served basis, but to be guaranteed admission to the park, an overnight package is strongly recommended. Call (814) 217-1111 for day pass availability.

Splash Lagoon is an all-inclusive resort featuring accommodations, entertainment, restaurants, and more, but its highlight is its indoor water park—over an acre of indoor water fun! Attractions include four twisting and turning body slides, a swirling body coaster for one or two riders, an 80,000-gallon activity pool, and two twenty-five–person whirlpools, one for kids and one for adults.

The newest cutting-edge waterslide in the country, Hurricane Hole is a one-person body slide, 125 feet long. Riders fly down a dark tunnel at speeds exceeding 40 miles per hour, then spin in the Hurricane Bowl before taking a midair plunge into the warm water below. Or you can try the Lazy River/Crazy River, a lazy river ride with an adventurous difference. Moms and dads can relax in the adults-only Paradise Cove hot tub, with beautiful murals on the walls, a waterfall, and massaging water jets to take the knots out of your muscles. Or the entire family can soak together in the Frog Pond.

Erie Art Museum (ages 8 and up)

411 State St., Discovery Square; (814) 459-5477; www.erieartmuseum.org. Open Tues through Sat year-round. Admission is $. Free admission on Wed.

The Erie Art Museum offers changing exhibitions, concerts, classes, and children's activities. During the first weekend of Aug, the museum hosts the Erie Art Museum Blues & Jazz Festival, which draws 10,000 people to Frontier Park for the Free event.

expERIEnce Children's Museum (ages 2-12)

420 French St., Discovery Square; (814) 453-3743; www.eriechildrensmuseum.org. Open year-round Wed through Sat 10 a.m. to 4 p.m., Sun 1 to 4 p.m. Closed Mon year-round and Tues during school year. Call or check the Web site to inquire about special holiday hours. Admission is $. Children under 2 enter free.

For small children the highlight of Erie is the expERIEnce Children's Museum, housed in an old livery stable. The museum is aimed at kids ages two to twelve, but those under age eight seem to enjoy it the most. According to one of the museum's curators, "This is a hands-on museum, which means that kids can come in and break things, and after they leave, we fix them."

There's a Gallery of Science on one floor and a Gallery of the Human Experience on the other. You can also see a simulation of a cave, in which children learn about cave painting, cave exploration, and fossils. At the Wegman's Corner Store, children can shop in a re-creation of a supermarket, complete with scanners, shopping carts, and very real-looking groceries. Youngsters may want to pick out a funny outfit from the costume closet and put on a show on a real stage. Toddlers and their parents are invited to story time, with beloved books and crafts, every Thurs.

Watson–Curtze Mansion and Erie Planetarium (all ages)

356 W. Sixth St.; (814) 871-5790; www.eriecountyhistory.org. Open Tues through Sun afternoons year-round. Call for current hours. Museum admission is $. Planetarium admission is $. Children under 2 are admitted free to both exhibits.

Kids of all ages love planetarium shows. Even toddlers will point out the moon and the stars. Call ahead for schedule of shows.

Erie Zoo (all ages)

423 West Thirty-eighth St.; (814) 864-4091; www.eriezoo.org. Open year-round. Call for admission prices and hours.

More than 500 animals representing nearly one hundred different species live in this fifteen-acre park. There's a children's zoo and a train ride around the zoo.

ALSO IN THE AREA

Wooden Nickel Buffalo Farm Restaurant and Shop (all ages), 5970 Koman Rd., Edinboro; (814) 734-BUFF; www.woodennickelbuffalo.com. Seasonal hours; please call ahead. Free admission. A herd of more than fifty buffalo roam on this fifty-acre ranch outside

Erie. It's quite a sight to see. Who knows, you might get inspired to get into buffalo farming yourself.

North East

About 20 miles east of Erie on US 20 is the historic village of North East. Take a walking tour of the historic district (brochures are available at local stores and museums).

Hornby School Museum (ages 4 and up)

11573 Station Rd.; (814) 739-2720. Open Sun 1 to 5 p.m. or by appointment. Admission is free, but donations are accepted.

If you call ahead and make arrangements, your children can experience what it was like to learn in a one-room schoolhouse built in the 1870s. Even the books and slates are original equipment.

Lake Shore Railway Historical Society Museum (ages 2 and up)

Corner of Wall and Robinson Streets; (814) 725-1191; http://lsrhs.railway.museum. Open Wed through Sun afternoons from Memorial Day to Labor Day. Call for exact hours. Admission free.

Here, you can see a variety of train equipment, including a Pullman car, a caboose, and a dining car. Located on a busy stretch of railroad track, the site practically guarantees that your children will get to see several modern trains pass by during your visit.

Where to Eat

IN THE COOKSBURG AREA

The Farmer's Inn. Two miles north of Sigel on PA 949, near Clear Creek State Park; (814) 752-2942. Restaurant, ice cream, bakery, gift shop, Amish furniture, horse-drawn wagon and pony rides, miniature golf, animal exhibits, petting zoo.

Gateway Lodge Country Inn and Restaurant, PA 36 in the heart of Cook Forest; (814) 744-8017 or (800) 843-6862. Dine by kerosene light. Staff dressed colonial-style. Breakfast and lunch daily. Dinner daily except for Mon.

Mama Doe's Restaurant, Shiloh Ranch Resort, PA 36, Cook Forest; (814) 752-2361; www.shilohresort.net. Fine dining and Italian cuisine. Breakfast, lunch, and dinner; daily specials, Saturday buffet. Also campground, cabins, and lodge.

Sawmill Restaurant, Intersection of PA 36 and PA 66 at the blinker light, Leeper; (814) 744-8578. Soft ice cream, fresh baked goods; home of the Sawdustburger. Open daily year-round, 6:30 a.m. to midnight (closes earlier in midwinter).

The Trails End, Cooksburg–Vowinckel Road, near Cook Forest State Park; (814) 927-8400. Steaks, seafood, sandwiches. Near theater and park attractions.

Vowinckel Hotel, corner of PA 66 and Cooksburg–Vowinckel Road, 5 miles from Cook Forest; (814) 927-6610. Homemade bread and pizza dough. Voted "Best Wings in Clarion County." Fireplace.

IN ERIE

Barbato's, 1164 W. Sixth St.; (814) 452-0100; near the Bayfront. Popular local chain with casual Italian specialties like pizza, calzones, and pasta.

China Garden Restaurant, 6801 Peach St.; (814) 868-2695.

Chuck E Cheese, 7200 Peach St., Summit Towne Center; (814) 864-3100.

Connie's Ice Cream, 6032 Peach St.; (814) 474-9996. Take-out ice cream homemade with the freshest ingredients.

Hoss's Steak and Sea House, 3302 W. Twenty-sixth St.; (814) 838-6718.

The Olive Garden, 5945 Peach St.; (814) 866-1105.

Pio's Italian Restaurant & Pizzeria, 815 East Ave.; (814) 456-8866. Pastas, pizza, and other casual Italian-style choices. Children's menu.

Pufferbelly on French Street, Fourth and French Streets, downtown; (814) 454-1557; www.thepufferbelly.com. Fine dining plus a children's menu in a restored 1908 fire station. Patio. The French Street Cafe next door offers sandwiches, coffee, and more weekdays from 7 a.m. to 3 p.m.

Sara's, Presque Isle (western end); (814) 833-1957. Seasonal restaurant with fresh-grilled hot dogs.

Smuggler's Wharf, 3 State St.; (814) 459-4273.

IN SHARON

Quaker Steak and Lube, 101 Chestnut St.; (724) 981-WING (9464) or (800) HOT–WING. The original location of the famous sports-car–themed chain is famous for—you guessed it—wings. Menu specials for those under ten. The decor is a motorhead's dream, from full-size Cadillacs to Chevys.

IN WELLSBORO

Wellsboro Diner, 19 Main St.; (570) 724-3288; open daily until 8 p.m. This 1939 all-American diner is a cozy, family-friendly stop.

Where to Stay

IN WELLSBORO

Comfort Inn Canyon Country, 300 Gateway Dr., Mansfield; (570) 662-3000 or (800) 822-5470. Conveniently located for events in Mansfield as well as touring nearby Pine Creek Gorge.

IN BRADFORD

Best Western Bradford Inn, 100 Davis St. South; (814) 362-4501 or (800) 344-4656. Open year-round. A good base for Bradford- and Allegheny Forest–area explorations. Outdoor pool.

IN THE ALLEGHENY NATIONAL FOREST AREA

Kane View Motel, US 6 East, Kane; (814) 837-8600; www.kaneviewmotel.com. The Allegheny National Forest is in the backyard of this convenient motel.

IN WARREN

Holiday Inn Warren, 210 Ludlow St.; (814) 726-3000 or (800) 446-6814; www.holidayinn.com/warrenpa. On-site restaurant, indoor pool, and a three-diamond rating from AAA make this a good choice for families exploring the national forest and other area attractions. Kids under twelve stay and eat free.

Super 8 Motel, US 6 and US 62 North; (814) 723-8881. Near major attractions and downtown. Continental breakfast.

IN THE COOKSBURG AREA

Clarion River Lodge, River Road in Cook Forest; (814) 744-8171 or (800) 648-6743; www.clarionriverlodge.com. Magnificent view of Clarion River. Guest rooms available. Open year-round.

IN PUNXSUTAWNEY

Pantall Hotel, 135 E. Mahoning St.; (814) 938-6600; www.pantallhotel.com. Beautifully restored Victorian hotel; restaurants on-site.

IN FRANKLIN

Quality Inn and Suites, downtown; (814) 437-3031 or (800) 535-4052. Free continental breakfast; restaurant, tavern, family plans.

IN OIL CITY

Arlington Hotel, 1 Seneca St.; (814) 677-1221 or (877) 677-1222. Kids stay free. Full-service restaurant, lounge, entertainment. Free continental breakfast.

IN THE CONNEAUT LAKE AREA

Days Inn–Meadville, just off exit 36A off I-79, Meadville; (814) 337-4264. Minutes from Conneaut Lake. Family restaurant on-site.

IN CLARION

Comfort Inn, I-80, exit 62, north on PA 68; (814) 226-5230. Free continental breakfast.

Holiday Inn of Clarion, PA 68 and I-80, exit 62; (814) 226-8850 or (800) 596-1313. Tropical courtyard with indoor pool, restaurant, and lounge. Kids stay and eat free.

Super 8 Motel–Clarion, I-80, exit 62; (814) 226-4550. AAA-rated; first-floor and non-smoking rooms. Free continental breakfast and local calls, cable television, outdoor pool.

IN ERIE

Erie has an impressive array of hotels and motels—with just about all the major chains represented. Most of the big-name places are equipped with indoor pools, definitely good news for families traveling in winter or when bad weather interrupts sightseeing plans. Here are a few highlights:

The Glass House Inn, 3202 W. Twenty-sixth St. (US 20); (814) 833-7751 or (800) 956-7222; www.glasshouseinn.com. A family-friendly, family-run colonial-style inn with outdoor pool and lots of room to play.

Marriott Residence Inn, 8061 Peach St.; (814) 864-2500. This all-suite hotel has kitchens in the rooms, an indoor pool, and a breakfast buffet.

Presque Isle Cottage Court, 320 Peninsula Dr.; (814) 833-4956. Located close to Waldermeer Water World and Presque Isle State Park. Apr through Oct.

For More Information

Pennsylvania Wilds visitor centers in Bradford and Lantz Corners; (800) 473-9370; www.pawilds.com

Endless Mountains Visitor Bureau; (570) 836-5431; www.endlessmountains.org.

Erie Area of Chamber of Commerce; (814) 454-7191 or (800) 542-ERIE; www.eriepa .com.

Mercer County Convention and Visitors Bureau; (724) 346-3771 or (800) 637-2370; www.mercercountypa.org.

Warren County Visitors Bureau, 22045 Route 6, Warren; (800) 624-7802; www.wcvb .net.

Pennsylvania's Great Outdoors Visitors Bureau, 175 Main St., Brookville; (814) 849-5197; www.visitpago.com.

Oil Region Alliance, 217 Elm Street, Oil City; (814) 677-3152; www.oilregion.org.

Potter County Recreation, Inc.; (814) 274-3365 or (888) POTTER–2; www.potter countypa.org.

Wellsboro Chamber of Commerce; (570) 724-1926; www.wellsboropa.com.

Index

A

AAMP Celebrates
Kwanzaa, 3
Aaron and Jessica's Buggy
Rides, 78
Abe's Buggy Rides, 78
Academy of Music, 26
Academy of Natural
Sciences, 17
Adventure Sports in
Marshalls Creek, 161
African-American Museum
in Philadelphia, 12
Ag Progress Days, 187, 196
Alburtis, 57
Allegheny Arms and Armor
Museum, 213
Allegheny Mountains
Convention and Visitors
Bureau, 132
Allegheny National
Forest, 214
Allegheny Portage Railroad
National Historic Site,
120
Allenberry Resort Inn, 97
Allentown, 58
Allentown Art Museum, 59
Altoona, 122
Altoona Curve, 124
Ambridge, 153
Americana Museum of Bird-
in-Hand, 80
American Civil War
Museum, 101
American Helicopter
Museum, 42
America On Wheels, 58
Amish Barn Restaurant, 79
Amish Country
Homestead, 79

Amish Experience/FX
Theater, The, 79
Amish Farm and House, 85
Amish Village, 82
Andorra Natural Area, 22
Andy Warhol Museum,
The, 137
Anthracite Heritage
Museum, 176
Antique Airplane
Restaurant, 103
Antique Motorcycle
Museum, 88
Arlington Hotel, 227
Army-Navy Game, 3
Arts and Crafts Fair, 187
Artworks at Doneckers, 77
Asa Packer Mansion, 178
Ashland, 180
Atwater Kent Museum, 11
Audubon, 44
August Wilson Center
for African American
Culture, 133
Avella, 154

B

Banana Factory, 63
Barbato's, 226
Bark Peeler's
Convention, 210
Barnes Foundation, The, 47
Barns–Brinton House, 40
bat hikes, 121
Battle of Brandywine
Reenactment, 38
Beach Lake Cafe, 183
Bear Run Nature
Preserve, 112
Beaver Stadium, 195
Bedford, 129

Bedford County Visitors
Bureau, 132
Beech House Creek Wildlife
Refuge, 167
Bellefonte, 200
Bellefonte Arts and Crafts
fair, 201
Bellefonte Historical
Railroad, 201
Bellefonte Historic
Cruise, 201
Bellefonte Museum for
Centre County, 200
Bellefonte/State College
KOA Campground, 202
Bellefonte Tourism
Commission, 203
Belleville, 193
Belleville Farmers Market,
187, 193
"Ben Franklin" and
Franklin's Friends, 15
Ben Franklin's Birthday
Bash, 3
Benzel's Pretzel Bakery, 123
Bernville, 74
Best Western Bradford
Inn, 227
Best Western Center City
Hotel, 35
Best Western Country
Cupboard Inn, 202
Best Western New Hope
Inn, 66
Best Western University
Center Hotel, 156
Best Western
Williamsport, 202
Bethlehem, 62
Bethlehem's Musikfest, 63
Betsy Ross House, 12

Bicentennial Observation
Tower, 223
Big Boulder Ski Resort, 178
Big Butler Fair, 148
Big Spring Film Festival, 187
Bird-in-Hand, 80
Bird-in-Hand Family Inn, 104
Bird-in-Hand Family
Restaurant, 79
Birdsboro, 74
Bishop White House, 10
Black Friday, 118
Blobfest, Phoenixville, 38
Blue Bird Inn, The, 103
Blue Cross River Rink, 17
Blue Knob All Seasons
Resort, 120
Blue Mountain Sports and
Wear, 177
Boal Mansion and
Museum, 197
Boalsburg, 197
Boathouse Row, 22
B.O.A.T. Inc., 222
Boat Rides at Wells
Ferry, 52
Boiling Springs, 96
Bonanza Steak House, 201
Bottle Works Ethnic Arts
Center, 120
Bowman's Hill Tower, 50
Bowman's Hill Wildflower
Preserve, 51
Box Huckleberry Natural
Area, 193
Boyd's Bear Country, 102
Boyertown, 73
Boyertown Museum of
Historic Vehicles, 73
Bradford, 212
Bradford County Heritage
Farm Museum, 206
Bradford County Historical
Society and Museum,
182
Brandywine Battlefield
Park, 40

Brandywine River
Museum, 39
Brandywine Valley, 39
Broad Top Area Coal
Miners Museum and
Entertainment Center,
129
Brownie's in the Burg, 183
Brownsville, 110
Brucker Great Blue Heron
Sanctuary, 219
Bryce Jordan Center, 195
Buca di Beppo, 66, 156
Buchanan State Forest, 131
Bucks County, 67
Bucks County Playhouse, 52
Bucks County River
Country, 53
Burges–Lippincott
House, 50
Burnside Plantation, 63
Bushkill, 165
Bushkill Falls, 165
Bushy Run Battlefield, 115
Butler, 148
Butler County Heritage
Center, 148
Byers' Choice Ltd., 55

C

Cabela's, 73
Caboose Motel, 219
Caddie Shak Family Fun
Park, 113
Caesar's Brookdale-on-the-
Lake Resort, 163
Callie's Candy Kitchen and
Pretzel Factory, 165
Camelback Ski Area, 163
Camelbeach Waterpark, 163
Camp Woodward, 200
Canoe Creek State Park, 121
Carlisle, 96
Carlisle Fairgrounds, 96
Carlisle Summerfair, 70
Carnegie Library of
Pittsburgh, 142

Carnegie-Mellon
University, 141
Carnegie Museum of
Art, 141
Carnegie Museum of
Natural History, 141
Carnegie Music Hall, 142
Carnegie Science
Center, 136
Carousel Water and Fun
Park, 172
Carpenters' Hall, 8
Cathedral of Learning, 142
Celebrate Erie Days, 206
Central House, 184
Central Market,
Lancaster, 86
Central Pennsylvania
Convention and Visitors
Bureau, 203
Central Pennsylvania
Festival of the Arts,
187, 194
Chaddsford Winery, 40
Chalfont, 55
Chamberlain's Canoes, 161
Chambersburg, 103
Chambersburg Heritage
Center, 103
Chambersburg Icefest, 70
Champion, 113
Chanticleer, 48
Cherry Crest Adventure
Farm, 80
Cherry Springs State
Park, 211
Chester County Tourist
Bureau, Inc., 67
Chester Springs, 41
Chester Springs Creamery
at Milky Way Farm, 66
Chestnut Hill, 33
Children's Discovery
Workshop, 188
Children's Living History
weekend, 107

Children's Museum of
Pittsburgh, 136
China Garden
Restaurant, 226
Chinatown, 26
Chocolatetown Motel, 104
Choo Choo Barn—
Traintown USA®, 82
Christ Church, 13
Christkindl Market, 191
Christmas in July, 107
Chuck E Cheese, 226
Churchville, 48
Churchville Nature
Center, 48
City Hall, Philadelphia, 25
City Island, 94
City Tavern, 15, 35
Civil War Reenactments
at Gettysburg National
Military Park, 70
Claes Oldenburg's
Clothespin, 25
Clarion River Lodge, 227
Claussville, 61
Claussville One-Room
Schoolhouse, 61
Claws 'N' Paws Wild Animal
Park, 168
Claysburg, 120
Clyde Peeling's
Reptiland, 189
Cocoa Nights Motel, 104
College Hall, 30
College of Agricultural
Sciences, 196
Colonial New Hope Walking
Tours, 51
Colonial Pennsylvania
Plantation, 46
Colton Point State Park, 207
Columbia, 87
Columbia–Montour Visitors
Bureau, 203
Comfort Inn Canyon
Country, 227

Comfort Inn, Clarion, 227
Comfort Inn Ebensburg, 131
Comfort Inn Johnstown, 131
Compass Inn Museum, 117
Coney Island Lunch,
131, 183
Congregation Mikveh
Israel, 15
Congress Hall, 7
Conneaut Lake, 219
Conneaut Lake Park, 220
Connellsville, 110
Connellsville Area Historical
Society, 110
Connie's Ice Cream, 226
Cook Forest Sawmill Center
for the Arts, 215
Cook Forest State Park, 216
Cooksburg, 215
Cooper Cabin, 148
Cooper's Seafood
House, 183
Corn Planting, 59
Cornwall, 75
Cornwall Inn, 104
Cornwall Iron Furnace, 75
Coryell's Ferry Historic Boat
Rides, 51
Coudersport, 211
Country Peddlers
Recreational Rentals and
Sales, 218
County Theater, 54
Courtyard by Marriott, 202
Courtyard by Marriott
Downtown, 156
Crawford Cabin, 110
Crayola Factory, 64
Cresson, 120
Crook Farm and Country
Fair, 212
Crown Plaza—
Philadelphia, 35
Crystal Cave, 72
Cyclorama, Gettysburg, 98

D
Daffin's Candies, 221
Daniel Boone
Homestead, 74
Daniel Weaver Company,
The, 75
Dan Rice Days in Girard, 206
Dave & Buster's, 17
David Wills House, 100
Da Vinci Science Center, 63
Days Inn Lewisburg, 202
Days Inn–Meadville, 227
Days Inn Penn State, 203
Declaration House (Graff
House), 11
Delaware County
Convention and Visitors
Bureau, Inc., 67
Delaware River, 160
Delaware River
Sojourn, 159
Delaware Water Gap, 160
Delaware Water Gap
National Recreation
Area, The, 160
Del Grosso's Park, 125
Derek's, 35
Derry One-Room School, 91
Devon Horse Show, 38
Dickens of a Christmas, 70
Dingman's Ferry, 166
Dobbin House Tavern, 103
Donegal, 113
Dorflinger–Suvdam Wildlife
Preserve, 169
Dorney Park and Wildwater
Kingdom, 60
Double Diamond Deer
Ranch, 216
Doubletree Guest Suites, 66
downtown Lancaster, 85
downtown Pittsburgh, 135
Doylestown, 54
Doylestown Inn, 54
Dozen Bake Shop, 156
Drake Well Museum, 218

Duquesne Incline, 141
Dutch Wonderland, 84

E

Eagle Iron Works and Curtin Village, 201
Eagles Mere, 181
Eagles Mere Ice Toboggan Slide, 181
Earth and Mineral Sciences Museum, 195
East Broad Top Railroad, 128
East End, Pittsburgh, 141
Eastern Centre County, 199
Eastern State Penitentiary, 20
Easton, 64
East Stroudsburg, 160
Ebeneezer Maxwell Mansion, 33
Eckley Miners' Village, 175
Edgar Allan Poe Evermore, 76
Edgar Allan Poe National Memorial, 27
Ed's Buggy Rides, 78
Ehrhardt's Lakeside Restaurant, 183
1852 Herr Family Homestead, 87
Eisenhower National Historic Park, 100
Electric City Trolley Museum, 174
Elfreth's Alley, 12
Elfreth's Alley Fête Days, 13
Elmwood Park Zoo, 45
Elverson, 41
Elysburg, 189
Endless Mountains Visitor Bureau, 228
Endless Mountains Visitors Bureau, 184
Entriken, 127
Ephrata, 77
Ephrata Cloister, 78

Erie, 221
Erie Area of Chamber of Commerce, 228
Erie Art Museum, 224
Erie Art Museum Blues and Jazz Festival, 206
Erie Maritime Museum, 222
Erie Otters hockey, 221
Erie SeaWolves baseball, 221
Erie Zoo, 224
Erie ZooBoo, 206
Everhart Museum, 175
expERIEnce Children's Museum, 224

F

Fabulous 1890s weekend, 206
Fairfield by Marriott—Lancaster, 104
Fairmount Park, 21
Fairmount Park Waterworks Interpretive Center, 20
Fall Festival, Forksville, 182
Fallingwater, 112
Fall Pumpkin Fest, 206
Falls City Restaurant and Pub, 131
Fallsington, 50
Falls Port Inn & Restaurant, 183
Farmer's Inn, The, 225
Farmland Fun, 83
farm vacations, 70
Farnsworth House Inn, 103
Farnsworth House Mourning Theater and Ghost Walks, 102
Fayette County Historical Society, 108
FDR Skatepark, 31
Fernwood Hotel and Resort, 166
Fireman's Hall, 13
Fireworks Capital of America Fireworks Festival, 151

Flood City Music Festival, 107, 120
Flying W Ranch, 215
Fonthill, 55
Forksville, 181
Fort Bedford Museum, 130
Fort Duquesne, 135
Fort Hunter Day, 70
Fort Hunter Mansion, 95
Fort Ligonier, 116
Fort Ligonier Days, 107
Fort Mifflin on the Delaware, 32
Fort Necessity National Battlefield National Park, 108
Fort Pitt, 135
Fort Pitt Museum, 136
Fort Roberdeau Historic Site and Natural Area, 124
Fox Chase Farm, 34
Frank Buchman House, 61
Frankfort Mineral Springs, 154
Franklin, 217
Franklin Court, 14
Franklin Institute, The, 18
Franklin Square, 4
Free Library of Philadelphia, 19
French Creek State Park, 41
Frick Art and Historical Center, The, 143
Friendship Hill National Historic Site, 108
Frost Entomological Museum, 195
Fulton County Tourist Promotion Agency, 132
Fun and Games, 172

G

Galeton, 210
Game Preserve, Lehigh Valley Zoo, 61
Gardners Candies, 125
Gateway Clipper Fleet, 140

Gateway Gettysburg, 98
Gateway Lodge Country Inn
    and Restaurant, 225
General Lee's
    Headquarters, 102
Genetti Hotel, 202
Gerenser's Exotic Ice
    Cream, 51
Gettysburg, 97
Gettysburg Battlefield bus
    tours, 97
Gettysburg Bike Tours, 97
Gettysburg National Military
    Park, 98
Gettysburg Train
    Station, 100
Giant's Hall, 125
Giggleberry Fair, 52
Gillingham Store, 50
Girard, 221
Glass House Inn, The, 227
Glenside, 48
Gravity Hill, 107, 130
Great Allegheny Passage,
    110, 111
Great Allentown Fair, 38
Greater Johnstown/Cambria
    County Convention and
    Visitors Bureau, 132
Greater Philadelphia
    Tourism Marketing
    Corp., 35
Great Essentials, 8
Great Pumpkin Carve, 38
Great Wolf Lodge, 163
Greene County Tourist
    Promotion Agency, 132
Green Hills Farm (Pearl S.
    Buck House), 56
Greensburg, 114
Greenville, 219
Greenville Canal
    Museum, 219
Greenville Farmers' Curb
    Market, 219
Greenville Railroad Park and
    Museum, 219

Greenwood Furnace State
    Park, 126
Grey Towers, 167
Groundhog Day, 206

H

Haines Mill, 59
Hamburg, 73
Hampton Court Inn, 183
Hands-On House, Children's
    Museum of Lancaster, 85
Hank's Place, 66
Hanna's Town, 114
Hans Herr House, 83
HarbourTown, 94
Harlansburg Station's
    Museum of
    Transportation, 151
Harley-Davidson, Inc.,
    Antique Motorcycle
    Museum, 88
Harmony, 149
Harmony Museum,
    The, 149
Harrisburg, 92
Harrison City, 114
Harvest Drive Family
    Restaurant, 79
Hawk Mountain
    Sanctuary, 71
Hawley, 167
Heart's Content, National
    Natural Landmark, 214
Heinz Field, 144
Heinz Memorial Chapel, 142
Hellertown, 62
Henry Schmieder
    Arboretum of Delaware
    Valley College, 55
Herb and Fiber Festival, 206
Heritage Center
    Museum, 86
Heritage Center of
    Lancaster County, 86
Herr Foods, Inc., 83
Hershey, 89
Hershey Gardens, 91

Hershey Highmeadow
    Campground, 104
Hershey Lodge, The, 104
Hershey Museum, The, 91
Hersheypark, 89
Hersheypark Christmas
    Candylane, 70
Hersheypark Creatures of
    the Night, 70
Hersheypark Stadium and
    Arena, 91
Hershey's Chocolate World
    Visitors Center, 89
Hesston, 127
Hiawatha Riverboat, 188
Hidden Valley, 114
Hidden Valley Four Seasons
    Resort, 114
Hidden Valley Resort, 107
Hills Creek State Park, 209
Hilltown, 56
historical reenactments,
    Independence National
    Historical Park, 10
Historic Bartram's
    Garden, 22
historic Bellefonte, 200
Historic Car Cruise, 187
historic Fairmount
    Waterworks, 20
historic Philadelphia, 5
Historic Williamsport
    Trolleys, 188
Historic Yellow Springs, 41
Holgate Toy Store and
    Museum, 213
Holiday Inn Express, King of
    Prussia, 66
Holiday Inn—Express
    Midtown,
    Philadelphia, 35
Holiday Inn—Historic
    District, Philadelphia, 35
Holiday Inn, Johnstown, 131
Holiday Inn of Clarion, 227
Holiday Inn Scranton–
    East, 183

Holiday Inn Select—Bucks County, 66
Holiday Inn Warren, 227
Holiday Inn, Williamsport, 202
Hollidaysburg, 121
Honesdale, 171
Hopewell Furnace, 41
Hornby School Museum, 225
Horseshoe Curve, 123
Horseshoe Curve National Historic Landmark, 122
Horticultural Center, Fairmount Park, 21
Hoss's Steak and Sea House, 201, 226
Hotel Hershey, The, 104
Houdini Museum, 174
Howard Johnson Inn Scranton, 183
Hoyt Institute of Fine Arts, 152
Hugh Moore Park, 65
Hummelstown, 91
Huntington, 126
Huntington Country Visitors Bureau, 132

I
Idlewild, 115
Independence Hall, 8
Independence National Historical Park, 5
Independence National Historical Park, reenactments, 10
Independence Seaport Museum and Historic Ships, 16
Independence Visitor Center, 5
Indiana County Tourist Bureau, 132
Indian Caverns, 125
Indian Echo Caverns, 91
Inn at Fordhook Farm, 55

Inn at Jim Thorpe, The, 178
Inn at King of Prussia by Best Western, The, 66
Inn at Starlight Lake, 172
Insectarium, 34
Intercourse, 78
Iron Horse Trail, 193
Italian Market, 31

J
Jack Frost Ski Resort, 178
James A. Michener Art Museum, 54
James A. Michener Art Museum—New Hope, 51
James Buchanan's Wheatland, 86
Japanese House and Garden, 23
Jeannette, 114
Jennie Wade House, 101
Jennings Environmental Center, 150
Jerome K. Pasto Agricultural Museum, 196
Jigger Shop, The, 77
Jim Thorpe, 176
Jim Thorpe Tourist Agency, 184
John Chads House, 40
John Harris/Simon Cameron Mansion, 94
John Heinz National Wildlife Refuge, 31
Johnnie's Restaurant and Lounge, 131
Johnstown, 117
Johnstown Flood Museum, The, 119
Johnstown Flood National Memorial, 117
Johnstown Heritage Discovery Center, 119
Johnstown Inclined Plane, 118

Josiah White II Canal Boat Rides, 65
July 3 Memorial, 107
Juniata River, 129
Just Ducky Tours, Inc., 139

K
Kane View Motel, 227
KatManDu, 35
Kayak Pittsburgh, 133
Kemerer Museum of Decorative Art, 62
Kempton, 71
Kennett Square, 39
Kennywood, 145
Kentuck Knob, 111
Keswick Theater, 48
Kimmel Center for the Performing Arts, 26
King's Gap Environmental Center, 96
Kinzua Bridge State Park, 215
Klavon's Cream Parlor, 156
Kleinfeltersville, 74
Knoebels Amusement Park and Campground, 189
Koziar's Christmas Village, 74
Kreider Farms, 80
Kutztown, 72
Kutztown Pennsylvania German Festival, 70

L
Lacawac Wildlife Sanctuary, 169
Lackawanna Coal Mine, 175
Lackawanna County Stadium, 175
Lackawaxen, 170
Lahaska, 52
Lakemont Park, 123
Lake Raystown Resort & Lodge, 127, 132

Lake Shore Railway Historical Society Museum, 225
Lake Wallenpaupack, 167
Lancaster, 84
Lancaster Barnstormers, 87
Lancaster, downtown, 85
Lancaster Newspapers' Newseum, 85
Lancaster Quilt and Textile Museum, 86
Lancaster Science Factory, 86
Lander's River Trips & Campgrounds, 170
Landis Valley Museum, 85
Landisville, 87
Land of Little Horses, 102
Langhorne, 48
Laughlintown, 117
Laurel Caverns, 109
Laurel Highlands Visitors Bureau, 132
Lawrence County Tourism, 151
Lebanon, 75
Lebanon Valley Rail Trail, 76
Le Bus, 35
Lehigh Gorge, 176
Lehighton, 176
Lehigh Valley Convention and Visitors Bureau, Inc., 67
Lehigh Valley Heritage Center and Museum, 60
Lenni Lenape Historical Society, 59
Leonard Harrison State Park, 207
Letort Spring Run, 97
Lewisburg, 190
Liberty Bell Center, 7
Liberty Bell Shrine, 60
Lights of Liberty, 11
Ligonier, 115
Ligonier Scottish Highland Games, 107

Limestone Springs Preserve, 77
Lincoln Caverns and Whisper Rocks, 126
Lincoln Train Museum, 101
Linvilla Orchards, 46
Little Buffalo State Park, 192
Little League World Series, 187
Little Pine State Park, 210
Little Red School House Museum, 149
Living the Experience, 86
Living Treasures Animal Park, Donegal, 113
Living Treasures Animal Park, Moraine, 152
Lock Ridge Furnace Museum, 58
Longwood Gardens, 39
Longwood Gardens Christmas Display, 38
Lost River Caverns, 62
Lower Yough, 111
Lulu's Noodles, 156
Luzerne County Tourist Promotion Agency, 184
Lycoming County Tourist Promotion Agency, 203
Lyman Run State Park, 210

M

Mack Truck Historical Museum, The, 59
Mall at Steamtown, The, 183
Mama Doe's Restaurant, 225
Manayunk, 33
Manhattan Bagel, 201
Manheim, 80
Mann Music Center, 3, 32
Mansfield, 208
Mansfield University, 208
Marathon Grill, 35
Maridon Museum, 149
Marriott Residence, 227

Martin Guitar Factory, 64
Mary Stolz Doll Museum, 165
Mattress Factory, 137
Mauch Chunk Lake Park, 176
Mauch Chunk Museum and Cultural Center, 177
McClure, 192
McConnell's Mill State Park, 150
McDade Park, 175, 176
McIntosh Inn, 67
Meadowcroft Museum of Rural Life, 154
Media, 46
Mellon Arena, 144
Memorytown, 183
Mercer County Convention and Visitors Bureau, 228
Mercer Museum, 38, 54
Merion, 47
Merrick Art Gallery, 152
Middle Creek Wildlife Management Area, 74
Middletown, 92
Middletown and Hummelstown Railroad, 92
Middle Yough, 111
Mifflinburg, 190
Mifflinburg Buggy Days, 187
Mifflinburg Buggy Museum, 191
Mifflin County Trout Hatchery, 194
Millbrook Marsh Nature Center, 196
Mill Grove, 44
Mill Run, 112
Millvale, 145
Milton Hershey School, 91
Monongahela Incline, 140
Montage Mountain, 175
Montgomery County Historic Sites, 67
Moon and Stars Cafe, 66

Moon–Williamson
   House, 50
Moraine State Park, 150
Moravian Historical
   Society, 64
Moravian Museum, 62
Moravian Pottery and Tile
   Works, 55
Morgan Log House, 57
Morris Arboretum, 33
Morrisville, 49
Moscow Country Fair, 159
Mountain Dale Farm, 192
Mountain Spring
   Carnival, 159
Mountain Trail Horse
   Center, 209
Mount Gretna, 76
Mount Gretna Lake, 76
Mount Hope Estate,
   Pennsylvania
   Renaissance Faire, 76
Mount Jewett, 215
Mount Pocono, 163
Mr. Small's Skate Park, 145
Mulberry Market, 35
Mulligan MacDuffer
   Adventure Golf, 102
Mummers Museum, 32
Mummer's Parade, 3
Museum of Indian
   Culture, 59
Musikfest, 38
Mutter Museum and
   College Gallery of the
   College of Physicians of
   Philadelphia, 28

N
National Association
   of Watch and Clock
   Collectors Museum, 87
National Aviary, 137
National Canal Museum, 65
National Constitution
   Center, 10
Nationality Rooms, 142

National Liberty
   Museum, 14
National Museum of
   American Jewish
   History, 15
National Riding Stables,
   Gettysburg, 97
National Road Festival, 107
National Toy Train
   Museum, 82
Nazareth, 64
Nazareth Area Visitor
   Center, 67
Nemacolin Castle, 110
New Bloomfield, 192
New Brighton, 152
New Castle, 151
New Germantown, 193
New Hall Military
   Museum, 9
New Hope, 51
New Hope and Ivyland
   Railroad, 52
New Hope Mule Barges, 52
New Hope Visitors
   Center, 67
New Milford, 172
Nittany Antique Machinery
   Show, 199
Nittany Grotto, 198
Nittany Lion Inn, The, 203
Norristown, 45
North East, 225
Northeastern Pennsylvania
   Bluegrass Festival, 159
northeast Philadelphia, 34
North Museum of Natural
   History and Science, 84
north Philadelphia, 28
North Shore and North
   Side, Pittsburgh, 136
Nottingham, 83

O
Ohiopyle, 110
Ohiopyle State Park, 111

Ohiopyle State Park Kentuck
   Campground, 131
Oil City, 218
Oil Creek State Park, 218
Oil Creek & Titusville
   Railroad, 218
Oil Region Alliance, 228
Old Bedford Village, 130
Old City Hall, 8
Old Economy Village, 153
Olde Town, 101
Old Jail Museum, The, 177
Old Mauch Chunk H.O.
   Scale Model Train
   Display, 178
Old Mill Village
   Museum, 173
Ole Bull State Park, 210
Olive Garden, The, Erie, 226
Olive Garden,
   Williamsport, 201
Olympia Candy Kitchen, 103
Omni Bedford Springs
   Resort, 132
Opera Company of
   Philadelphia, 26
Oralee's Golden Eagle
   Inn, 131
Original Waffle Shop, 202
Outdoor World–
   Pennsylvania Dutch
   Country, 104
Outdoor World Scotrun
   Resort, 183
Outer Limits, 217
Outhouse, The, 81

P
Packwood House
   Museum, 190
Pantall Hotel, 227
Paoli, 44
Paradise, 83
Parker Dam State Park, 211
Parkway attractions, 17
Patch Town Day, 159

Path of Progress Heritage
Route, 107
Pat McMullen's
Restaurant, 183
Paton, 122
Peanut Bar and
Restaurant, 103
Pearl S. Buck House, 56
Peddler's Village, 38, 52, 53
Pendergrass Tavern, 130
Penfield, 211
Penn–Brad Oil
Museum, 212
Penn Relays, 3
Pennsbury Manor, 49
Penn's Cave, 199
Penn's Landing, 3, 15
Penn State Creamery, 194
Penn State Ice Pavilion, 195
Pennsylvania Academy of
the Fine Arts, 25
Pennsylvania Dutch
Convention and Visitors
Bureau, 70, 85
Pennsylvania Farm
Show, 70
Pennsylvania Farm Vacation
Association, 71
Pennsylvania Lumber
Museum, 210
Pennsylvania Military
Museum and Twenty-
eighth Infantry Division
Shrine, 198
Pennsylvania Renaissance
Faire, 70
Pennsylvania's Grand
Canyon, 206, 207
Pennsylvania's Great
Outdoors Visitors
Bureau, 228
Pennsylvania's Northeast
Territory Visitors
Bureau, 184
Pennsylvania State Laurel
Festival, 206

Pennsylvania State
Parks, 179
Pennsylvania Trolley
Museum, The, 154
Pennsylvania Wilds visitor
centers, 228
Pennypacker Mills, 57
Peter J. McGovern Little
League Baseball
Museum, 187
Peter Wentz Farmstead, 56
Philadelphia, 1
Philadelphia Convention
and Visitors Bureau, 35
Philadelphia Flower Show, 3
Philadelphia Folk Festival,
38, 57
Philadelphia Marriott West,
The, 67
Philadelphia Museum of
Art, 19
Philadelphia Orchestra, 3
Philadelphia PHLASH bus, 4
Philadelphia Trolley
Works, 4
Philadelphia Zoo, The, 29
Phipps Conservatory, 143
Phoenixville, 45
Pike County Historical
Society, 166
Pike to Bike Trail, 131
Pine Creek Gorge, xi,
206, 207
Pine Creek Outfitters, 208
Pine Creek Trail, 208
Pine Crest Cabins, 216
Pine Crest Yacht Club, 168
Pine Grove Cabins, 184
Pioneer Tunnel Coal Mine &
Steam Train, 180
Pio's Italian Restaurant &
Pizzeria, 226
Pittsburgh, downtown, 135
Pittsburgh Hilton &
Towers, 156
Pittsburgh, North Shore and
North Side, 136

Pittsburgh's East End, 141
Pittsburgh Symphony, 145
Pittsburgh Zoo, 144
Pittston Tomato
Festival, 159
Plain & Fancy Farm, 78, 79
Plaza and Court of King of
Prussia, 44
Please Touch Museum, 1
PNC Carousel at Schenley
Plaza, 142
PNC Park, 144
Pocono Action Sports, 168
Pocono Cheesecake
Factory, 165
Pocono Environmental
Education Center
(PEEC), 166
Pocono Indian
Museum, 165
Pocono Inn, 183
Pocono Mountains, 163
Pocono Mountains
Convention and Visitors
Bureau, 184
Pocono Raceway, 173
Pocono Super 8 Motel, 183
Pocono Whitewater
Rafting, 178
Point Marion, 108
Point Pleasant, 53
Point State Park, 135
Portersville, 150
Potter County Recreation,
Inc., 228
Powdermill Nature
Reserve, 116
PPG Aquarium, 144
Presque Isle Cottage
Court, 228
Presque Isle State Park, 221
Pride of the Susquehanna
riverboat, 94
Promised Land State
Park, 167
Pufferbelly on French
Street, 226

Pumpkin Fest, 107
Punxsutawney, 217
Punxsutawney Chamber of
    Commerce, 217
Punxsutawney Groundhog
    Zoo, 217
Punxsutawney's Groundhog
    Day, 206
Pymatuning Deer Park, 220
Pymatuning State Park, 220

Q
Quaint Corner Children's
    Museum, 123
Quaker Steak and Lube, 226
Quality Inn and Suites,
    Franklin, 227
Quality Inn, Stroudsburg,
    183
Quality Inn & Suites,
    Lancaster, 104
Quiet Valley Living
    Historical Farm, 162
QVC Studio Tour, 42

R
Raccoon Creek State Park
    and Wilderness
    Reserve, 153
Rachel Carson
    Homestead, 147
Radisson Lackawanna
    Station Hotel, 174
Rafting on the
    Youghiogheny, 111
Rail Expo at Steamtown
    National Historic
    Site, 159
Railroaders Memorial
    Museum, 122
Railroad Museum of
    Pennsylvania, 81
Rails-to-Trails, 105
Ramada Inn on Market
    Square, 104
Ramada Inn State
    College, 203

Raystown Lake, 105, 127
Reading, 72
Reading Public Museum, 72
Reading Terminal Market,
    26, 35
Red Caboose Motel, 104
Red Lobster, 202
Red Rock, 180
Richland, 77
Ricketts Glen State
    Park, 180
Ridley Creek State Park, 46
Ringing Rocks, 65
Rittenhouse Square, 27
Riverboat Queen Fleet, 4
RiverFest, Scranton, 159
River Rink, 17
River's Edge Cafe, 131
Riverside Stadium, 94
Riverview Cafe, 156
Roadside America, 73
Roasting Ears of Corn, 59
Robert Indiana's *Love,* 25
Robertsdale, 129
Rockhill, 128
Rockhill Iron Furnace, 128
Rockhill Trolley
    Museum, 128
Rodin Museum, 19
Roebling's Delaware
    Aqueduct, 171
Ronks, 80
Rosenbach Museum and
    Library, 27
Rupp House History
    Center, 101
Ryerss Library and
    Museum, 21

S
Sandcastle Water Park, 146
Sarah Street Grill, The, 183
Sara's, 226
Sawmill Restaurant, 225
S. B. Elliot State Park, 211
Schenley Park, 141,
    142, 143

Schnecksville, 61
Schriver House
    Museum, 100
Schuylkill County Visitors'
    Bureau, 184
Schwenksville, 57
Scotrun, 163
Scott Arboretum of
    Swarthmore College, 46
Scranton, 173
Searight Toll House, 108
Second Bank of the United
    States, 8
Seldom Seen Tourist Coal
    Mine, 122
Senator John Heinz
    Pittsburgh Regional
    History Center, The, 139
Sesame Place, 48
Seven Points Marina, 127
Seven Points Marina/
    Houseboat Rental, 132
Seven Springs Mountain
    Resort, 113
Seven Springs Resort
    Spring Festival, 107
Shannon Inn and Pub, 162
Sharon, 220
Shartlesville, 73
Shaver's Creek
    Environmental
    Center, 197
Shawnee Inn & Golf
    Resort, 183
Shawnee Mountain, 162
Shawnee Mountain
    Lumberjack Festival, 159
Shawnee Place Play and
    Water Park, 161
Shawnee River
    Adventures, 161
Sheraton Society Hill, 35
Shoe Museum, 29
Sight & Sound Theatre, 82
Sinking Valley, 124
Skytop, 163
Skytop Lodge, 164

Slifer House Museum, 190
Smith Memorial Playground and Playhouse, 24
Smokey Bones Barbeque & Grill, 66
Smuggler's Cove, 183
Smuggler's Wharf, 226
SoakZone, 115
Society for Contemporary Craft, 138
Soldiers National Museum, 102
south Philadelphia, 31
Splash Lagoon Indoor Waterpark Resort, 223
Springdale, 147
Springhill Suites, 156
Spruce Creek, 125
Stackhouse Park, 120
Stagecoach Tavern, 50
Starlight, 172
State Capitol Building, 92
State College, 194
State College Super 8 Motel, 203
State Museum of Pennsylvania, 93
Station Square, 139, 140
Steamtown National Historic Site, 173
St. Mary's, 213
Stone Valley Recreation Area, 196
Story Book Forest, 115, 116
Stourbridge Line Rail Excursions, 172
Strasburg, 81
Strasburg Rail Road, 81
Strip District, Pittsburgh, 138
Stroudsburg, 160
Sullivan County Fair, 182
Sullivan County Sleigh Ride and Rally, 182
Summer concerts at Penn's Landing, 3

Sunoco Welcome America! Celebration, 3
Super 8 Motel–Clarion, 227
Super 8 Motel, Warren, 227
Susquehanna Valley Visitors Bureau, 203
Swarthmore, 46
Swigart Museum, The, 126

T
Tales of the Great Flood, 118
Tanglwood Ski Area & Winter Park, 167
Tannersville, 163
Tarentum, 147
Tavern Restaurant, The, 202
T&D's Cats of the World, 191
Temple University Dental Museum, 28
Thomas T. Taber Museum of Lycoming County, 188
Three Rivers Heritage Trail, 144
Time of Thanksgiving, 59
Timothy Lake, 183
Tioga Central Railroad, 209
Tioga Trail Rides, 208
Tionesta, 215
Tipton, 125
Titusville, 218
Todd House, 10
Tom Ridge Environmental Center, 222
Tour-Ed Mine and Museum, 147
Towanda, 182
Town Criers, 7
Trails End, The, 225
Triple "W" Riding Stables, 168
Trough Creek State Park, 121
Trout Hall, 61
Troxell–Steckel House, 61
Troy, 206

Troy Fair, 206
Tuscarora State Forest, 193
Tussey Mountain Ski Resort, 199
Tuttleman IMAX Theater, 18
Tyler Arboretum, 46
Tyrone, 125

U
Uniontown, 108
United States Hot Air Balloon Team, 44
University of Pennsylvania Museum, 29
University of Pittsburgh, 141, 142
Upper Black Eddy, 65
Upper Delaware River, 170
Upper Delaware Scenic and Recreational River, 170, 171
Upper Yough, 111
U.S. Army Heritage and Education Center, 96
U.S. Mint, 12
USS Becuna, 16
USS Lawrence, 16
USS Olympia, 16

V
Valley Forge, 43
Valley Forge Convention and Visitors Bureau, 67
Valley Forge National Historical Park, 43
Victorian Christmas, Bellefonte, 187
Victorian St. Peter's Village, 41
Vinnie's Italian Eatery, 202
Volant, 151
Vowinckel Hotel, 225

W
Wachovia Science Park, 19
Wagner Free Institute of Science, 28

Wagner–Ritter House, 120
Waldameer Park and Water World, 222
Walnut Street Bridge, 93, 94
Warren, 214
Warren County Visitors Bureau, 228
Washington, 154
Washington County Historical Society's Lemoyne House, 155
Washington Crossing, 50
Washington Crossing National Historic Park, 50
Waterfront, Philadelphia, 15
Water Gap Trolley, 161
Water World, 45
Watson–Curtze Mansion and Erie Planetarium, 224
Wayne, 48
Wayne County Fair, 172
Wayne County Historic Society Museum, 171
Weaver's Lebanon Bologna and Baum's Bologna, 75

Weavertown One-Room Schoolhouse, 80
Wellsboro, 207
Wellsboro Chamber of Commerce, 228
West Chester, 42
West Homestead, 146
West Mifflin, 145
Westmoreland Museum of American Art, 114
west Philadelphia, 29
Wharton Esherick Studio, 45
Whitaker Center for Science and the Arts, 92
Whitefield House Museum, 64
White Haven, 176
Wild and Scenic River Tours, 170
Wildflower Music Festival in Hawley, 159
Wildflower Reserve, 153
Williamsport, 187
Willow Street, 83
Winslow Hill, 213
WK&S Railroad Line, 71

Wooden Nickel Buffalo Farm Restaurant and Shop, 224
Woodloch Pines Resort, 169
Woodward Cave and Campground, 200
Worcester, 56
World's End State Park, 181
Wright's Ferry Mansion, 88

Y
Yellow Breeches River, 96
Yellow Springs, 41
Yogi Bear's Jellystone Park, 112
York, 88
Yough Plaza Motel, 131

Z
Zane Grey Museum, 171
Zippo/Case Visitors Center, 212
ZooAmerica North American Wildlife Park, 90

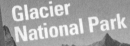